WE PLA
ON

ANDY BRASSELL

WE PLAY ON

Shakhtar Donetsk's
Fight for Ukraine,
Football and Freedom

ROBINSON

ROBINSON

First published in Great Britain in 2023 by Robinson

1 3 5 7 9 10 8 6 4 2

A CIP catalogue record for this book
is available from the British Library

ISBN: 978-1-47214-806-3 (hardback)
ISBN: 978-1-47214-807-0 (trade paperback)

Typeset in Palatino LT Std by SX Composing DTP, Rayleigh, Essex

Printed and bound in Great Britain by Clays Ltd, Elcograf S.p.A.

Papers used by Robinson are from well-managed forests
and other responsible sources

Robinson
An imprint of
Little, Brown Book Group
Carmelite House
50 Victoria Embankment
London EC4Y 0DZ

An Hachette UK Company
www.hachette.co.uk

www.littlebrown.co.uk

To Michelle, Gabriel and Roman,
the (my) world's greatest front three

Contents

Foreword by Darijo Srna

When the final whistle went during our penultimate Ukrainian Premier League match of the season against Dnipro-1 (we won 3–0 to clinch the title), I felt empty. Empty because I'd already been through every emotion.

I had been living for that day. This championship was the most important, for me, in the history of Ukraine. Why? Because one year before, when the war started, nobody even expected that we could play the Ukrainian championship. And one year and three months later, we were Ukrainian champions and we were going directly into the Champions League group stage again.

In the meantime, we had lost the whole coaching staff from before the war. We had also lost fifteen foreign players – thanks to FIFA. We began to rebuild the team. We started to play with a lot of young players. They felt some pressure, which is normal. When it was close between Dnipro, Zorya and us towards the end of the season, I never once said to the team, 'We must win.' I wanted to take away the pressure from them. I just said, 'Let's play our game. If we play our game, with our spirit, we will win the championship.' The team and the club, the coaching staff – they deserved that. All of us together, we deserved to win this championship.

The matchdays we have now, with no crowds, when the air raid siren can go off at any time and we have to go and hide in the bunker . . . that has become normal for us. It's difficult. People are dying and we're playing football – we didn't even really celebrate our win.

This is a victory not just for Shakhtar. This is a victory for Ukrainian fans, for Ukrainian football, because we are back in the Champions League. We want to show to the world that we are alive. That we are strong. Not just us – the whole of Ukraine. We are continuing to play. We are continuing to win. And this is our biggest victory: that we are here today. We are alive. We are supporting each other.

My job as sporting director has changed a lot since 24 February 2022. I've changed a lot. We've all changed a lot. War changes everything. But for me, Shakhtar is not a job. It's my football family. I arrived as a player in 2003 and, ever since, everything that I had to do for my club, for my second country, for my president, for my friends from Shakhtar, I did. With money. Without money. I will always do it.

I'm happy to have been with my team in Kyiv when the rockets arrived. My wife and my children respect that Shakhtar are my football family, and they are with me in every moment, because they understand the importance. All my best friends are there and we go through this together.

I have lived through three wars: the first in Croatia in the 1990s, then in 2014 in the Donbas region, and now. I have lived through this with Shakhtar. I know how it is to have to leave your house; how it is to have to leave your city, your country. Because of that I'm three times stronger with them, because they are my friends. And I'm so happy to be to be part of this chapter, because in this last year, we've shown each other how much respect and love we have for each other in this difficult moment in time.

Before the war, I thought that I couldn't love Shakhtar any more than I did. But now that love has deepened. I want to stay here my whole life. I'm a professional, but I'm also an emotional person. It's not a question of money. Shakhtar is much more than money. Shakhtar is family. Shakhtar is strength. I hope that, reading this book, you will begin to understand the spirit of the club and the power of playing on. It is our legacy.

Introduction

Ukraine is everywhere. The peace symbol remains painted in the centre circle of Bundesliga pitches, and in March 2023's Copa del Rey edition of El Clásico, a supporter near the front of the stand in the Bernabéu brandished a large Ukrainian flag, seen by viewers in hundreds of countries around the world. And that's what this is about – visibility.

The world's understanding is that Ukraine has been at war since 24 February 2022. Ask anybody connected with Shakhtar, and they will tell you that they have been at war for much, much longer. They left their home city of Donetsk in spring 2014. That's why, every time Shakhtar defied the odds with their European results in their adopted home of Warsaw in 2022–23, it mattered. It's also why it mattered every time they won a trophy or a big European match – and there have been plenty, with the team having reached two Europa League semi-finals and two rounds of 16 since 2015. And it mattered when they sold a player of renown to one of Europe's elite.

When the legendary Milan coach Arrigo Sacchi said, 'Football is the most important of the least important things,' maybe this is what he meant. Or maybe he couldn't even have imagined how important football could be in a setting like this, an unthinkable setting, a worse-than-worst case scenario, as the Shakhtar legend Darijo Srna put it.

I have written and talked about (mainly European) football for almost two decades and few subjects have made me examine the way I approach my work as forcefully as this one. As you will read in the coming pages, Shakhtar started to become a regular feature in my work orbit in around 2007, as they began to make their presence felt in the Champions League – and what a presence it was. Making a film about Shakhtar with the *Guardian* in 2015, however, changed my view of this club forever.

Football often looks like such a glamorous life but this club and its players were stuck in a netherworld. They were just coming to terms with leaving their city and making a new base in Kyiv, with flights to home games in Lviv, by the Polish border. The treadmill of uncertainty and endless travelling felt like a holding pattern. Neither they, nor I, could have any idea how long it would last for.

It was an extraordinary situation and it put the club and, I suppose, the game in a different light for me. As people who write and talk for a living we should always choose our words carefully but I sometimes wonder if we do, particularly in a football context. So the words we use all the time in referring to matches, results and even boardroom meltdowns – 'disaster,' 'catastrophe', 'tragedy' – are thrown about with little thought given to what they truly mean. I suspect I have been guilty of that in years past.

'Hero' is also an overused and often melodramatically employed epithet in football. It's the hero of the hour; a goal-scorer, a maker of a last-ditch block, the player who takes one for the team in picking up a card and 'sacrificing' him or herself for the greater good ('sacrifice' is another of those ill-used words). In a wider sense our 'hero' might be a long-serving player who gives everything to the club, perhaps putting the possibility of moving onwards and upwards to one side to stay loyal.

But these (mainly) men who represent Shakhtar are something else. I came to know this through extensive conversations with them – and those who used to be in their positions and have since moved on. Conversations in Ukraine, Poland, France, England and Turkey in hotels, on training pitches, deep in the recesses of stadiums after matches, and over Zoom calls, as we all do nowadays. It is sometimes hard to get words from football people; the media-trained are paranoid about giving anything away, while the uber-motivated want to be on the training field or on their laptops and phones analysing their opponents and their own games for incremental gains, rather than talking about their actions to journalists. Not so here. They had stories to tell and a cause that the world must continue to hear. Many times they wanted to talk. On other occasions, I suspect, it was the last thing they wanted to do, but they were open and frank all the same.

But I can really say that these people – Igor Jovićević, Taras Stepanenko, Sergei Palkin, Darijo Srna, Yuri Sviridov, Andrei Babeshko, Oleg Barkov and all of Shakhtar's players and staff – are heroes for the fortitude, humility, grace and determination with which they carry themselves, going above and beyond what anyone could expect of any hero. I can say the same of those journalists like Andrew Todos and Iryna Koziupa, who cover countless miles.

These people will simply not be beaten. It has been an honour to tell their story.

1

The Escape

'You can't mix sport and politics. But this time, you have to. We must. Because Shakhtar lost two homes in eight years. And Russian teams – they are still there. They are still playing. It's impossible for them to play World Cup, European Championship, Olympic games. It's impossible. It's not their [the sportsmen's] fault, but it's not our fault. We lost our home because of them [Russia].'

Darijo Srna, Shakhtar Donetsk sporting director,
6 February 2023

Tension is tension, and war is war. You might have an idea in your head that point one can always naturally develop into point two, but the speed with which that journey takes place when it does – or that it happens at all, depending on your perspective – is shocking.

'One day before, on [February] the twenty-third,' remembers Darijo Srna, 'I was having dinner with my friend in a restaurant, everything was full, we were enjoying ourselves. The twenty-fourth in the morning, you cannot . . .' The Shakhtar Donetsk sporting director usually speaks as he thinks, rattling along at pace, efficiently and neatly layering the strata of any subject, regardless of its complexity. Here, even he needs to stop, to absorb, to consider, to try and find the words. 'You see how scared people are.' He makes himself restart. 'Going out of the city with their children, billions of cars on the street, traffic . . .' There is just too much to process, too much to explain and too much to comprehend. Perhaps it will never be possible to do so.

On 24 February 2022 at approximately 4 a.m. Kyiv time, Russia's all-out offensive on Ukraine began. In what Russian president Vladimir Putin historically and infamously described as a 'special military operation', the capital, plus the cities of Kharkiv (another former home of Shakhtar) and Kherson were targeted by the Russian military, with airstrikes aimed at taking out Ukrainian military infrastructure and border protection in particular. It was the worst-case scenario made reality, with an extraordinary abruptness.

Russian–Ukrainian confrontation was not new. The Euro-maidan protests of November 2013, against the reneging of then-president Viktor Yanukovych on his promise to sign an association agreement with the European Union, had turned violent in the weeks and months that followed. The situation reached its nadir in February 2014 when police snipers started taking shots at peaceful demonstrators in the city's Independence Square, killing scores of them. A Ukrainian move towards a tighter relationship with Europe had pushed Putin, who had never truly accepted the break-up of the Soviet Union, to brutal action. In that same February Crimea, the Black Sea peninsula to the south, was occupied by Russia, and continues to be.

Outside Ukraine, it was often described as 'unrest', 'turbulence', 'instability', but not always recognised for what it truly was. Invasion. War. The *Fourcast*, Channel 4's weekly world news podcast, actually did acknowledge the holding pattern of Russia in Ukraine when it assessed the possibility of a full-blown invasion in its episode on 12 February 2022. 'There's no major invasion of Ukraine by Russia right now,' outlined host Kiran Moodley with a hint of fatalism, while correspondent Paraic O'Brien spoke of continuing border skirmishes 'bubbling away under the surface, a grinding, low-level, cold war [which] is psychologically difficult to process.'

But 2014 had been the year when life changed for Shakhtar. By May the Crimea situation was near replicated in Donbas, the south-eastern, 45,000-square-km region pressing into the Russian border, of which Donetsk is the de facto capital. Taking advantage of the instability following Euromaidan, Russian-funded separatists violently wrested control. The club, its staff and players hurriedly packed up and fled Donetsk, never to return, and setting Shakhtar on their current, itinerant path.

In 2022, the Russian invasion was full and uncompromising. It would not just be Shakhtar and the clubs from the eastern part of the country, such as the smaller Olimpik Donetsk, who in 2021 had been forced to withdraw from the Ukrainian Premier League (UPL) citing a lack of funding, that would be profoundly affected. For some, the moment, when it arrived, was hard to fully believe. They needed to be sure. 'We woke up to the sounds of explosions,' Shakhtar captain Taras Stepanenko tells me. 'Before [this] everyone in Ukraine, I think, was watching the news, saying something could happen, that a lot of Russian troops were [moving towards] the borders of Ukraine.' Then came the noises that woke millions of Ukrainians from their slumbers. 'My wife said to me, "My dear, the war has started." But I said, "No, maybe you're wrong, maybe it's some problem in the factory or the energy power plant, I don't know."' Reports coming through via online news sites and first-hand accounts on social media removed all doubt. 'But then we started to read the news and we knew that, yes, Russia had invaded Ukraine.'

'That day was terrible,' Israeli midfielder Manor Solomon, who spent the 2022–23 season on loan at Fulham, says. 'I woke up, and the other players woke up, to the sound of explosions. It was a nightmare.' As the possibility of a Russian offensive built, Shakhtar had sought to set the minds of Solomon and his fellow overseas players at relative ease. They had, after all, experience of dealing with extraordinary events. 'The club . . . told us that everything was going to be OK and we will be safe,' he says, 'and if something happens, they will rescue us and they will get us out. But in the end, it was a different story.' The sheer speed and brutality of it all caught everyone by surprise.

Others had seriously feared war, but not expected the scale of attacks that were quickly becoming apparent. 'It was authentically chaos,' recalls Igor Jovićević, then the head coach of Dnipro-1 and now in charge of Shakhtar. 'Because you speak about it [the prospect of war], you feel afraid, that there could be an invasion by the Russians, but you think maybe subconsciously that it could be Donbas again, but not so deep [into the country].' Yet here it was not just in Donbas but in Kyiv, Kherson, Dnipro (some four hundred kilometres southeast of the capital).

One of Jovićević's predecessors, the Portuguese coach Paulo Fonseca, was in Kyiv at the time with his Ukrainian wife and their son. 'At the time rumours were swirling about the possibility of Russia invading Ukraine,' he tells me, 'but we thought it probably wouldn't happen, or [if it did] it may happen again in the region of Donbas, in Donetsk, in Luhansk, but we never imagined it could be the whole of Ukraine. I remember I was on holiday, and there was more and more news on the matter and I said to my wife that we had to go back to Ukraine to see what we should do, because things were getting dangerous there. And my wife, who had gone through the experience of Donetsk, where she is from, was convinced nothing was going to happen, but said, "Let's go back to see."'

They had no idea of the 'really, really tough' situation that lay ahead of them. The Fonseca family's experience of the suddenness of it all chimes with Srna's. 'So we went back four days before the war started,' he says. 'I found Kyiv the same as when I lived there. People were extremely calm, the city was normal, living their normal everyday lives, and everyone was very confident in relation to what may transpire, saying nothing would happen here. If problems were going to occur, it would be in the region of Donbas and Donetsk and Luhansk, but here . . . nothing would happen here. So during those days the atmosphere was extremely calm. Even so, I thought, OK, let's spend some time in Portugal and let's take the family, that's what I told my wife. So we prepared things and booked our flight for the twenty-fourth of February at ten o'clock in the morning.

'We went to bed extremely late,' he continues, 'preparing everything for the journey, and the only thing I remember, at around five o'clock in the morning, was that I was woken up by the sound of the falling bombs. We lived in an apartment on a very high floor from where you can see almost the entire city. I went to a window, looked out, and saw that the war had started. We have a young child – at the time he was about to turn three – and we entered in panic, like I think everybody did, and my first concern was how we were going to get out of there. Looking out of the window, I saw all the cars coming out of their garages, everyone trying to escape, to flee. I managed to arrange a vehicle and, after speaking to some people, they advised us to go in the direction of Lviv, towards Poland, and try to get out that way. We got in the car, but when we arrived in the city centre it was a standstill because of the traffic.'

For Shakhtar it was time to do a headcount – and to take refuge. 'Firstly, I started to send messages to family, relatives, friends,' Stepanenko recounts, 'to see if they were in a safe place, and if they were OK. In Kyiv we were in a house and my sons slept on the second floor. We took them, we went into the basement and stayed there for three days. [We knew] Russian troops were really close to Kyiv and we didn't know if they were coming into the city. So it was better for us to stay there.'

The skipper's situation was different to that of many of his teammates. Having revolutionised Ukrainian football with their large-scale import of (mainly Brazilian) overseas players over the previous fifteen years or so, Shakhtar had a cosmopolitan squad, which at the time included seventeen non-Ukrainian players (fourteen of whom were Brazilian). Ever since the 2014 departure from Donetsk, the club's administrative base, offices and home had been the palatial Hotel Opera in downtown Kyiv, the property of multi-billionaire club owner Rinat Akhmetov. It was always going to be true north for everyone connected with the club needing somewhere to go when crisis point was reached.

'In Hotel Opera myself and my staff were there,' details Roberto De Zerbi, Shakhtar's head coach at the time, 'plus thirteen or fourteen Brazilian players and their families. A total of 40–45 people, with of course also journalists from BBC and CNN.' While the gathered parties eventually began to work on a what-next plan, it was initially about community, company, and a sense of comfort. 'I have never been before in such a situation,' De Zerbi continues, 'so myself and my staff were just trying to help and support Brazilian players to leave the country and at the same time to organise for us a plan to leave.'

Shakhtar is a rock-solid club, with experience beyond what any club should really have to have given events since 2014. They are consistent in management, board level personnel and outlook. They are pragmatic and practical. But as Srna suggested, even they were blindsided by this. This was something else. Everything and everyone, however, was still in a spin. 'The first day,' Stepanenko says, 'nobody knew what to do. It was a total mess.'

His situation was different. Unlike the overseas players, Stepanenko hadn't gone to the Opera, staying hidden away with his family and keeping in touch down the line. 'I just had a video call with De Zerbi,' he said, 'and he asked where we were staying, and if we were safe. The Brazilian players were in the Opera, waiting for a rescue from Kyiv, because already all flights were cancelled. You could only leave Kyiv by bus or by car [at that point]. But there were huge problems with [finding] petrol, and it was a really stressful situation.'

Everyone, no matter how sanguine, had their moment of doubt. Srna's was different to many others. He is Shakhtar royalty, having arrived as a twenty-one-year-old and given the club nigh on two decades of almost continuous service – give or take a year in Italy with Cagliari in the final season of his playing career – as a player, assistant to Portuguese coach Luís Castro and now sporting director. He has been through every state with the club, but even before, his life was rarely easy. Born in spring 1982 in modern-day Croatia to a Bosniak father and a Croat mother, his experience of war and displacement stretches back to childhood and the break-up of Yugoslavia. 'I'll be honest with you,' he tells me. 'I wasn't afraid on February the twenty-fourth when they started bombing at four in the morning. I had fear when I started to hear the sirens. The sirens put me back in the 1990s in Croatia, when I was a nine-year-old kid.'

He quickly found his own way to perspective. 'I wasn't in such a huge panic because,' he says, 'first of all, my family wasn't with me. My family was in London. And more or less it was OK for me. But on the other side you hear my daughter and my son; they're calling me and saying, "Daddy, Daddy, we are waiting for you at home." On the other side you have fifteen [overseas] players, one with a six-month-old baby . . . I cannot leave them.' And he didn't.

Everyone under the Shakhtar umbrella tends to look to Srna and CEO Sergei Palkin for leadership, and that's what they got. De Zerbi, a leader of men, stood up too, despite having moved to Ukraine less than a year before to take on his first head coaching job outside Italy. With his family not having come to Kyiv with him, he was subject to similar pressures to reassure relatives, feeling helpless at home, as Srna was. He resolved to stay until his players had safe passage. 'My family didn't understand my choice,' he acknowledges, 'because before the war started they were [already] pleading for me to come back home, especially my nineteen-year-old daughter everyday was telling me, "Dad, come back home." During the first days of war there was desperation mixed with anger, but when I came back home my daughter understood what kind of tight relationship there was between me and my players.'

De Zerbi's assistant, Enrico Venturelli, was in a parallel situation, also having to explain the situation to remote, fraught family. 'I was living in Kyiv with my girlfriend – she is Ukrainian – but of course in Italy my family was so worried, particularly my father,' he nods. 'When in your life you have a commitment, you have to keep it until the end. This is my view about life and business, because it's too easy to be happy when everything is fine, and then run away when there is any trouble. So I was committed until the end. I stuck to my position, I followed my head coach, and then [when the time came] we left all together.' De Zerbi cuts in on Venturelli, keen to underline his assistant's loyalty. 'Enrico learned the lesson well, and because of this I kept an opinion about him in my mind – he is a top man and if I have the chance to bring him with me, I'll do it. And I did it.' The pair now work together in England, at the Premier League club Brighton and Hove Albion.

For all, the survival instinct began to trump the sense of bewilderment. Some took it into their own hands. One of the Brazilian contingent, winger Tetê, wasn't going to hang around and let the situation play out. He had arrived in Ukraine as a teenager from Grêmio and adapted quickly. Far from the Brazilian cliché, he liked the cold, for one. 'The first night I arrived,' he told *L'Équipe* in September 2022, 'it was -18°C and I slept all night with the window open.' His new teammates thought it was hilarious. They quickly grew to like him. He settled well, shining in the UPL and Champions League alike, and met and married a Ukrainian woman, Tania.

Despite having turned twenty-two little more than a week before the invasion, Tetê was every inch a grown man. He had to be, growing up in a tough part of Alvorada, adjacent to Porto Alegre in Rio Grande do Sul, in southern Brazil. Like many young footballers from tricky backgrounds, he had been quickly pushed into a leadership role in his family, but he was comfortable with that. He was not loud or brash, but he was decisive. When he signed his first professional deal, he moved his parents out of Alvorada and into a house 'a hundred times better,' as he revealed to *Globo* in a 2019 interview. He bought them a home in a smart southern suburb of nearby Porto Alegre.

In a moment of crisis, he again took the bull by the horns. 'It was kind of a scary moment,' he admitted in his self-produced documentary *Eu Sou O Furacão* (*I Am The Hurricane*, a reference to his nickname) in early 2023. 'We already knew that they were about to invade. We could hear the bombs from our house but,' he cracks a smile, 'I was still playing video games.' Playing video games had always been his release valve from moments of pressure, and a big one was coming.

'I was calm,' he continued, 'because we're the ones that are responsible for our families and if we pass that panic to the people around us, they would have got more scared for sure. So I tried to keep them calm. In three or four hours, I decided. Let's get the car with my family and go and cross the border.' Once the couple reached Poland they found a hotel and Tetê quickly joined a local gym to stay in shape. Those daily workouts would be his routine for two months, punctuated by him and Tania buying, preparing and handing out boxes of food and hygiene essentials for refugees arriving from Ukraine. He later signed a short-term deal with French club Olympique Lyonnais, with his Shakhtar contract suspended as part of FIFA's ruling of 8 March, which allowed foreign players in Ukraine and Russia to sign for other clubs without penalty until 30 June. When he was thrown on for his Lyon debut as a late substitute against Angers, Tetê hadn't touched a football since leaving Ukraine. Two minutes later he collected a Malo Gusto pass with his left foot, then curled a sublime winning goal into the far corner. No drama, just action.

While Shakhtar had attempted to reorder the unfathomable in the Opera, the centre of their world for almost eight years, the rest of Ukrainian football began their own scramble towards some sort of salvation. 'Last year I was here,' says Jovićević, who was then leading Dnipro-1 through their mid-season training camp in Antalya, the coastal city in Turkey where many of the UPL clubs go to ready themselves for the resumption after the substantial winter break. Antalya is where he is now putting Shakhtar through their paces in familiar surroundings, a welcome crutch of continuity in a world without much of it. Sitting on a sofa in the team's hotel lobby he is even more of a vivid, garrulous and engaging speaker than Srna but, just like his sporting director, you can see him take a second after his words to compose himself, to try and settle the insanity of everything that has happened in the previous twelve months. Has it only been a year? It barely seems real.

'On 23 February we were leaving here,' he remembers, winding back to the same backdrop in the previous year when much was comparable to now, but when so much was different. 'We had to go back to Ukraine because on the twenty-seventh, we had our first game [of the UPL resumption] against Desna. We decided to go back three days before the first official game for adaptation, because it was snowing [in Ukraine].' Many UPL teams were in the same boat – in Turkey enjoying palatial facilities as they geared up for a season restart like any other, on the surface at least. Yet amongst the players and the staff the talk was inexorably flowing in one direction. The potential invasion was on most, if not all of their minds.

'In the last days in Antalya we were reading that the invasion could be happening,' Jovićević says. 'We were calling back [to

Ukraine] to ask, "What's happened?" and told, "Don't worry, the championship will go on."' The squad completed the camp, returned home – and then it happened. 'So we arrived back on the twenty-third to Dnipro and at 5 a.m. on the twenty-fourth we heard the first bombs. It was a shock,' he says, despite the build-up. The saving grace for Jovićević from his perspective, as with Srna, was that his wife and children live back in the Croatian capital, Zagreb, where he made his initial steps in the game as a fêted young player from the renowned Dinamo academy. He was alone.

'I lived in the training centre of Dnipro,' Jovićević recalls, 'and I heard *boooch* [he makes the noise of a huge explosion]. There were a few bombs at five o'clock. We went to the bunkers and we were there until ten o'clock, and you were reading on the internet that the war had begun.' The mood of the group, as with Shakhtar, was one of confusion at the dizzying pace of events. 'For a few hours we got together as a team,' he continues, 'and decided what to do, but it was a panic.'

Dnipro-1 also had a diverse staff with diverse needs – and varying levels of consular assistance from their respective embassies. Keeping it all together was a challenge but, Jovićević recognises, they had a strong guiding hand from club president Yuriy Bereza, a former member of parliament and commander in the Dnipro Battalion, a volunteer police unit set up in the wake of the violence in 2014. The plan clicked into place. 'We had twelve foreign players in the team,' Jovićević details, 'some Spanish coaches on the coaching team, and we took a few cars from the club. On the advice of the president we headed west, and left Dnipro.'

Shakhtar's operation was on an even bigger scale. The Croatian embassy had advised Srna to leave. The Brazilians were still waiting for definitive direction from theirs. Srna was getting assistance from his friend Aleksander Čeferin, the UEFA president, but it wasn't happening quickly enough. The former made it plain to the latter that he wouldn't be going anywhere until he was sure that his players were out safely. Čeferin came through for him. 'After two days ...' – just how long those days felt is apparent as Srna unconsciously stretches in his seat – ' ... Čeferin helped a lot. The president of the [Ukrainian] federation, Andriy Pavelko, helped a lot, and we found a way to get all the players out of Ukraine.'

It wasn't just Shakhtar looking after their own. Dynamo Kyiv players Vitinho and Carlos de Pena were with them in the Opera. After a while, their number also included Fonseca and his family. Trying to get out on the packed roads was proving a futile – and extremely anxious – experience. 'There is a road that goes to Shakhtar's training centre,' says Fonseca, 'and you could see the kilometres of queues and the cars weren't moving. And then, when I was in the queue, Vitaliy [his former assistant and interpreter] and Darijo Srna called me and said, "Coach, don't try and leave today. It's impossible. You won't be able to get out of here. The Brazilian players and the Shakhtar coaches are there. Go there, see what you can do."'

They arrived to find an atmosphere barely calmer that the one outside. 'When I got there, De Zerbi was there with his coaching team,' he relays, 'the Brazilian players were with their families, with everyone a little bit in panic. The Hotel Opera has a room, on the basement floor, where we had dinner. It was a large room, and as the alarms were always going off that's where they asked people to sleep, so we all took our mattresses and we slept there, but everyone was in panic because there was a lot of contradictory information. Some said Russia were going to enter into Kyiv, bring down the government, and then there would be no more problems. On the other hand, we felt that the Ukrainian army was defending Kyiv, so there was a lot of doubt.'

That uncertainty made Fonseca take the initiative, like Tetê had. 'On the second day I decided to contact the Portuguese embassy, as I knew the people there, to try and understand how they were getting Portuguese citizens out of Kyiv. They said a van had already left, but the next day another van would be leaving in the direction of the border, and I said to my wife we had to risk it. We had to risk it in the embassy's vehicle. Maybe we'd have luck. So my wife, my son and I and my wife's family left Kyiv heading towards Moldova, on a journey that lasted more than thirty hours, without stopping, lots of traffic, even at night, sirens always going off. Other people were also in the van, some Portuguese people.' The frightening speculation continued on the way, though. 'We could hear at the front they were saying, "We can't go this way because they're attacking there, we have to go that way." And after around thirty hours without stopping we arrived near the border with Moldova, from where we afterwards managed to leave through Romania.'

The Brazilians had been feeling similarly stymied, with limited help from back home. Júnior Moraes, the most senior of the players from Brazil, got the footballers and their families – a twenty-strong group – together in the lobby of the Opera, where they recorded a message on his phone to send out to the world, asking for help from the Brazilian government. It was the club, with the help of UEFA and FIFPRO (the world players' union), that figured out the best possible plan in the circumstances.

On Saturday 26 February, the foreigners left the Opera for the train station with Brazilian flags hung up on the inside of the bus windows to indicate neutrality. From there, it was a sixteen-hour train journey to Chernivtsi in the country's west. If leaving Kyiv, the feeling of moving, provided some initial relief, it didn't last long. Getting out of the capital meant seeing what was happening to the rest of Ukraine out of the train window. 'It was horrific,' said Pedrinho, when he eventually landed back home in São Paulo. '[We saw] some terrible images, and towns absolutely destroyed. I had my four-month-old daughter in my arms and just wanted her to be all right.' Every time he called his family, 'I said goodbye to them, because I was saying to myself that could be the last time that I heard their voices.' On arrival at Chernivtsi, a bus to Moldova and another to Romania saw them to safety.

Then came the moment for Srna to start his own journey, which he did by road. He shared space with three of his coaching staff and a full tank of extra petrol in the back for refills. 'I started to drive at twenty to seven in the morning,' he recounts. 'I drove, like, thirty-four hours. Until the border. My players . . . they decided to go by train, I decided to go by car. They started one day after me, by train, and we arrived more or less at the same time.' He idly taps his phone against the table as we sit opposite each other at the Hotel Cullinan Belek in Antalya, as if trying to jolt himself from momentarily zoning out. 'We arrived in Moldova. And Roberto [De Zerbi], he went by train to Lviv, and then by car to Budapest.' Repeating it is a mantra. It still carries a huge ring of surrealness to it.

'This was a difficult period,' Srna continues, still trying to make sense of it. 'Really. I have the photos in my head, videos, but it's difficult to explain in words.' Seeing Srna struggling to describe something is quite a disarming experience. To listen to him one senses that the trauma is less the undertaking of the journey and more the witnessing of others going through it – on foot, with children and any belongings they could carry. Srna refocuses, and then shakes his head. 'This guy [Putin] doesn't do anything good for the world.' Even if Srna has known more than his share of hardship he is well aware that his status and career make him more privileged than many. Yet in that moment – *these* moments, we should say – it was clear that no amount of money or status could have protected him, them, you, anyone, from this.

Tetê, Júnior Moraes, Dentinho and Shakhtar's Brazilian clan had never appreciated the sense of community created by them and their predecessors as much as they did over those two long, long days in the Opera. 'We heard the noise of fighter jets, the noise of bombs,' former Barcelona defender Marlon, who De Zerbi brought over with him from Sassuolo, told reporters when he finally landed back in Rio de Janeiro with his family. 'It was a horrible situation. But there were

17

people that were willing to take risks, such as Júnior Moraes, who went out to get food, and nappies for children.'

They, at least, made it out thanks to the club's and Čeferin's efforts. Other Brazilians in Ukraine – there were a total of thirty-two registered to UPL clubs at the beginning of the 2021–22 season – were left to fend for themselves, with their embassy in Kyiv offering little assistance. Lucas Rangel, a Brazilian forward playing for Vorskla Poltava – about three hours north of Dnipro – made a dash for it in his car, taking two Brazilian Poltava-based clergymen and the mother of an acquaintance's girlfriend with him.

Like so many others, Rangel took the long way round, he told *The Mail On Sunday*'s Josué Seixas at the time, attempting to avoid Kyiv while the Russians attacked the capital. Using social media updates to keep him abreast of a rapidly changing situation, he let his family back home know where he was when reception was available, all the time terrified by the sound of aircraft overhead. After various detours, Rangel and his travelling companions ditched the car and walked the final five hours to the Polish border, in temperatures as low as -8°C. He finally made it home to his wife and children in Alvorada – Tetê's home city – via flights from Poland and Portugal.

Jovićević's journey was even longer. He quickly tallies it up in his head. 'It was about sixty hours, maybe,' he estimates. 'Sixty hours without sleep. We had got to the [Dnipro team] hotel, and we wanted to leave in the night, but the government and President Zelenskiy [declared] a curfew, from 7 p.m. to 7 a.m. When it's dark, it was forbidden [to go].' Like Tetê and his family, Jovićević and his travelling companions decided to make a break for it. 'On the second day,' he says, 'we went anyway.'

There are only eight-and-a-half years between Jovićević and Srna – the coach is the elder at forty-nine – but there are significant differences between the generational experiences of the two Croats. As conflict ripped Yugoslavia apart in the early '90s, deeply affecting Darijo's childhood, Igor was exiting stage left to make his way in European football as the Balkans' *wunderkind* of the time. After an extensive battle for his signature in 1991 ('Milan, PSG, Auxerre . . . ' he lists the clubs offering him the Earth) he was whisked away by Real Madrid when in Verona, on the brink of signing for local club Hellas, the 1985 Italian champions. 'A team come in the hotel in elegant suits,' he says, eyes widening, 'and then you see them. Michel, Emilio Butragueño, Hugo Sánchez, [Robert] Prosinečki. This is Real Madrid.' Jovićević's father Čedo had coached Prosinečki at Dinamo, breaking the ice. 'Pedro Zapata, the vice-president, invited me to go back to Madrid with them,' and the seventeen-year-old was inking a five-year deal with Castilla, the club's B team.

So while Srna was living his childhood in partial dread in a fracturing nation, the teenage Jovićević was in Spain living out every kid's dream. While the former was – unfortunately – well prepared for the worst by his most formative experiences, all of this horror was new for the latter. 'So in the morning we went west,' Jovićević continues, 'to Lviv. By then they'd started bombing the bridges. So [from there] you could go to Romania, Hungary, Slovakia, to Moldova but part of it

[Transnistria] is Russian.' The calculus was complex, and real life or death, rather than theory.

'In my phone I have all these villages,' he taps his phone animatedly. 'All these villages that don't even exist in Google Maps. If you make a wrong' – he turns his hand one way and another, indicating a tricky route – 'you are dead.' As dystopia morphed into fear, desperation and exhaustion, it felt like a journey without end. 'So these sixty hours for us . . . we went over to the Romanian side. It was like ten years.'

Some didn't have to endure that ordeal, but were hit with different levels of complication. Farès Bahlouli, the Lyon-born former Monaco and Lille midfielder, was having the season of his life for Metalist Kharkiv in the Persha Liha, Ukraine's second tier, when war was declared. Metalist were due to come back from their own winter training camp in Turkey on the day that Russia invaded. Bahlouli and his teammates' last sleep before flying back was interrupted by urgent news from Ukraine. 'We heard that things were a bit hot back home [in Ukraine],' he told beIN Sports's *Football Show* of 15 March 2022, 'but nobody really believed [anything was going to happen]. We were woken by calls at 4 a.m. by family members, from the president, from some of the staff who had stayed back in Ukraine. So we found out our city had been bombed and that Russian troops had invaded our town. This is how we got wind of it, and we were in total shock.'

Like so many others, Bahlouli left a life he had built – and a career he had rebuilt in Kharkiv, having failed to fulfil his potential at a cluster of prestigious French clubs – behind at a stroke, because he had to. 'I have my apartment, my clothes, some personal effects, my kids' stuff, my wife's things,' he said. 'I was pretty much there for a year-and-a-half so I was quite settled. We left everything. But they're only possessions. When I see my [Ukrainian] teammates who've left behind their families, their wives, their children, who are hiding down in the Metro stations, who are refugees, who are scared at each siren when it sounds . . . I feel lucky compared to my teammates and most Ukrainians.'

In relative terms Bahlouli *was* lucky, flying home via Paris. Some of his teammates were in an extra level of purgatory in the days immediately after the invasion, trapped and unable to go home to loved ones with flights cancelled and a no-fly zone not shifting in a hurry. Not to mention the new level of reality that would await them if and when they finally did get there. 'They're stuck in Turkey,' Bahlouli said at the time. 'They can't go back to their country, because each man of between eighteen and sixty is obliged to stay in the country, to take up arms and help their country.'

Journalist Adam Crafton spent a few months embedded with Shakhtar, making the award-nominated podcast series *Away From Home* for *The Athletic*. He too makes the distinction between the experience of the war and its immediate consequences for foreigners and for Ukrainians. 'That was a three- or four-day trauma for those international players and their families,' he points out to me, 'and that got a lot of attention. Everyone was just talking about these international players, the Brazilian players. How do they get out? And then you stop and think, Shit, this is actually going to be the next few years for all the players that they're leaving behind.'

Those Ukrainians already in their own country, like Stepanenko, were dealing with something else entirely. As we sit over tea in a basement café at the Cullinan, a gentle hush falls over the table as the captain takes a breath and considers what the difference was in the experience for him and for his international colleagues: 'I think it was awful for them and for us,' he begins to tell me, 'but for them they understood that it was really dangerous to stay in Kyiv and they wanted to leave Ukraine. But they understood when they [got away] they could go home, and they could stay in a safe place in Brazil. But for Ukrainians, you knew that Russians were in your country, they wanted to destroy your life, they wanted to take your country under their control and it's real war in your country. You know that people will die, and you know that you have to move to a safe place.'

The fight for them, tragically, would continue. A different kind of fight to that on the frontline. 'A player can help Ukraine on the football pitch but he doesn't know anything about armies, guns or war,' Srna told the *Guardian*'s Nick Ames in March 2022. 'It would be his decision but maybe it's better if they volunteer with things like offering food and supplies, while using their platforms to make their voices heard. All of them are involved in humanitarian action now.'

For the foreigners, now physically removed from the drama, a feeling of emptiness was about to set in, having left teammates, friends and dreams behind. 'I felt dead inside,' shrugs De Zerbi. 'In reality, the Shakhtar wound is still open. It's the human aspect [that counts most]. Due to the war we had to leave the country, to leave Kyiv, which is a fantastic city, but which during the war and under the shelling was full of checkpoints, and there was a ghostly silence during day and night. We left on Sunday afternoon by train, and the city was absolutely different than what I remember [it] was before the start of the conflict.'

What followed was a period of stasis that footballers just don't have. While Tetê put himself through his paces in a Polish gym, Solomon made the most of time with his family back in Kfar Sava, central Israel. He had left his country for Ukraine at age nineteen, and after being thrown into an unimaginably bad real-world situation, he had the opportunity to decompress and spend rare and valuable moments with those who meant the most to him – the sort of rare time to assess and be grateful for what you have. And after such an ordeal, Solomon felt especially grateful for everything. 'In this period, I knew that I would be without football,' he reflects, 'and without my team. But I said, OK, one benefit that I can take from this is that now I [can be] close to my parents. I'm with my friends. So I don't know when again I'll be able to spend so long in my home.'

Back in Ukraine, Kyiv and Shakhtar were left looking for leaders to guide them back into the light. Srna and Palkin were involved, taking their lead from Akhmetov, the man whose money and vision always made it happen. 'He lost around 60 per cent of his business,' Palkin tells me, with Mariupol particularly badly hit in the opening days and weeks of the war, which Akhmetov told Reuters in April 2022 was 'a global tragedy'. Mariupol, in the south of the Donetsk Oblast, which the Ukrainian government estimates has lost around 75 per cent of its population since the beginning of the full-scale war, was also the home of iron and steel mills owned by Metinvest, one of Akhmetov's main companies.

That the transformation has been so pronounced, so horrific, is now abundantly clear to the world after Google Maps recently changed their imagery of the region, as Paul Niland, a Kyiv-based British businessman and writer tells me. Mariupol is razed. There is simply nothing left. It had been a source of pride to its people and its region, having become the regional capital after the annexation of Donetsk. It was not just industrial but had become pretty, and it had become green, with investment in public parks building on its natural location on the Sea of Azov. The Ukrainian ambassador to the United Nations shared an article that Niland wrote on the destruction of Mariupol on his social media, linking it with a photograph of António Guterres, the UN secretary-general, shaking hands with Sergey Lavrov, Russia's Minister for Foreign Affairs. The sheer depth of his rage, his indignation, was palpable. 'What the Ukrainian ambassador wrote when he shared my piece,' says Niland, 'was, "Dear UN colleagues, The next time you shake hands with a member of the Russian delegation, bear this in mind. Mariupol is one of the worst war crimes of the twenty-first century."'

Akhmetov has pledged to rebuild Mariupol, whatever it takes. And it will take a lot. Metinvest has ceased all production and come to an agreement with various creditors. It employed 35,000 people in Mariupol. 'Of these,' CEO Yuriy Ryzhenkov told *NV Business* in September 2022, 'about half have made contact with the group. Most of them have left for Ukrainian-controlled territory. Unfortunately, currently, we have no contact with the other half.' Ryzhenkov also estimated that steel products with a value of more than $150 million were stolen from the port by Russian invaders. So Akhmetov really will have to start again. 'He could live anywhere in the world that he wants to,' says Srna with no little admiration, 'but he [has decided] he won't leave Ukraine.'

Ready to start again, whenever the end of all this might be. Akhmetov had built Shakhtar from the ground up once. Doing it again would be an almighty challenge but in the meantime, it would take all his – and his trusted staff's – considerable ability to keep it all going.

2

The Barcelona Of The East

The first time is easy to remember. It was 3 October 2007, on a pleasant early autumn evening in Lisbon. Not balmy, but certainly no more than light sweater weather on the cusp of the city's Segunda Circular. The football was such, though, that it was easy to feel a remnant of summer headiness.

Shakhtar had arrived at Estádio da Luz, an atmospheric arena even when only two-thirds full, to face Benfica, a traditional giant of the European game, in the Champions League. It was a partisan backdrop, marginally offset by a cluster of just under a thousand visiting supporters boxed off high in the south-west corner; a number boosted by blue-and-yellow flag-waving locals, with a significant swathe of Ukrainians moving to Portugal to live and work at the time, often in construction.

An opening stanza of the match that flitted from one end to

the other settled into Ukrainian poise and passive domination, with the visitors bagging the decisive (and only) goal of the game just before half-time. It was, in retrospect, typically Shakhtaresque. Brazilian midfielder Jádson smashed the ball into the net above two defenders hurriedly stationing themselves on the goal-line, after his compatriot Fernandinho drew the goalkeeper, Quim, and squared it to his teammate.

That was my first time seeing Shakhtar Donetsk in the flesh and looking back at the footage now it is familiar yet other-worldly, a pattern of play at once expansive and yet deliciously simple. Once Benfica lost the ball in midfield Shakhtar moved with stealth and speed. Răzvan Raţ charged from the left into the sort of underlapping run that would become increasingly popular among full-backs in subsequent years, ferried it to Fernandinho, and the midfielder could easily have shot himself, as many would have. Instead, in synergy with his team, he knew the extra pass made the goal a near inevitability. You watched it unfolding in the Champions League but equally it looked like the work of a highly accomplished five-a-side team, the sort that is not just talented but whose players know each other like the back of their own hands, who leave you gasping gritty air and struggling to compose yourself and to recalibrate your thoughts. Pass, pass, pass, extra pass, goal, all seemingly in the blink of an eye, and all on their own very specific terms.

Over a decade later, in a portacabin on a building site in south-west London, the face of Joe Palmer, by then the chief executive of AFC Wimbledon, lit up at the mention of Shakhtar's helter-skelter 3–3 draw at Benfica in the Europa

League the night before. The result saw them through to the competition's last 16, after they found a way back from 3–1 down. 'That was the old Shakhtar,' smiled Shakhtar's former Executive Director of Strategy, Commerce and Marketing, citing their movement of the ball, their brightness, their adventure. The image of it was enough to momentarily lift the weight of grey skies and a prodigious workload, a welcome nod to good times in the past, running down a thread from 2007 and leading to 2020.

He was right. It really was the old Shakhtar. When Covid-19 interrupted the season a few short weeks after we spoke on the site – almost five months elapsed between the two legs of the club's round of 16 tie against Wolfsburg, in Lower Saxony and Kyiv respectively, which had been the reward for beating Benfica – it turned football, as well as the world at large, upside down. Perhaps modern Shakhtar, used to carrying on regardless through a slew of intolerable disruption, were better equipped than most to deal with it.

Either way, the club ended up doing what it always did – succeeding. When the Europa League reconvened in a final 8 format in one place, mirroring the Champions League, in August (while the senior competition was self-contained in Lisbon, the Europa League final stages were held in north-west Germany between Gelsenkirchen, Düsseldorf and Duisburg), Shakhtar were there, present and correct. After thumping a fellow European perennial in Basel in the Gelsenkirchen quarter-final, they ran out of steam against Inter in the last four, eventually ceding 5–0 in Düsseldorf.

No matter. It had been a good run, and a second Europa

League semi-final in four seasons, a remarkable achievement for a club without a home to call its own. Maybe even a bigger achievement than the UEFA Cup victory of 2009, making Shakhtar only the second Ukrainian club to win a European trophy after Dynamo Kyiv and the only one to do so since the break-up of the Soviet Union? 'Actually yes,' says Sergei Palkin, when posed the question. 'We can say when we go through in the Champions League under [Paulo] Fonseca [to the round of 16 in 2017–18], and then to the [Europa] semi-finals, that's the biggest.'

Just how astonishing Shakhtar's ability to do that was – to maintain a dynasty in the most unforgiving of circumstances – will probably only truly be absorbed in the fullness of time. The groundwork Rinat Akhmetov, Sergei Palkin, Mircea Lucescu and the rest laid set a standard so beyond previous expectations for an eastern European club post-1992, when *perestroika* and *glasnost* met the beginnings of serious commercialisation of the European game, that much of their latter-day successes are wrongly assumed and under-appreciated, a continuation of the reputation and the name. Shakhtar just doing what they always do.

Shakhtar was formed in 1936 but named Stakhanovets at the time, after the prevailing Stakhanovite cultural movement. Alexei Stakhanov, a miner and Soviet poster boy for productivity, lent his name to the movement in the 1930s. He was born in Izmalkovsky District (then Lugovaya) in Russia, but became famous for his mining work in Donbas. The team did exactly what it said on the tin. A team of pitmen. Even when, in 1946, the name was changed to Shakhtar (literally, 'Miner'), that connection was retained. The origins, and the links to home, loom large.

Local and regional pride meant everything in Soviet times in particular, when individualities were ignored in favour of the wider collective. Back then, Shakhtar were a relative minnow, not only trailing behind the Muscovite giants of Spartak, Dynamo and CSKA that dominated the Soviet Top League, but also Dynamo Kyiv – thirteen-time champions between 1961 and 1990, more than any of the big three from Moscow (Spartak, CSKA and Dinamo) managed. The Dynamo society of multi-discipline sport clubs was created in 1923 with branches all over the Soviet Union and, post-World War Two, in other Eastern Bloc countries. The legacy of this is apparent in Romania's Dinamo Bucharest or the former East Germany's Dynamo Dresden, for example. In the post-war Soviet Union, members of Dynamo clubs tended to be from the MVD, the Ministry of Internal Affairs, or the KGB, the Committee for State Security.

Kyiv had particular significance for the Soviet Union, its rich black soil intensively farmed and its production of wheat, oil and sunflowers helping to make it 'the breadbasket of Europe,' as the *Financial Times* coined with familiarity in a report on the country's agriculture in April 2022. Kyiv became the capital of Soviet Ukraine in 1934 and its natural resources made it a target for Nazi colonisers shortly after and, thus, a focus of tragedy and atrocity.

As Kyiv recovered after the war, Dynamo had renown far beyond the Soviet Union, latterly thanks to the stewardship of groundbreaking coach Valeriy Lobanovskyi (who had represented both Dynamo and Shakhtar in his playing days as an imaginative winger). An educated man with an analytical mind, Lobanovskyi rewrote the rule book, coupling a versatile, pressing-led game with high standards of fitness and diet expected of his team to meet his tactical demands. It was aided by scientific and statistical support and facilities from a team of experts that the likes of Shakhtar could only dream of. In the two of his three spells in charge of Dynamo that fell in the Soviet era, Lobanovskyi guided the club to eight Soviet championship titles, six Soviet Cups and two European Cup Winners' Cups. Oleg Blokhin (1975) and Igor Belanov (1986) both won the Ballon d'Or under his tutelage.

For Shakhtar it was comparatively slim pickings. There were a couple of second-place finishes in the Soviet Top League and a run deep into the European Cup Winners' Cup in 1984, before a goal by Porto striker Mickey Walsh five minutes after coming on as a substitute in Donetsk ousted Shakhtar at the quarter-final stage. So it was the Portuguese club who eventually made it to a first European final. Walsh went on to smash in a memorable winner for the Republic of Ireland against the Soviet Union in a World Cup qualifier at Dublin's Lansdowne Road later that year.

As the 1980s came to an end and momentum gathered around a Ukrainian independence movement, Dynamo would regularly wear shirts in the yellow and blue of Ukraine as an alternative to the club's traditional white. Dynamo's 2022–23 third kit, yellow with blue collar and trim around the sleeves, pays germane homage to this.

After independence in 1991, everything changed. Ukraine declared itself an independent nation in August and the Soviet

Union ceased to be in December. The structure of the new Vyshcha Liha, the first post-Soviet football championship in Ukraine, was agreed on 10 September 1991 by a Football Federation of Ukraine (FFU, now known as Ukraine Association of Football, or UAF) committee. It wasn't simple. About fifty different options for structuring Ukrainian club football were put forward, Vladimir Mylenko wrote on *football.ua* in 2010. Eventually, a format was agreed by which nineteen teams were invited to take part: the six 'biggest' clubs from the Soviet Top League, including Dynamo and Shakhtar, and a clutch of others from the all-Ukrainian competitions. The twentieth spot was claimed by FC Temp Shepetivka after they won November 1991's two-legged Ukrainian Cup final against Veres – the first post-independence, all-Ukrainian competition.

The teams were organised into two parallel groups of ten, with the winners of each group facing each other in a championship final. It ran from March to June, establishing an independent competition before the league switched to the autumn–winter–spring format favoured by most of Europe's major leagues for 1992–93, which began on 15 August 1992, with a single league of sixteen teams playing a more traditional double round-robin.

The league, then, was different, and so were Shakhtar. They would only finish outside the top four once from the independent league's inception onwards – finishing tenth in 1995–96, a chaotic and unprecedented season for the club. The Donetsk-born businessman Akhat Bragin had become the club's first president shortly after independence, but his era came to a dramatic and shocking end on Sunday 15 October

1995. Shakhtar were at home to Tavriya and just a few minutes after kick-off, a bomb was remotely detonated in the Central Stadium Shakhtar, instantly killing Bragin, his brother, several bodyguards and a female server. A huge plume of smoke rose from the west stand amid scenes of chaos and panic. The power of the explosion was such that 'eyewitnesses claim that the remains were scattered in a radius of 30 metres,' according to BBC Ukraine's Lina Kushch at the time.

It was the culmination of several attempts on the life of 'Alik the Greek' as he became a target for rival business clans in Donetsk in a wild, anarchic and frequently criminal post-Soviet economic landscape. His wife and children seldom ventured beyond the confines of the fenced-off Lux Hotel on the outskirts of the city, and he was ferried around in an armour-plated Mercedes.

Out of this most horrifying of scenarios, modern Shakhtar was born. Rinat Akhmetov was Bragin's friend and associate and could easily have been there with him when the explosion went off. He missed it by a whisker, and when the post-Bragin landscape settled, it was Akhmetov who succeeded him as club president and as controller of the coal mines and steel mills that had been the main source of Bragin's wealth. This set Akhmetov on his way to becoming Ukraine's richest man.

Time passed without a conclusion to the case; ex-police officer Vyacheslav Synenko, who had left Donetsk for Greece in 1999, was implicated by the confession of a gang member. After an international warrant was issued for his arrest, Synenko was apprehended in March 2004 in Athens, where he was working as a house painter. Synenko was sentenced to life in prison in 2005 after being extradited back to Ukraine, but the conviction was later overturned on appeal.

So rumour and insinuation about Akhmetov, and his progression up the food chain after Bragin's death, were allowed to fill the vacuum created by the lack of closure. He is not a widely quoted public figure outside his own channels, but he addressed the accusations of his involvement in Bragin's death when speaking to the *Kyiv Post* in December 2022. Akhmetov called the implication 'a lie, and this lie causes me great pain.'

He recounted the scenario from 1995, and what a near-miss it had been for him. 'Akhat and I were five minutes late for the match,' Akhmetov recalled. 'He jumped out of the car and ran to the stadium without waiting for me. The explosion was about five seconds later, no more. It thundered as soon as I opened the door of my car. When your best friend dies in front of your eyes, and you realise that [you missed] your death [by] five seconds, and after that you are accused of something, it is very painful and unfair.' He finished his statement in clear, emphatic fashion: 'I have never been associated with any criminal organisations. I have never been prosecuted, and no criminal charges have been filed against me.'

What is undisputed is that the president's influence on modern-day Shakhtar pervades every aspect of the club, and it stretches far beyond the financial. The money is no small thing, of course. Akhmetov currently covers huge losses that the club incurs as well as funding various humanitarian programmes, and he remains by far Ukraine's biggest taxpayer. As well as his personal liabilities, his umbrella holding company System

Capital Management (SCM, a familiar Shakhtar shirt sponsor from down the years in the Champions League) paid over UAH 73 billion (£1.67 billion) in tax in 2022 despite the war, according to Ukraine's Interfax news agency.

Before the conflict, the whole world could see where the money was going. It was right there on the pitch building the team of his – and many others' – dreams, with a clutch of glamorous talent from Brazil making its way to Donbas. When we think of Shakhtar's Brazilian influence we think of Mircea Lucescu, the much-loved Romanian coach who arrived at Shakhtar in May 2004 after a four-year spell in Turkey, firstly with Galatasaray and then with Beşiktaş.

A polyglot who speaks fluent Portuguese, Lucescu's vision and personnel skills laid the groundwork for the perfect storm as Shakhtar sought to build something spectacular on the pitch. He had been adored in Turkey and his impact on Shakhtar was stellar, with the team taking the step to the next level and doing something which had historically seemed impossible – they put Dynamo Kyiv in the shade. The Italian Nevio Scala, famed for his time at Parma and Borussia Dortmund, had broken through the glass ceiling by guiding Shakhtar to a first league title in 2002, but establishing domination would need more than eye-catching names. It would need a bold philosophy and a striking image all of their own.

In the decade after Lucescu arrived, Shakhtar won eight Ukrainian Premier League titles, five Ukrainian Cups, seven Ukrainian Super Cups and that historic UEFA Cup. He won the last of those Ukrainian Cups in 2016, with Shakhtar beating

Zorya Luhansk 2–0 in the final, which was Lucescu's curtain call after a twelve-year period in charge.

They also captured the imagination beyond the borders of Ukraine with their invention and swagger. While Dynamo continued to lean mainly on Ukrainian players supplemented with a few choice foreign imports, Shakhtar were spectacularly exotic. After Lucescu was installed the pace of demographic change was quick. He took charge of the Ukrainian Cup final on 30 May 2004, thirteen days after his appointment, and his starting line-up for the 2–0 win over Dnipro contained six Ukrainians, three Romanians, a Pole and a Croatian (Brandão, the sole Brazilian, was on the bench). For the following year's showpiece, in which the holders were deposed by Dynamo after a tight final, the eleven contained two Brazilians, Matuzalém and Brandão, with two more on the bench, Jádson and Elano. The team that won the historic UEFA Cup in Istanbul four years later, meanwhile, was replete with five Brazilians and only three Ukrainians.

The beginnings of the Brazilian enclave certainly predated Lucescu. Brandão, the towering centre-forward, was the first to arrive in 2002. He would serve the club for six-and-a-half seasons, becoming a prolific scorer in domestic and continental competitions, before leaving for Olympique de Marseille in January 2009. Yet the acceleration of the programme, and of Akhmetov's dream made flesh, was real under Lucescu. And every successful coach needs not just support, but a go-between. Lucescu got to know Franck Henouda in Turkey, when the former was coach of Galatasaray and the latter was involved in the deal to bring in striker Mário Jardel – the scorer of a phenomenal 170 goals in 175 games for FC Porto before making the move to Istanbul – to beef up his side for a Champions League campaign, having inherited a UEFA Cup-winning side from Fatih Terim. The transfer was a typical piece of Henouda business.

Having spent his twenties working for Club Med, Henouda made contacts in Paris and Brazil, and had the idea of exporting players from the latter to the former. Harvesting young talents from Brazil, he aimed to make the powerhouses of Paris Saint-Germain, Marseille and Bordeaux their destinations. Then, in 1998, a golden opportunity fell into Henouda's lap which changed his destiny. Brazil's World Cup-winning goalkeeper from 1994, Claudio Taffarel, was scheduled to sign for PSG, but when that fell though, Henouda was able to set him up with a move to Galatasaray instead. It represented a fork in the road. 'From there,' Henouda told *Footballski*'s Pierre Vuillemot in September 2015, 'I started to explore, and I brought quite a few Brazilians into Turkey.'

The pair stayed in touch. Lucescu was just getting his feet under the table when he enlisted Henouda's help for the team he aimed to build. He would get young Brazilians on board who were easier to mould and ambitious to grab an opportunity in Europe. Sticking with players of the same nationality wasn't a coincidence or an obsession with a particular strand of football culture. It aimed to create an instantly coherent blend, with little room for cultural or linguistic misunderstanding. The eventual result was that Shakhtar had a personality that had never before been seen in Ukrainian football. Yet if the experienced coach was the shepherd of the project, it stemmed directly from the passion of the president, according to Sergei Palkin. 'If we're talking about the philosophy of our club, the strategy of our club, the sport side of it,' he emphasises, 'the key person who changed everything was the president.'

'Originally,' he continues, 'he very much likes attacking football. If he could win every game but without playing attractive football, he wouldn't. So that's why we went into the Brazilian market. And it was the president who went and got Lucescu, because he also likes these players very much and . . . can I just take this?' As if by magic, at that moment Akhmetov calls Palkin for his daily update. As I discover over the coming weeks and months, this is a common occurrence; you'll be deep in conversation with somebody connected to Shakhtar, and the president will call them. Even now, with the realignment of priorities and life taking over, Akhmetov is intimately involved with club business. His investment on a financial level is undeniable, but his employees frame him as a visionary, not just a provider of means. Palkin finishes up his conversation with Akhmetov, comes back to me and apologises. 'It's like I said to you, he calls me every day.'

Darijo Srna concurs. Some presidents have an interest, some a need to be heard and to intervene. With Akhmetov, it was beyond enthusiasm, and more of an obsession. In a report for ESPN in 2015, Brett Forrest wrote that an SCM employee told him that Akhmetov would 'refuse to discuss' company business on matchdays, such was his focus. The sense was that everything else in SCM would have to take its place in the queue, behind Shakhtar. So rather than Lucescu unilaterally imposing his own vision of the game, ingrained in him by his formative years as a player back home in Romania and cultivated over an itinerant career, he was selected with Akhmetov's idea of how things should be mapped out in mind.

For Srna, who arrived from Hajduk Split as a midfielder, Akhmetov's influence on how he developed on the pitch, and how his career unfolded, was explicit. The president suggested to him that his future was at right-back, a position he had played 'a couple of times' for Hajduk and Croatia, 'but with a back three,' so more as a wing-back. 'As part of a four, it's very, very different. At the beginning I was not so happy,' he says from beneath an arched eyebrow.

'The president said to me, "Darijo, you are playing midfield but I could buy another hundred midfielders like you. But a right-back like you? I could only find two or three in Europe." And that was the main point for me. I had a lot of problems defensively at the beginning but for me, the best form of defence is attack, and that was the motto in my head.' Casting Srna (at least ostensibly) as a defender was really just another way for this voracious team to get another attacking player on the pitch. 'Probably 65–70 per cent of the games, I was in attack,' Srna shrugs. 'If you look at the full-backs we bought since, it's always thinking about attack, because we play this kind of football.'

That kind of football was developing quickly. 'We all grew up together,' Srna says of this heavily South American-flavoured team. He hints that maybe if he hadn't been redeployed, he might have struggled to find a spot in midfield. Instead, the new credo propelled him to greater heights. 'When you're surrounded by amazing players,' he says without a hint of arrogance, 'that's when you start to become an amazing player.

'José Mourinho has a different style than us but Lucescu, [Roberto] De Zerbi have our style. [Paulo] Fonseca has our style. We are choosing typical coaches for our style of the game.' Lucescu wanted everyone to be able to play so even the defenders he chose, like Yaroslav Rakitskyi, were assured and cultured on the ball. 'And he's one of only two defenders because the full-back . . . ' Srna makes a whipping hand motion of them flying off into the middle distance, as if taken by the joy of being part of it all over again. Technical excellence was a given but even if Shakhtar's game was based on territorial domination, there would be no sterile possession. Incision was always at the forefront of the mind, even if that might sometimes be risk-inherent. Everyone was involved. Fernandinho, for example, is most widely celebrated as the key defensive midfielder in his time at Manchester City. At Shakhtar he was wild and free, a raging bull of a midfielder, reminiscent of a young Roy Keane at Nottingham Forest, before he went to Manchester United and embraced a similar sort of caretaker role as Fernandinho later would in the blue half of the city. 'We're so open,' remembers Srna. 'We play such offensive football and with this, we get amazing results.'

The pinnacle of those results was in spring 2009 on the way to the UEFA Cup, a momentous first European trophy for the club. Before the final was the second leg of the semi, a titanic step in itself – for Shakhtar beat Dynamo in an all-Ukrainian tie not just to reach the Istanbul final, but to show the world that more than one club spoke for Ukraine and its football. Donetsk's Olimpiyskiy was packed to its 24,300-capacity, the fans seemingly all feverishly waving the orange club flags left on their seats. It was some atmosphere.

'It was . . . ' He struggles to find the right adjective. Incredible? 'Yes.' When Ilsinho drifted in from the right, deftly steered the ball inside Dynamo defender Ayila Yussuf and placed his left-footed shot around Stanislav Bogush with conviction, it was the eighty-ninth minute and the ultimate exclamation point. That winning goal, and that night, was the moment not just when Shakhtar showed the world that they had the upper hand on Dynamo. 'For us at the time,' says Srna, 'it was more important to beat Dynamo than it was to win the final. But when you arrive in the final – they only ever remember who won the final. And if we had lost against Werder, we didn't do anything.' They also showed, with that fervent stadium fit to burst, where they were going. They needed to move up to the next stage, to go bigger and better. 'They were already building the new stadium across the way,' Srna remembers. 'I think it was destiny that we went into the new stadium with the UEFA Cup.'

It had been a tie that gripped Ukrainian football from the beginning. The first leg in Kyiv had been a struggle after Dmytro Chyhrynskyi's own goal gave the hosts the lead. 'It had been a very tough match,' remembers Lucescu, '[especially when] they scored the first goal. Fernandinho, he managed to make it 1–1 and get us a draw.' The midfielder slid in from close range after Willian's cross – not a typically easy-on-the-eye Shakhtar goal, but worth its weight in gold. 'That's incredibly [important], because I'm sure that if we didn't win this tie,

Dynamo Kyiv could have also won [the UEFA Cup],' Lucescu says, 'because they had a very good team in that period. They had big players.' Ilsinho's goal, according to Lucescu, was a fork in the road for the club. 'We were at the beginning of our career in Europe,' he says. 'The interest in what we did was incredible on the streets of the town, but the stadium was not [always] full. But we did it without experienced players. They managed to play at this level because they trained very well and they became a very good team playing very good football, spectacular football. Because of this, we got attention from everywhere in Europe. Arriving at such a high level in Europe was very difficult, but we succeeded.'

The final itself was almost a Shakhtar promotional film, set perfectly for them to show their swagger to anybody out there not already aware of it. Against Thomas Schaaf's Werder Bremen, equally brave in their approach if a little diminished from their sensational double-winning side of 2004, the game to-ed and fro-ed at a dizzying speed. It was replete with the sort of pleasure that the tension of a final often prohibits. We were glad to get thirty minutes extra, with the surrounds of Fenerbahçe's iconic Şükrü Saracoğlu Stadium giving the occasion an extra mania. 'It's incredible,' enthuses Lucescu, '[even if] we didn't play at the Galatasaray stadium. Turkish supporters are incredible, and they helped us very much during this final.' Still hugely popular in Istanbul from his time on the European side of the city, catching up with familiar company had a price. 'I bought about five hundred tickets to give to my friends in Istanbul,' he laughs. Shakhtar needed the extra support, with 'the stadium full and [with] so many Werder Bremen supporters. But the others, Turkish and Ukrainian, were with Shakhtar. We had a very good year.'

It was remarkable to get that far after a challenging opening to the season – one that might have seen coaches with less credit in the bank than Lucescu lose their jobs. The team managed just one win in their first nine games. 'We started badly in the championship because we made some transfers that didn't immediately work out,' he concedes, 'but we did very well in the Champions League. We lost against Barcelona when they didn't really play fair with us,' – Lucescu rarely lets a previous perceived slight go, even years down the line – 'as it was 1–0 for us after eighty-five minutes.' Then Yevhen Seleznyov went down with an apparent head injury. 'We put the ball out,' says Lucescu, still indignant, 'but they didn't give it back.' Not only that, but the visitors carried on the game without Seleznyov having received any treatment. As Lionel Messi tapped in the equaliser at the back post, three Shakhtar defenders were pointing to Barça to put the ball out.

Lucescu was, by his own admission, incandescent with rage. 'It's not possible,' he insists. 'Even with it being the beginning of [Pep] Guardiola's coaching career.' He did at least get the last word in the sixth and final group game at Camp Nou. 'After, we won the second match in December in Barcelona, 3–2,' he smiles, 'and carried on in Europe into springtime.' That gave Shakhtar the platform to thrive after dropping down to the UEFA Cup. It had not been easy getting past Tottenham Hotspur, CSKA Moscow and Marseille on the way to the last four confrontation with Dynamo.

In Istanbul Luiz Adriano exchanged goals with Werder Bremen's Naldo, a powerful free-kick with which Shakhtar goalkeeper Andriy Pyatov might have done better, so the game went to extra time. When the indefatigable Srna burst down the right for the umpteenth time, seven minutes into the first period of the extra thirty, his cross found Jádson. The busy midfielder sidefooted towards the corner, it slipped through Tim Wiese's grasp, and Shakhtar had their trophy.

Yuri Sviridov, now Shakhtar's director of communications but yet to start work at the club at the time, had flown over from London for the game as a fan. He describes it as 'one of the best moments of my life.' If edging Dynamo in the semi had been hugely satisfying, this, he believed, was where the bragging rights really were. 'We had started chasing them,' he reflects, '[and] we won a championship for the first time in 2002. We became like a real competitor for them, but the only way in which we were different from them [was] we hadn't won an international trophy. Dynamo had two Cup Winners' Cups and a UEFA Super Cup in '75, and '86. We needed this just to become equal to them on an international stage. And twentieth of May is [the] day when it happened in 2009. And I think it's one of the most crucial days in our history.' It was the recognition of what they'd built, the growth of their philosophy and it also gave Shakhtar their next step; access to that August's UEFA Super Cup, where the UEFA Cup winners would face the Champions League winners – none other than Barcelona.

The Barcelona connection is important. In the years following Guardiola's appointment as coach they leapt in global profile. A club that didn't become European champions for the first time until 1992 was the first name on the lips of football fans two decades later. Why? It was remarkable in that it was based on style and philosophy as much as it was substance and silverware.

Real Madrid had an advantage from way back, with their fabled president Santiago Bernabéu one of the key figures behind the establishment of the European Cup in the 1950s. His club then went on to lift the first five editions, before Benfica finally broke the hegemony in 1961. Barcelona were the losing finalists on that occasion, but wouldn't reach another one for twenty-five years, when Terry Venables's team lost on penalties to Steaua Bucharest in Sevilla's Ramón Sánchez Pizjuan Stadium. It is harder to think of a sounder foundation to be Europe's preeminent club.

For Barcelona, it was always about philosophy (like Shakhtar under Akhmetov) and a large part of that was about a particular ethos: *Mes que un club*, the phrase which is still written into the seats in Camp Nou's east stand. Barça was never just about the trophies but the idea of what the club represented. That it stood for Catalonia and its sense of self, though, had limited exportability. Johan Cruyff and his establishment of what the club meant on the field changed things. He respected and honoured the club's traditions (even naming his son Jordi after the region's patron saint) but was, with his former Ajax coach Rinus Michels, largely responsible for the aesthetics that made FC Barcelona something to believe in on the pitch as well as off it.

The 2009 UEFA Super Cup brought the masters and apprentices face to face. That Shakhtar and Barça met in

Monaco – back in the days when the Super Cup was the jewel in the crown of a one-venue, European football season curtain-raiser, a gala week – was more than the normal ceremonial obligation of Champions League winners versus UEFA Cup winners. It was a barometer of exactly what was happening at the cutting edge of the European game. If the casual fan was unaware of what linked the two beforehand, it was made explicit on the night.

Lucescu had been here before. His first trophy at Galatasaray was the UEFA Super Cup, won in August 2000 against Real Madrid thanks to a Jardel brace, with the winner an extra time golden goal. Yet if the Madrid side that Lucescu faced was a formidable opponent in name, they were not exactly the greatest side ever to don the famous white. Despite brushing domestic competitors Valencia aside in the Champions League final in Paris that spring, they had finished a miserable fifth in La Liga, with Deportivo La Coruña winning a first championship. They needed the intervention of UEFA and the RFEF (*Real Federacion Española de Fútbol*) to allow them to defend their trophy, bumping fourth-placed finishers Real Zaragoza down into the UEFA Cup.

With Florentino Pérez taking over as president from Lorenzo Sanz that very summer, the first incarnation of the *galácticos* was only just taking shape. Luis Figo arrived that summer in a blockbuster transfer that was Pérez's central election promise, and the Portuguese made his Real Madrid debut against Lucescu's Galatasaray in Monaco. Zinedine Zidane would not arrive until 2001, Ronaldo made the move to the Spanish capital directly after firing Brazil to the

World Cup in 2002 and David Beckham rejected Barcelona to move to the Bernabéu in 2003. So the version that Lucescu's Galatasaray faced were noble opposition, but far from the full manifestation. More *galáctiños*, perhaps.

The Barcelona that Lucescu's team lined up against nine years later were wolves in wolves' clothing, not that of sheep. They were the real deal and then some, a side who even then brimmed with history-making resonance. Their line-up in Monaco in 2009 could be named blindfold by many. Valdés; Dani Alves, Puyol, Piqué, Abidal; Yaya Touré, Xavi, Keita; Messi, Henry, Ibrahimović. Shakhtar, however, were not cowed.

'We tried to play our football, even against them,' Srna points with his index finger. 'That's the point.' Lucescu is even more emphatic about it. 'We deserved to win,' he told UEFA's Eugene Ravdin in 2016. 'But the most important thing for us was that every year Shakhtar managed to reach the same high level of performance. We never went below that level.'

'We respect Barcelona so much and they respect us as well,' continues Srna. 'After that I spoke with Pep at Manchester City – he had wanted to bring me to Bayern Munich, so I spoke to him a couple of times – and he really fell in love with Shakhtar.' It's not hard to imagine, bearing in mind Guardiola's almost-childlike, obsessive instinct for the game at its beautiful best. 'With the style, with the players,' Srna says as he lists the qualities that drew the then-Barça coach in. 'He bought two players from Shakhtar for himself – Fernandinho and Douglas Costa. We [Shakhtar and Barcelona] are moving in the same direction of how football must be.'

The Super Cup was often seen as a glorified exhibition

match, a clause to be fulfilled before the start of the European season, the support band that must be endured before the headliners. Not for Shakhtar. It was their opportunity to trade blows with the best. 'It was a very difficult game for us because we were playing one of the best teams in the history of football. We conceded a goal two minutes before the end, by Pedro, and . . . ' – his eyes widen ever so slightly and he starts to list the stars, drumming his hand off the table as he delivers each one of the legends – 'Ibrahimović, Xavi, Dani Alves, Keita, Piqué, Puyol . . . an amazing game. But we were proud we played this Super Cup in Monaco. We were so close but anyway, it was a huge experience for us and a huge step forward for us.'

Does Srna think Guardiola was surprised by just how good Shakhtar were? 'No. Guardiola [already] respected us a lot, because even before that we beat them in Camp Nou 3–2, we lost 2–1 in Donetsk and [further back in 2004] we beat them 2–0 in Donetsk when Messi played his first [Champions League] game, at Olimpiyskiy Stadium.' He takes a half-pause of the rapid-fire replay in his head for us both to absorb the fact, a pleasing one. 'Messi played his first game in the Champions League against Shakhtar. There's some sort of connection there.'

That connection is real, rather than just perceived. It goes beyond style and into needing to stand for a certain set of football values, where artistic merit is at least as important as results. Not just the idea that controlling the process will eventually lead to tangible success, but that the process itself is something to be aspired to and celebrated. It was later on, after Shakhtar had created the strong sense of self which made them an easily identifiable part of elite European football's culture, that this need for a bespoke, house style came to be seen as a commercial necessity, rather than just something which was aesthetically desirable. In Martí Perarnau's 2014 book *Pep Confidential*, a first-hand insight into Guardiola's first season at Bayern Munich, it is acknowledged that the premier brand in German football needed something more to truly conquer the world at large; it needed to establish a Bayern brand of football, and the trilogy of coaches starting with the Dutchman Louis van Gaal, continuing with Jupp Heynckes and ending with Guardiola himself, would lead them to that holy grail.

It was not initially planned like that at Shakhtar; it was more organic. 'Everything started from taste, football taste but yes, from there we started to build our strategies,' Palkin confirms. 'We have what we have [today] because of this. Because of this we now know how to buy and sell talent. We are not changing this. Of course, the war influences things because not everybody wants to come. If you're talking about foreigners, it's difficult to bring them to Ukraine in this moment.'

Overseeing the construction of a new stadium four hundred yards away from the loved but tired old counterpart AFC Wimbledon had left as a top-flight club in 1991 was a tiring but satisfying task. It was also very on-brand for Palmer, who looked to approach challenging puzzles from different angles. Before pitching up in EFL League One to guide Wimbledon back to their spiritual home at Plough Lane, he had worked at Sheffield Wednesday. He had streamlined their commercial operation, experimenting with the club producing their own kit to drive down consumer prices and simultaneously raise profit margins. Before that, he had spent five years in Ukraine, trying to help close the gap between the country and western Europe off the pitch, as Lucescu and the team had on it.

Palmer's role for Shakhtar had been different to his subsequent ones in English football, and not just in terms of scale. In 2009 he was arriving at a club with one foot already in a new dimension, buzzing with excitement and possibility having just moved into the state-of-the-art Donbass Arena on the back of winning that first European trophy. Palmer had had his horizons broadened by Sviridov, then studying international sports marketing at Birkbeck, a research wing of the University of London, based in the city's Bloomsbury district. The pair aimed to set up a sports marketing company together, and they travelled to Ukraine with the aim of exporting business there. In their discussions with various clubs it was recognised that Shakhtar needed some out-of-region help in presenting their burgeoning brand, with their on-pitch reputation spreading like wildfire. Palmer took a job there and Sviridov, a Donetsk native and a Shakhtar fan, returned to work at the club the following year. 'It was a huge responsibility,' Sviridov says. 'It was my club and I didn't want to fail.'

What Palmer wasn't prepared for was the sheer scale of the Shakhtar operation, as he detailed when talking to me for the *Football Ramble*'s *Ramble Meets* in 2019. 'In terms of full-time staff you're talking 450 people,' he said, 'which is five times more than most football clubs. One of the best training bases in Europe, one of the best stadiums in Europe, but no sense of really how to articulate it.'

Yet they realised they needed to, or the president did. 'Akhmetov was the perfect owner in that sense,' Palmer nodded. 'Often finding foreign strategists to take his businesses to the next level.' It became a virtuous circle. That foreign talent not only helped to build the brand, the concept, the extension of the soul, but it helped to solidify an identity that would attract further foreign talent, even when means were diminished and when life was harder.

The image on the pitch is what sold the concept to Roberto De Zerbi. The by-now traditional Shakhtar approach synced with his strong ideas on the game in terms of a front-foot attitude and pushed him to accept the head coach's job in 2021, replacing Luis Castro. It was a new dawn on both sides. For De Zerbi, it was a first post outside of Italy – he had spent most of his playing days back home too, save a couple of years in Romania with Cluj towards the backend of his career – and not in one of Europe's most visible leagues like France, one of the nations from which he attracted interest. For Shakhtar, it was a break from the stream of *lusofone* (Portuguese-speaking) coaches that followed Lucescu, to aid communication and cultural click with the large Brazilian portion of the dressing room. It was brave. They were betting on tactics trumping talking, in the short term at least. Both parties were making a leap of faith.

Not that De Zerbi was a stranger to Shakhtar's guiding on-pitch principles. His teams were always bold, attacking and liked to have the ball, a clear prerequisite with his new team.

At Sassuolo – where his role in the development of players including Domenico Berardi, Manuel Locatelli and Giacomo Raspadori, all of whom contributed to Italy's memorable Euro 2020 win – De Zerbi made himself attractive to a lot of clubs. His ability to augment players' value was certainly something that chimed with modern Shakhtar.

The connection was there too with Guardiola, who had briefly played in Brescia, De Zerbi's hometown, towards the end of his playing career. Like the Catalan coach, De Zerbi was a disciple of Marcelo Bielsa, the iconic Argentinian tactician with a poet's heart and a scientist's eye, who demanded a Stakhanovite work ethic. Press, man-to-man mark and attack – always. When De Zerbi was fired by Palermo in 2016 he got a message to Bielsa, asking him if he could come to northern France and observe some of the old master's training sessions at Lille. He was welcomed with open arms.

Bielsa was hardly at the apex of his storied career at the time. He was let go after just thirteen league games in charge amid chaotic scenes, with his expensively assembled side struggling at the foot of the table and myriad stories in the French media of poor discipline within the squad (the relationship between Bielsa and Lille would end up in the courts, with the coach claiming almost €20 million in compensation for what he claimed was unfair dismissal). But the door had been opened and an imagination had been fired.

You imagine peak Srna would have loved the buccaneering of playing in one of De Zerbi's better sides. When it became clear the coach was going to leave Emilia-Romagna, there was interest from all over Europe – from elsewhere in Italy but also France (where Lyon were particularly keen) and England. Yet straight away, there was an acquiesce between the Italian coach and the by-then deposed Ukrainian champions. 'The first main point in common was the style of play, which goes through the players,' De Zerbi says from his office at Brighton and Hove Albion's training centre in Lancing, 'and Shakhtar's players were very close to my idea of football. It was the same ten years ago when Willian, Douglas Costa, Fred, Fernandinho were playing in Shakhtar.' If Shakhtar were determined to win the race for De Zerbi, convinced of his suitability, it quickly became clear that the feeling was reciprocated. De Zerbi was totally sold on the president, and remains so. '[Shakhtar's] identity goes on and on,' De Zerbi continues, 'because Rinat Akhmetov is a real football expert. He loves to see Shakhtar winning but more than that he loves to see Shakhtar playing good football. That was exactly the point in common we found straight away.'

Despite winning the Ukrainian Super Cup, De Zerbi never quite got it going for Shakhtar in Europe in his all-too-brief, war-truncated spell in charge. 'I think we deserved more points,' he says of his group stage campaign in which they came mightily close to beating his countrymen from Inter. It continued a theme that sometimes plays on Srna's mind. 'We didn't have any luck in the Champions League,' he ponders.

It wasn't just in the Champions League that they were lacking a rabbit's foot. In 2007, two years before they finally got their hands on the UEFA Cup, they were a whisker away from knocking out holders Sevilla in the round of 16. The Andalusians' goalkeeper, Andrés Palop, headed in a Dani

Alves corner to equalise in the last of four minutes of stoppage time at the Olimpiyskiy, and Sevilla went on to win in extra time on their way to retaining the trophy. Yet Shakhtar's football, their convictions, eventually found a way.

Palmer's enthusiasm on that grey South London day reminded me just how these Shakhtar teams stay in your head – and your heart. Once you've had a taste of how good it can be, it's quite moreish. The season after Istanbul in that same competition, now rebranded as the UEFA Europa League, Shakhtar had made a trip to London, to play Fulham. Their first half display was hypnotic, like Barcelona at their best, as the cold February breeze blew in from the Thames and we (and Fulham) were enchanted again. 'We saw some of the finest football ever played at Craven Cottage,' wrote Fulham blog *HammyEnd.com*, 'but it wasn't courtesy of the men in white. The metronomic passing and mesmerising movement of Shakhtar Donetsk will live long in the memory . . . the Ukrainian outfit were absolutely incredible but somehow lost a game they were utterly controlling thanks to a bolt from the blue by Fulham's much-maligned number nine.'

Yes, remarkably that ended in defeat despite the fact that, according to *HammyEnd.com*, 'their ball retention was almost unparalleled as they worked wonderful triangles right across the pitch.' Bobby Zamora's thunderous second-half winner, smashed in off the underside of the crossbar as he ran onto Zoltán Gera's delicious roulette flick, was a goal that Lucescu might have really appreciated under different circumstances. Roy Hodgson's team would eventually make it all the way to the Hamburg final, drawing the second leg at Donbass to go through, before being edged out in extra time by Atlético Madrid – but the impression was made, just as it was on so many other occasions. 'There is not a Fulham supporter I know that doesn't say that Shakhtar were the best team we faced en route to the final,' says ESPN broadcaster and Fulham fan Archie Rhind-Tutt.

It was an impression they left everywhere, from Braga to Barcelona, a sense of having been witness not just to a winning team, but of having seen some sort of cultural happening. When people saw Shakhtar with no prior knowledge or preconceptions, Sir Bobby Robson's description of Hungary's whirlwind 6–3 victory over England at Wembley in 1953 sprung to mind. 'They were men from Mars as far as we were concerned,' he memorably ventured, capturing the sense of sheer wonder and bewilderment they bestowed on spectators and direct opponents alike. When Shakhtar met Barcelona in the Super Cup in 2009, they joined the dots in front of the world. From peripherals in the provinces to the full glare of European football's bright lights in little more than a decade. That's where Shakhtar were, with that series of stunning first impressions all over the continent now put into some sort of context. Success was something for the club, and something special at that. The aesthetics? They were everything.

3

Lucescu

'I thought we would celebrate your birthday at the Donbass Arena, together with fifty thousand fans, where we would chant "thank you" from the bottom of our hearts. If someone asks me "what would you say about Mircea Lucescu?", the first time I would say, "He is a great friend of mine." Mircea, I greet you on your birthday and wish you Happy Birthday, and let your dream, our common dream, and the dream of all our fans come true as soon as possible – I want us to return together as soon as possible to the Donbass Arena.'

Extract from open letter by Rinat Akhmetov, Shakhtar Donetsk owner, 29 July 2015 – Mircea Lucescu's seventieth birthday

'He did a lot of good things for us. He arrived at an important moment, we won so many titles with him, we lived the most beautiful time in our careers – Donbass Arena, Donetsk, our stadium, our city. Honestly, I respect him for everything that he did for Shakhtar.'

There is a caveat. When somebody connected with Shakhtar is discussing Mircea Lucescu, there is almost always a caveat.

'But I cannot understand,' says Darijo Srna, 'why he went to Dynamo Kyiv. I will never understand why he went there. This is something that . . . it's not fair. But it's his decision.

56

I respect it, but I don't like it.' It is Srna who speaks about it most directly, characteristically enough, without inference or subtext. Elsewhere, it's just a feeling that you get.

Sergei Palkin, reflecting on Lucescu's reign at Shakhtar, is keen to draw focus from the credit for those titles just resting with the coach. 'If you're looking at the philosophy of our club,' he argues, 'the strategy of our club – I'm talking about the sporting side of it – the key person who changed everything is this president. He [always] really liked attacking football. If, for example, he can win all the matches but not play attractive football . . . he doesn't want to go in [this direction]. Why did we jump into the Brazilian market? Because Brazilians do everything it is possible to do with the ball.'

It isn't only Palkin who says this to me. The view from the outside is clear. That Lucescu's twelve years in Shakhtar are almost unparalleled in the modern game. That he shaped the club from provincial also-rans to a club of continental importance, renowned over Europe and the world, their excellence received almost on a word-of-mouth level. To hear him not talked of as the architect of it all can feel a touch jarring. Yet he is no longer revered at the club that he helped take from the shadows into the light, that he helped introduce to greatness. To say Shakhtar want to airbrush him from history isn't quite right – and for them to offer credit to Akhmetov is both fair and normal. He's the president, an icon and a transformative figure and after his energy and resources lifted the club into the orbit of European football's good and great, his enthusiasm, his drive, his feeling for the club has kept it alive over a mounting tally of fallow years.

'He gave it all,' says Srna. 'All his love, all his money, all his patience.'

But nobody here is tripping over themselves to eulogise Lucescu or to give him credit. And we know why, and there's something very sad about that. Lucescu is now an old man. He turned seventy-eight in the summer of 2023 and his son Rāzvan (himself in his early fifties) is an established coach in his own right, having bossed the Romanian national team (like his father) before finding success in Saudi Arabia and Greece. In the latter nation, he led the northern giants PAOK to a first league championship in thirty-four years in 2019. At this stage, Lucescu senior should be putting his feet up and basking in his achievements. That is not his way, but it is not really an option either.

Crossing the divide is taboo. Wartime solidarity is real, even extending to the hardcore in the stands. 'Since 2014,' says Anglo–Ukrainian football journalist Andrew Todos, 'there's been a bit of a truce between all Ukrainian ultras anyway, because they combined together saying, "we're not going to scrap and fight each other" – unless it was like some sort of six versus six in a forest somewhere which was agreed upon. They weren't going to do like fighting in stadiums amongst fans because [they're saying], "we need to combine against a common enemy."' Any sort of truce has not, however, made the Shakhtar–Dynamo rivalry disappear, and it has barely even tempered it.

Lucescu was never blind to that of course, intimately knowing what works for Shakhtar, what doesn't and what grinds the gears of the club and those around it. He could have only expected one sort of reaction from the Shakhtar side when agreeing to Dynamo's proposition in July 2020. He got that blowback straight away, with Dynamo's ultras maybe even more unhappy that a figure so closely associated with their biggest rivals had arrived than those that were part of Shakhtar were about a club legend defecting, albeit not directly.

Four days on from his appointment, Lucescu announced to Romanian newspaper *Gazeta Sporturilor* that he was withdrawing from the deal he had made with president Ihor Surkis. 'Unfortunately, I decided to give up the possible collaboration with Dynamo Kyiv,' he wrote. 'I thank Surkis's family for the trust given and [for] the invitation, but it is impossible for me to work in a hostile environment, without the support of the ultras, who the club badly needs in these moments.' Surkis played a straight bat, said that he hadn't received any news from Lucescu saying that he wouldn't stay, and carried on regardless. The two reconvened and agreed that they would work together.

It is an unusual late career twist for a hitherto universally praised coach, made an honorary citizen of Donetsk in May 2009 – nine days after Shakhtar won the UEFA Cup – and presented with a Romanian coach of the decade award at a gala ceremony in Bucharest in December 2013. Only Sir Alex Ferguson has more major club trophies to his credit than Lucescu's thirty-eight. Yet remarkably, if Lucescu had never even left Romania – which seemed his likely fate when he was a young man, given the country's regime at the time – his strike to European football's gong would still be resonating.

To some this will seem an unlikely claim, given his twelve transformative years at Shakhtar, famously built on a raft of Brazilian talent. Not to mention Lucescu's worldliness, as a polyglot and a hoarder of cultural experiences from all over the world. Yet the seed of his long love affair with Brazilian football comes from the 1960s when Nicolae Ceaușescu's reign was already fully underway, if yet to reach its worst authoritarian excesses. At that time, Romania was not open but it was a communist country that realised that cautiously fact-finding from cultures outside its borders had its benefits. Ceaușescu's 1968 visit to France to meet with Charles de Gaulle, who he greatly admired, and de Gaulle's return visit to Romania in the same year, fostered a closeness.

The French president believed that the two could make strides to an open, free Europe and Romania, 'aiming to affirm its autonomy in front of Moscow and pursue its national-communist project, seemed to lean closer and closer to the West,' according to Cezar Stanciu in a 2013 article for Cambridge University Press, 'The End of Liberalisation in Communist Romania'. Richard Nixon visited Bucharest in 1969. This spirit of guarded curiosity is how Angelo Niculescu, the coach of Romania's national team, persuaded the Romanian Communist Party to let his team undertake a tour of Brazil before the 1970 World Cup. The then-24-year-old Lucescu, his captain, had also played for him at Dinamo Bucharest.

'I loved Brazil and the players so much,' Lucescu enthuses, speaking to me down the line from Kyiv, but the swell of excitement in his voice making it sound as if he was in the same room. 'We played a tournament there in Maracanã. I won the

60

best player and they gave me a radio-operated Volkswagen after we played against Vasco da Gama, Flamengo and Independiente [of] Buenos Aires! And they played very, very well. And after this, during the World Cup, the president of Fluminense [Francisco Leitão Cardoso Laport] sent a letter to the [Romanian] embassy and after to the Minister of Sport to invite me – because it was impossible in that period to leave the country – to play three months in Fluminense. They didn't let me go.'

The fire had been lit under Lucescu, though. This set the foundations too for long into the future. 'I loved Brazilian football so much. I loved their training, their skilful [ways] and at the same time I started to learn Portuguese, because I realised that they couldn't learn [my] language, and it was much, much easier for them if I could speak Portuguese than if they [tried] speaking [mine]. This also made me very, very close to them and their families. For this, I [created] very good relationships in this period. And they played such good football. Fantastic football.'

It always comes back to the football, and the build-up to the 1970 World Cup proved to be a watershed for the Romanian game and for Lucescu. Still, the extent of his immersion in the whole experience is clear. 'When I spoke to my Brazilian players, I told them that I know Brazil much better than you,' he laughs, but he isn't joking. He knows this continent-sized country from top to bottom. The twenty-something Lucescu saw it all, he tells me – Natal, Fortaleza, Recife in the north. São Paulo state. Coritiba, Florianópolis in the south. After visiting with the national team he went again later with Dinamo Bucharest.

It was a place and a culture which connected with Lucescu on a personal and on a professional level, and he consumed everything he could. 'I knew the country; the culture, the arts and everything.'

If the experience had opened Lucescu's mind in broader terms it had made him, and coach Niculescu, think about a different approach for Romania on the field. Niculescu hadn't especially wanted the national team job. He felt the pressure would be unbearable, especially following on from poor results and performances, but also guessed he would be upsetting the Party if he refused. Yet even drawn into an almost impossible group containing reigning champions England, favourites (and eventual winners) Brazil and 1962 finalists Czechoslovakia ('they were a very, very good team in Chile,' emphasises Lucescu), Niculescu's team gave an excellent account of themselves during the three matches in Guadalajara. Romania lost to a solitary Geoff Hurst goal against England, beat the Czechs and went down 3–2 to Brazil in a thrilling third game that still bristles ('We don't speak about it'), even if Lucescu did swap jerseys with Pelé afterwards – a prize he framed at home, never washing it.

'And the process we took from their style of playing . . . that's what they call *temporizare* in Romania.' The literal meaning in English is something akin to 'delaying', but the idea was to control possession and control the tempo of the game. 'Let's use what we are good at,' says noted Romanian football journalist Emanuel Rosu. It was a proactive rather than a reactive strategy, based on looking into what Romania did have at their disposal instead of fretting about what they lacked. Romania had taken inspiration from the Brazilians but from now on they were going to do things on their terms, not anybody else's.

The visit to Brazil before the Mexico World Cup had been as much of an epiphany for Niculescu as it had been for Lucescu. Closed borders meant the Romanians were cocooned from the world outside. Moreover, before Niculescu took them to Mexico, they hadn't qualified for a World Cup for thirty-two years. With no foreign football on television they were far from cosmopolitan. They had been stranded on their own metaphorical island for much of the 1960s. Now they were starting again, and facing such celebrated opponents was almost a liberation. Success need not be measured in results, because they were almost too much to hope for. Being competitive was the main aim. Niculescu knew his players were largely not fast, strong or aggressive. They would have to find a way to lean into their own qualities rather than hope to magically absorb somebody else's. Brazil had flipped a switch in a few willing minds.

The concept of *temporizare* was born and it worked. 'Angelo Niculescu created this style,' Rosu details. 'He used to walk the ball to pass the ball. He used to get everyone involved and to launch attacks at the right moment. They had very clear views on when they should attack. And Lucescu was the guy who understood it best.' It was all about the power of the collective, to the extent that Nicolae Dobrin, 'the biggest player from Romania until Gheorghe Hagi,' as Rosu describes him, was left out by Niculescu in one of the most contested decisions in Romanian football history. In a 2011 interview with *Gazeta Sporturilor*, the coach explained he wasn't sold on Dobrin's commitment, judging that he 'came to Mexico to have fun and feel good'.

When Niculescu passed away in June 2015 at the age of ninety-one, the tributes recalled that in the years directly before his death, both FIFA and UEFA acknowledged him as 'the inventor of tiki-taka,' as Romania's *ProSport* put it. In other words, his team were the forefathers of the dream that Barcelona would later sell to the world. 'With the technical quality, the skilful quality of our players,' Lucescu says, 'we could pass it and [we could] win. Football based on passing. We left a very good impression in Guadalajara. We know we lost, yes, but we did very well with a young team, a very young team. I was the captain of this team. And from this, I wanted my teams to play like this. Like Brazilian players.'

The idea of the World Cup as a high watermark has stayed with Lucescu. He delights in the circle being completed in the way that by 2018, two years after his own Shakhtar exit, Brazil were taking on the world with a clutch of his protégés. 'I thought Shakhtar became the most Brazilian team in Eastern Europe, maybe in all Europe,' he smiles, 'because in the last World Cup in Russia, we had five players. Shakhtar had five players there in the group of twenty-three.' Two were still at the club, Taison and Fred, though the latter was on the brink of a £47 million transfer to Manchester United. Elsewhere in the squad were Douglas Costa, Fernandinho and Willian. His players remain his players after they've gone, just as Shakhtar remains part of them.

'He had a really big influence on my career,' Fernandinho told me in a 2016 television interview for *UEFA Champions*

League Weekly. 'I spent eight years working together with him. There's a lot of things I know today that I learned from Mircea Lucescu. He was someone really important in my tactical development, and in my technical development. I arrived from Brazil young, only twenty years old. It's not just his tactical intelligence though, but his experience. It's always an education.'

If the experience of 1970 set in stone Lucescu's main principles for the coming decades, it wasn't just the World Cup that coloured his enduring vision of the game. It was his personality as a player. Lucescu had been a tricky, touchline-hugging winger for most of the 1960s and 1970s, and that transferred to how he wanted to play as a coach – and he moved into the latter discipline before leaving the former, as player–coach at Corvinul Hunedoara in early 1979. The Lucescus had moved almost 400km to the north-west at the request of his wife Neli, following the devastating Vrancea earthquake of 1977, which hit the capital hard. Yet it was inevitable that Lucescu would end up back at Dinamo at some point and he did, in 1985, where he could apply his principles at an even higher level.

'Even with Dinamo Bucharest in 1990 we played like [Shakhtar],' he says, 'because it was my way. I was convinced [at the time that] this was the future of football, and now it's very coordinated. That was what I said when I was a player. Playing for Dinamo Bucharest, our centre-forward Dudu Georgescu won the Golden Boot of Europe twice, because I was a player who crosses very well.' He searches for a comparison, and he is not falsely modest. 'If you remember

[Ricardo] Quaresma or [David] Beckham – like them. Thirty goals, just from my crosses. And after, when I became coach in Dinamo Bucharest, we won the Golden Boot twice again with [Dorin] Mateuț's forty goals [in 1989] and [Rodion] Cămătaru [in 1987], with our attacking football.'

He doesn't dwell on this period but it was a golden one for Romanian football, building on Steaua Bucharest's European Cup win, beating Barcelona in the final in May 1986. The following month, Dinamo beat the newly-crowned Steaua in the Cupa României final to win Lucescu his first major silverware as a coach. His work at the club in the years that followed left many Romanian commentators – and Lucescu himself – forever wondering what might have been. The revolution was a huge step forward for people's lives, but it quickly became clear that Romanian football would struggle to carry on its upward curve in continental competition. In 1989 and 1990 Dinamo reached the quarter-finals and the semi-finals respectively of the European Cup Winners' Cup. Then came the revolution and players were able to go abroad, which they did, in huge numbers. Nine of the eleven that started Dinamo's 6–4 win over Steaua in the Cupa României final in May 1990 left that summer for clubs in Spain, Germany, Greece and Turkey. The Dinamo dream of a European Cup of their own would be frozen in time forever. 'I think that was the biggest missed opportunity in Lucescu's career at club level,' Rosu reflects.

The revolution also provided the opportunity for Lucescu to indulge his own suppressed wanderlust. In the summer of 1990 he headed to Italy, to Pisa, beginning a relationship that again would endure beyond his actual presence there. Italy covers most of Lucescu's career in the 1990s, as he continued to Brescia, Reggiana and Inter afterwards. Yet the attachment stayed with him when he moved on. He was on holiday in Italy, the great and lasting love of his western European odyssey, when an insistent Rinat Akhmetov sent a private plane to Verona to pick up Lucescu and bring him to Donetsk. 'It was the second year,' Lucescu describes, with Shakhtar having made a big play for him in the summer of 2003, after his first season at Beşiktaş. He opted to stay. This time was different. After he arrived in Ukraine, 'immediately they announced that I shall be the new coach.'

It meant cutting ties with Beşiktaş, which wasn't easy. 'I had to write a letter to Beşiktaş, telling them that [I was going],' he says, with a hint of sadness. 'They changed the president Serdar Bilgili who brought me in, and at the same time there was this proposal from Shakhtar, from Akhmetov. For more than a year I've seen how the life is there,' – the original offer piqued Lucescu's interest enough for him to keep in touch with Shakhtar's fortunes – 'how the team is, how the coaches have been there, because I came immediately after [Bernd] Schuster.' Before Schuster had been the respected Nevio Scala, who won Shakhtar their first UPL title in 2002.

However much Shakhtar and Akhmetov had gone the extra mile to get their man, it represented a big risk for Lucescu. He was adored at Beşiktaş, having arrived in 2002 from Istanbul rivals Galatasaray with a point to prove. 'He followed Fatih Terim [at Galatasaray], who was a legend,' remembers Ibrahim Altinsay, a high-ranking television executive who was on the

Beşiktaş board at the time. Despite winning the title in 2002, the Galatasaray board decided to get rid of Lucescu. 'And he was a little bit sour about his firing,' Altinsay says. 'So he wanted to show everybody that that he wasn't just a one-time success.'

The pressure was on the president, Bilgili, and his board to get their appointment right too. They were heading into Beşiktaş's centenary season on the back of a failed appointment in the returned Christoph Daum, which had seen them finish only in third place, sixteen points off the top. A title, therefore, would be more important than ever, 'the jewel in the crown,' as Altinsay puts it. 'We needed a coach that would make us champions,' he says flatly. 'At that time, we didn't have time to build up [to make a decision] and Galatasaray fired Lucescu. The honorary president of the Turkish Federation, Şenes Erzik, then said, "Why don't you think about [him]?" Well, I mean, we said, "Why not?" It's his experience. He made Galatasaray successful with very little budget, with unknown players, foreign players.'

This in itself was a break with mainstream Turkish football culture. Presidents liked to spend big on aging stars to get supporters onside. Lucescu preferred to use his resources with prudence. He may have been a trophy signing for Beşiktaş, but he wasn't interested in getting any of them in his playing squad. In his contract talks with the club it was clear he already had a plan. 'He just asked players for his system,' says Altinsay, 'but when we were starting negotiations he says [about suggested players], "Don't do it, don't do it, it's very expensive. Don't spend the money. I'll find you another alternative." And we were very much prepared [to spend].'

Lucescu had his guys he trusted, just as he would in Donetsk later on. Antônio Carlos Zago, the former Roma centre-back who had been a stalwart for him at Beşiktaş, came in as his assistant at Shakhtar in 2013. For the forward part of his Beşiktaş team, he had also favoured familiarity. He set his sights on Sergen Yalçın to pull the strings from attacking midfield, as he had done for him at Galatasaray, despite misgivings from some concerned about his fitness and particularly his weight. 'He was a very skilled player,' remembers Altinsay, 'and he was free so [Lucescu] said, "I'll make him play". And he scored the winning goal for the title at the end of the season.' The following year, in October 2003, Sergen scored twice at Chelsea, handing the eventual Champions League semi-finalists their first home defeat under the ownership of Russian billionaire Roman Abramovich. It was the first time Beşiktaş won a Champions League game outside Turkey and they did it in some style. Altinsay tells me that Lucescu sat on the flight home to Istanbul bemoaning the things his team hadn't got right. 'He didn't celebrate anything. He wanted to control the game from the first to last minute. Even without the ball.'

His attention to detail was unremitting, whatever the situation. Having already shown a coach's scope for analysis as a player, Lucescu was insatiable now he actually was a coach. Yet this made him collaborative rather than dictatorial. 'I'm going to help the coach,' Zago said after touching down in Ukraine. 'I'm also going to help the new players to adapt. Obviously Lucescu is going to set the tasks, but two heads are better than one.' He had been there before. When Lucescu arrived at Pisa he had inherited a fitness trainer, Adriano

Bacconi. The two clicked immediately and the coach had a plan in mind for his new colleague. He wanted to quantify stats into a more tangible way of judging player performance, so had the idea of putting the data into a computer. He had his fitness coach put the players through their paces during the day and crunch their numbers at night.

'Each [analysis] followed a player,' Bacconi told *Gazeta Sporturilor* in a 2011 interview, 'and noted all the movements, passes and lost balls. I processed them at night, and on Monday morning I transferred them to Excel. There were no big video cameras then – everything was analogue. For two years I did exhausting work.' Lucescu's demands on Bacconi were considerable, but he and his boss were breaking new ground.

'He's the brain behind the [first] football analytics projects,' confirms Rosu. 'He invented the modern way of analysing football games regarding stats. He hired two guys from the technical university [of Pisa] and to move everything to computers. Imagine that in the 1990s! It was absolutely crazy.' Lucescu and Bacconi went into business, creating the program Football Athletic Results Manager (FARM). When the pair moved to Brescia in 1991, they allied the statistical analysis to video montages, which had voice recognition. In 1994, the Italian football federation, the Federazione Italiana Giuoco Calcio (FIGC), approached Bacconi on behalf of Arrigo Sacchi for help preparing Italy for that summer's World Cup. For the first time, the team began to use live statistics during games.

Later that year, Lucescu and Bacconi stepped up their partnership, each investing $35,000 to develop FARM's successor, Digital Soccer. A large part of Italian football's elite was convinced by Lucescu's vision of the future of analysis and tactical preparation. Clubs like Juventus, Lazio and Inter all expressed an interest. When Lucescu returned to Romania in 1997, he and Bacconi dissolved their partnership though they stayed in touch, and the former even later asked the latter to work with him in Turkey, an invitation that he was too busy to accept. By the time Bacconi sold the remainder of his shares in 2006 – having sold 60 per cent of them to the Panini group in 2000 for a reputed €2 million – he was doing video analysis for Marcello Lippi's Italy, who were on their way to winning the World Cup in Germany. Lucescu's idea had grown beyond the realms of what many – certainly Bacconi – had imagined, and shaped best practice in the game.

The curiosity without end, the desire to find out more about more and more things that shaped Lucescu's destiny from the late 1960s, is something that never left him. He is still that person, looking to discover and innovate, holding dear his preferences of the past while remaining open to the new. He is digital and analogue at the same time, reinventing the course of how things are done yet still filling journals with ideas, thoughts and plans in the most old school way possible. 'I still have the notebooks,' smiles Altinsay. 'The first thing he was . . . he was examining the opponent in great detail. Perhaps more than the coach of that team.' Elsewhere, handwritten notes defined Lucescu. One of the most upsetting aspects for him of being forced to leave Donetsk in a hurry was having to leave behind manually written files and documents. Going back years, they detailed not just his methods and his teachings, but how he had come to that way of thinking. Whereas others pore over old photos, Lucescu's notes reminded him of where he'd been, what he'd done and everything he'd achieved. They were at once reference and nostalgia, a validation of his work. 'The rupture was really abrupt,' recounts Rosu. 'He always spoke about the memories he was left with from Donetsk and the fact that he could probably never go there again in the future.'

Lucescu had made the most of the freedom that he had so craved in the latter stages of the Ceauşescu era. After the chance to go to Fluminense came and went in 1970, there had been other moments. 'In 1984, after the Euros in France,' he confirms. 'Yes. European Championships in France. I was invited by [Francis] Borelli, the president of Paris Saint-Germain. Again. I asked my boss [at the Romanian Federation] to ask the minister to let me go. My wife was with me too. I only wanted to see how it was . . . in a big club. I didn't know. They didn't give us permission to all go.' (His son Răzvan, then fifteen years old, was back home.)

It's one of the reasons why, post-revolution, Lucescu became such a Romanian icon. 'He was the guy with the foreign touch, you know?' Rosu remarks. 'You guys don't have the same thing because you always had this open culture, but for us to have success abroad was something really special. He was the image of a guy who was having success abroad in management, which is not a small thing because when he coached in Italy, the three teams he coached there . . . it was the best league in the world. Even though he didn't get to the highest level [immediately] he did get to Inter later, which says a few things about his reputation there. He got to meet [Diego]

Maradona. He got to coach Ronaldo at Inter, [Diego] Simeone at Pisa, and he had a big influence on so many players that we know well today like [Andrea] Pirlo and many, many others. He's a guy who people have a lot to learn from. He's the very definition of a teacher. You know, he's influencing them not only on the pitch, but in their way of life and their character.'

There is a clear divide between Lucescu and many modern coaches, though. In a world in which coaches of all different styles and personalities, from Pep Guardiola through Thomas Tuchel to José Mourinho enjoy stoking their own myths, Lucescu does not. He has self-worth without really feeling the need to build his own legend – which, perhaps, is why he's occasionally been taken for granted.

'He's an adaptable guy,' says Rosu of Lucescu's ability to roll with the punches. 'He goes to places and adapts his style to the local culture he's confronted with. He's not a guy who says, "Look, I came here and now everything is going to change and you're doing this and this and this." He's not Guardiola. He likes open football.' There is philosophy and a set of beliefs but there is not micro-management. It's more practicality.

Neither is Lucescu hoarding the credit. 'I want to tell you,' he insists, 'that President Akhmetov, he raised up this team because, as I told you, he is very intelligent and succeeds in [all aspects of] organisation and development.' So when Lucescu talks about the early years at Shakhtar 'when we were making the team', he does really mean 'we'. With his preferences and Akhmetov's, it could have been an all-Brazilian team had it not been for the Ukrainian Premier League rule requiring the presence of four domestically qualified players in the eleven.

The regulations actually worked in their favour, though, in a combination of native and overseas qualities that meshed well, a bit like when Guardiola brought his ideas to Bayern Munich and combined them with more traditionally German values of tempo and athleticism.

'I knew that to be a very successful team,' explains Lucescu, 'we needed to put the Ukrainian players in defence. Goalkeeper, defence and defensive midfield player, and the others Brazilian. We trained with some Ukrainian players at the back and we combined that with an attack that maintained the Brazilian technique, the velocity, the rapidity in attack. The defensive, physical preparation of Ukrainian players was really good in this period.' It was about union, though, rather than division.

The Ukrainians in the squad realised that the environment around them was changing but also that they could benefit from it, as Lucescu sought a global standard. Taras Stepanenko, arriving from Metalurh Zaporizhzhia in a dual transfer with his friend Serhiy Kryvtsov in the summer of 2010, was making a big step up but Lucescu, he says, made him feel like he belonged at once. 'When I came to Shakhtar he gave me a feeling of importance,' he says, 'like for him I'm the player who can really help the team. He believed in me, and I felt it from the first time I met with him.'

Not that Stepanenko had it easy from his new coach. He acknowledges there were frustrations, even 'problems' when he didn't immediately become an automatic pick for the first team. When Lucescu did give him the go-ahead, it had been worth the wait. Stationed as the midfielder sitting in front of the defence, Stepanenko had a ringside seat as Shakhtar's Brazilian armada put opponents to the sword. 'When I first came to training,' he recounts, 'I just realised these players are on another level. These players played such quick football, with one or two touches, and I really needed time to adapt to this. Step by step I adapted to play with these great players like Fernandinho, Willian, Douglas Costa, Teixeira, Darijo Srna. With the new knowledge, the new approach in training, I started to help the team.'

For Stepanenko, though, the main advantage of working with Lucescu was on a mental level. 'He taught me a lot about how to win trophies, how to be professional, how to win big matches. His strong mentality helped me throughout my career. There are four points [you need] to succeed – mentally, technically, physically and tactically. If you have a strong mentality, you're a player for Lucescu.' Such was Stepanenko's commitment to his coach's ideals and to the overall project that he began to learn some Portuguese, to communicate with some of his overseas teammates with greater meaning.

Language is a recurrent theme with Lucescu. From the time before the Mexico World Cup, when he began to master Portuguese as a way to connect with players and people he admired and sought to know with greater depth, it has been a central tenet of his journey to learn and discover. When you ask those who know him what his secret of finding such synergy with Brazilian players is, the first response is always the same. 'First of all he speaks the Portuguese language,' answers Palkin. 'He likes Brazilian players and he knows how to connect with Brazilian players. To find the keys to open the doors with Brazilian players . . . sometimes it's difficult. Lucescu knows how to do it.'

This partially explains his almost instant connection with Akhmetov after arriving. The president targeted Lucescu for a reason; he wanted to bring not just success but thrilling, recognisable football that became part of the club's very fabric. Akhmetov had the same motivation as Beşiktaş fans. He would connect with Lucescu because he wanted to be excited as much as he wanted to win.

'I think that the president wanted me because I put Dynamo Kyiv out [of the UEFA Cup],' he says with a hint of mischief. The numbers from those ties in winter 2002 come to mind quickly. '3–1 in Istanbul. 0–0 in Kyiv in -11°C. That was incredible.' Akhmetov knew that winning and creating a Shakhtar brand of football would not be easy; introducing something new and dynamic to a provincial, traditionally working-class landscape.

'He is incredibly intelligent,' enthuses Lucescu. 'He analyses absolutely everything. He saw that I did very well in Turkey – winning with Galatasaray, winning with Beşiktaş – and working in eastern Europe, it's not so simple. It's difficult for all the coaches coming from western Europe. I don't remember one being successful. Maybe Dick Advocaat at Zenit. Juande Ramos? Here in the east there's not [always] the same professional level organisation. When I came [to Shakhtar], I was surprised by the organisation, though.'

On the football side, Akhmetov was enthusiastic and driven, but not arrogant or assuming. He was always keen to learn from Lucescu. 'I remember after the matches in Donetsk,' he grins. 'We stayed for about two hours after each match to speak about football, really, and to stay together [and talk]. And then to sing karaoke with him. He said every time that before he didn't drink and with me, he started to drink some wine.' Lucescu's love of Italian culture was coming in useful socially as well as professionally, it turned out. 'We became good friends from there.'

On those nights, Lucescu and Akhmetov discussed the future and grand plans for Shakhtar. They spoke of the latter's plans to expand the club's infrastructure with a new, dedicated, state-of-the-art stadium on the agenda. They spoke incessantly of the team. Not just of the Brazilian dream, but of Lucescu's other speciality – bringing through young players of various backgrounds, which would lean into both men's desire for a dynamic type of football.

'I told him it's better to take young players,' Lucescu says, 'because they can remain with us for a long time, five or six years if we take them [early enough]. It's because of the experience I had in Turkey . . . you don't see young players. [It's mainly] older players, big names, of thirty, thirty-two years old. All the teams there have big, big debts. It's incredible. They pay a lot of money out in contracts, but after one or two years, they have to be changed. In Turkey, this is my experience. I said, "No, we don't do it like this. We have to take more young players and bring them up like I did in Dinamo Bucharest." If not for the revolution, Dinamo Bucharest could easily have won the Champions League. We were very, very good. I had eleven players in the [Romanian] national team in the World Cup in Italy in 1990.'

When Lucescu was making his case to Akhmetov, his record backed him up. 'With my experience,' he continues, 'I convinced the president to start doing this because until I went there, he took players but he didn't understand that in football, he has to buy and to sell, not only to buy to be on the circuit of [top level] football. When I came there were players who finished their contracts and went before we could sell them. No more.'

Akhmetov's part of the plan was to take the club to the next level in terms of infrastructure. While Lucescu was refining the plan on the pitch, his president was going to build an arena worthy of his super team. 'He said to me that he wants to build a monument,' Lucescu explains. 'I had also said to him, "President, if you want to be in Europe, we have to have a good stadium," because the stadium we were playing in [Olimpiyskiy] was not a good enough level. They [the public] said, "How many spectators do you think we will have?" I said, "Maximum of thirty thousand." [Akhmetov] said, "No, I shall make a stadium of 55,000." He was right, because after it was full, for Champions League games.'

Seeing the plans for the new arena, Lucescu knew he had to build the team to fill it. 'If you want spectators,' he argues, 'you have to take Brazilian players, to bring the people to the stadium for the beautiful game they can give to them. And we took Matuzalém first.' The just-turned twenty-four-year-old midfielder arrived from Brescia, the coach's old club. 'My present,' he smiles. 'The president, Gino Corioni, was a very good friend.' The pair spoke in Brescia and then Corioni and Akhmetov met and negotiated in Paris. A deal was struck for

€8 million, and Shakhtar had a game-changer. '[Matuzalém] was the best player in Ukraine. From then [Akhmetov] was convinced that the Brazilians can do something for us and we started to take more young players.'

As with his strategy at Beşiktaş, Lucescu was picking choice targets rather than wanting his board to spend indiscriminately, and as with Beşiktaş he wanted the club to be lean, to think of the future, to run like a business. Smart and sharp worked for him. It wasn't just a question of means. For Lucescu, gluttony would make creating a successful culture more difficult. 'The first one we sold was [Anatoliy] Tymoshchuk [in February 2007],' he details. 'I convinced him [Akhmetov] to let Tymoshchuk go to Zenit, for a lot of money. $20 million. They had wanted to sell him for $3 million. We now know what this $20 million is worth. They [Shakhtar] understood that this is a future [plan], bringing players, developing them, getting good results to improve [the club's] image and [to improve] the value of the players. Then, sell them and buy another, because they can't all stay there more than five, six, seven years like Fernandinho, Willian, Douglas Costa, Alex Teixeira.'

That golden quartet were the full manifestation of Lucescu's vision of spotting young, developing players, getting good service out of them and then selling them at maximum value. 'We took them at, say, nineteen and they left at twenty-five, twenty-six at the latest,' he says, pointing out the model extended beyond Brazilians. 'We also sold Dmytro Chygrynskyi to Barcelona, and [Henrikh] Mkhitaryan to Dortmund. And after, you see what a career he [Mkhitaryan] had, as well as Tymoshchuk and other players. This is when I started to make a really professional team.'

That team started to gather respect, and a name, under Lucescu. He cherishes memories of his battles with Pep Guardiola and Barcelona. If Shakhtar and Barcelona have some sort of cross-continental connection, then their two most famous coaches are at the heart of that. 'Of course I appreciate Guardiola very much,' Lucescu clarifies. 'I was Brescia coach and, after I left, Guardiola came [towards the end of his playing career] and they lived in the same apartment where I was before for a year. Really. Yes, it's incredible. When we played the Super Cup final in Monte Carlo against Barcelona, where we lost 1–0 but only after 120 minutes, we spoke about it and how incredible it is. It may be coincidence. But he's a coach that I admired very much.'

If that was some sort of pinnacle in late summer 2009, a wider coming out party for Shakhtar as they announced their level to armchair football fans across the globe, Lucescu's mind stretched back to before the UEFA Cup final. To the ultimately unsuccessful Champions League group stage campaign in autumn 2008 that deposited his side in the lower-tier competition in the first place. 'Oh, boy. I don't know what could have happened if we didn't lose that match against Barcelona [in Donetsk].' They had led for a long time on that night, courtesy of Ilsinho just before half-time. They were heartbreakingly picked off, twice, by Lionel Messi in the closing stages. 'To [go down] 2–1 in the space of five minutes, in the last moments of the game . . . ' he laments, 'because we dominated. We had another opportunity to score. We've been much better than them. I think that the team could have got to a very high level in Europe.' It speaks volumes for Lucescu's ambition that he still thinks of how they could have bettered that year's European champions, one of Guardiola's best two sides ever, a gold standard of club football, rather than ending up with the UEFA Cup, which they did so well to make theirs in a historic season.

He regrets none of it, of course. 'It was a fantastic experience,' he purrs, and not just because of the longevity, and laying roots. 'Donetsk was like London for me because I was successful there. When you are successful and all, it's beautiful. Life is beautiful. If you have no success . . . maybe Madrid can still be Madrid. But after a while you'd realise how sad you are.' There is genuine affection for a city in Donetsk that many non-natives have found unremarkable, but it all comes back to the same thing – equating place with triumph.

That geographical connection, that grounding, was such that it was perhaps inevitable that the move away would shake even someone as experienced and canny as Lucescu. He chooses not to blame the end of his Shakhtar reign on the move away from Donbas, on the upheaval, on the necessary recalibration of such a well-functioning club on the fly. 'There's always the need to find a different way, not only in Shakhtar, [not only] in Donetsk, but everywhere in the world. To continue to be successful, it's so, so difficult, because you have to change every time. The players remain the same but you have to shift your discourse, your way of speaking. You have to change all the time, to find motivation, [to keep things] different, not only from the football perspective but from all the other parts of our life experience. And you have to bring something [new] every day. In the final stages of a championship campaign, it's not a problem for the players to play every three days. Physical problems end, because it's only physical. But for the coach, it's so difficult because it's mentally tough, and you have to have the force [of will] to remain at this level.'

It's the first time during our conversation that this hive of ideas, possibilities and innovations sounds slightly tired. He frames it by going back to an admired peer. 'To Guardiola again,' he pivots. 'He has an incredible passion to continue, to remain at this level, but has the possibility to change the players. Taking the best players. Do I have this possibility? No. [I have] to do the same thing with the same players. And sometimes they get into a routine and you have to know how to lift them up again, to not let them drop off. It's much, much more difficult than when you have the possibility to change the players, to buy what you want.'

That luxury was not afforded to him and, he believes, the shifting conditions hastened his eventual departure in 2016. 'Things changed. The Brazilians arrived at the level that they started to play in the national team. The big clubs started to ask them to come. They came to me to help them to go to the big clubs in western Europe. Fernandinho, Willian and Douglas Costa and Luiz Adriano. So in these situations, I realised that it's impossible to keep these players here. I spoke with the president asking him to find a solution, to let them go and to bring other players in.'

If those were first world problems at Shakhtar as the balloon went up and Lucescu – and the club – just had to hold onto the rope, not looking down, the current situation is a far harsher reality. The principles endure, but the sporting outlook, as well as the real life one, is tough. 'When you are making a team with young players it is more difficult,' he sighs. 'What is our team like now in Dynamo Kyiv? Only with academy players? It's not easy because competition between the players disappears. They are two friends starting from thirteen years old to play together. They are two friends. Or not, as it's not always possible in a team. You have to maintain big levels of competition amongst the players. It was difficult but it was also so beautiful.'

And there were beautiful moments. In October 2020, at seventy-five years, two months and twenty-one days, Lucescu became the oldest coach in Champions League history in Dynamo's match with Juventus at the Olimpiyskiy. Andrea Pirlo – who had been given his Serie A debut for Brescia by Lucescu in 1995, two days after his sixteenth birthday – was on the opposing bench. That Brescia link again. There was even more to come, as fans started to come back into stadiums after lockdowns, and in spring 2021 Dynamo clinched the league and cup double. Yet again, Lucescu was the victim of his own success. Three of the starters in May 2021's cup final win over Zorya Luhansk were gone by January 2023. Vitaliy Mykolenko (who went to Everton), Viktor Tsyhankov (to Girona) and Illya Zabarnyi (a €20 million sale to Bournemouth) all left to send their coach back to the drawing board, again.

When asked how moving from Donetsk all those years back in 2014 changed the club's way of working – changed his way of working – Lucescu tries to take the drama out of it, being thankful for small mercies of scale, compared to some of his previous homes. It is clear, though, that he missed Donetsk after Shakhtar went – a manageable, compact city, and his own private kingdom to an extent. 'That was very good there,' he reflects, 'but very good because I didn't lose time on the roads. No, like when I've been at Internazionale – from Milan to Appiano Gentile [Inter's training ground], which is an hour-and-a-half away. It's a very, very big traffic burden, but in Donetsk it's fifteen minutes to the training centre. Perfect. So making the training easily, discussing with [colleagues] and after living your life normally. Not living in the car. It was the same thing [heavy traffic] in Istanbul. It's so difficult.' Lucescu likes his own space to work and to think. On the road, constantly in transit, thrown into the post-Donetsk situation of living and training in Kyiv and playing in Lviv (at least initially), it wasn't the same. While keeping football in Ukraine going in the present day is a duty and a privilege, it is also exhausting for a man who is already a veteran of Ukrainian football.

'It's very difficult,' he sighs. 'It's not easy to play matches without supporters, because football is made for supporters.' Having endured games behind closed doors during the height of the pandemic, that is now being reprised for even more tragic, deadly reasons. '[The fans] bring enthusiasm and motivation to the players,' Lucescu continues, 'and they put pressure on the players. Now, there is not that. Not at all. We have to make very, very long journeys – for example, to go to play in Uzhhorod, it's eleven hours by train. Seven hours by bus to Lviv. And it's not easy. It's very difficult after we play the Europa League each week in Poland, in Kraków, and then go from Kraków to Kyiv, because we have to play outside [Ukraine] for Europa League. With the championship in Ukraine, we are giving supporters this sensation that the life can continue, but playing two times a week, nine hours apart is not easy.'

While some – mainly the Romanian Embassy – tried to persuade him to go back to Bucharest when war fully broke out in 2022, Lucescu never considered staying away. 'I'm staying here because I couldn't leave,' he says. 'It was very nice when I came. I was invited here, I've been successful and now when these big difficulties [come], to leave seems to be something abnormal, something not good. Not only for them, for me, for me. I remain hoping that all this situation will change one day and life will go back to normal. And at that moment, I shall say, "OK, I helped this. I did this."' He has already done his share, and more. Does he look back now at what he did at Shakhtar and think, especially with the turbulence that Ukraine has suffered since, that yes, he did something amazing there?

'It's this, for sure,' he agrees. Without even being asked, he starts to defend his decision to join Dynamo; a natural reflex after the years of consternation. 'When I decided to come to Dynamo Kyiv it was four years after [leaving Shakhtar], not immediately. After four years, the president of Dynamo [Surkis] asked me to come and discuss it with me, because they didn't win the championship for about five years. He wanted me to help them.'

Lucescu is well aware of what he did at Shakhtar, and that it can never be taken from him. 'Those twelve years are part of my emotions. It's my nostalgia, my souvenirs, my memories. They remain in me, and nobody can change that now. Nobody can ask me to change it. But I'm a professional coach and it's normal that where I work, I give my all. And after, you see that we [Dynamo] won immediately. A league championship, a cup. A super cup. With Dynamo Kyiv, Shakhtar had twenty-three points advantage one year before and the year I came we won with eleven points [more than them]. With the same team, the same players. But it's important [to impact] the mentality of the players, to realise how important it is to bring them along with you, to convince them that they can do it. Afterwards it got more difficult, because the war started and it was very difficult for Dynamo Kyiv. They lost eleven players. And we couldn't take another single one because there was no money. It's difficult without support, without spectators. You have publicity, but no sponsors. Anyway, we have to continue. We have to remain here, because the brand [has to keep going], even Shakhtar, for us to remain at the high level. We must not renounce. Because this war will finish one day. And it's important to restart at the same level that we left. Yes.'

When you feel his passion for Ukrainian football, and Ukraine as a country, it is sad to consider that Lucescu might not be there for the rebuild. His mind is still alive with ideas but he feels uncharacteristically weary. That won't do, because he will never stop being excited by new ideas, and by new possibilities, part of the same attitude that benefitted Shakhtar for so long.

Even back in Romania he was a student not just of the game but of people, of culture, of history, of life in all its forms. 'When he played against a big coach,' notes Rosu, 'or when coaches and big teams were coming to Bulgaria or to Hungary, he used to travel and watch them play and spend the night talking about football and learning about their philosophies.' The way that Altinsay sees it is that Lucescu always 'had the Schopenhauer philosophy' – asceticism, the belief in abstinence to focus on the spiritual. In Lucescu's case, abstinence from cashing in, following the easiest path to the top but staying true to his principles and his ideals, expanding his mind and his palette. Moreover, Altinsay frames Lucescu's approach in terms outside football nomenclature. 'We talked about philosophy, we talked about history, we talked about art,' he remembers.

When he left Istanbul, Lucescu received a gift from Altinsay. 'It was a lithograph of the area that the Romanians lived in in Istanbul. And he gave everybody a silver plate with our names and signatures on it. It's very valuable to all of us. Those were the good days.' The good memories endure. 'We played fantastic football,' he beams, 'We scored the most goals. I mean, after twenty years you can see when you go to the stands. You can see the Beşiktaş stripes with the names of Sergen [Yalçın], [Federico] Giunti, Zago, Óscar Córdoba, on the backs. Look at Turkish football now,' he sighs. 'It wasn't a dream or anything. Sometimes I don't believe it. We really experienced these things.'

'He's a guy who never stopped learning,' says Rosu, 'and never stopped adapting. Never stopped putting brick on brick on brick and building himself. That's what he even does today with computers, with WhatsApp, with all the things that determine his way of playing now, even now, because he's even updating as we speak. He's trying to become more modern to align himself to the new methods of playing football and coaching. This is the type of guy he is.'

He is not always the perfection that he craves, perhaps. But his path is necessary, as he sees it. Mistakes, missteps and failed experiments are all part of remaining relevant for so long. So in Lucescu's mind, choosing to return to Ukraine and to take up with Dynamo, the forbidden frontier from a Shakhtar perspective, makes some sort of sense. Treading the path of innovation and discovery, blocking out voices warning that it was too risky, too wild – that is Lucescu all over. That burning need to achieve the best, whatever it took, worked for Shakhtar for so long – and perhaps, if we're honest, it is a philosophy that still lingers at the club now, years after his departure.

4

The Brazilians

Akhmetov and Lucescu had set the table. Now they needed their guests to come in their droves. We're not just talking about the fans here, though when Lucescu told me about the idea of 'bring[ing] the people to the stadium for the beautiful game', the president and coach were convinced their vision of the most stylish Shakhtar possible was a central pillar of that. What they had to first build together was the environment for the Brazilian talents they both dreamed of to arrive and to thrive. They had to clear the cornfield, essentially, to even start building the baseball diamond. Assembling their own version of the Houston Astros would come much later.

If we fast forward from the first post-match meetings between president and coach to autumn 2020, it was clear the philosophy of Lucescu, enabled by Akhmetov's dreams and desires, was alive and well in the club's DNA. The belief in the Brazilian way was as strong as it ever had been; long after Lucescu, long after Donetsk and the Donbass Arena and after years on the road. Even without any fans to fill the stands, with Covid-19 keeping supporters out of Champions League fixtures and most European domestic football at that time. Our nomadic version of Shakhtar were humbling Real Madrid, the perfect union of Brazilian flair and scintillating football inspired by Brazilians. Even after everything, the dream and the ideals endured.

Those ideals had been demanded by Akhmetov and fulfilled by Lucescu. His command of Portuguese was a good starting point but his devotion to a football belief system was even more important in creating the Shakhtar we know. 'I prefer attacking football,' he says with a tone that borders on the non-negotiable, failing to understand why anyone would want anything else. 'Very [strong] combination play, very modern. If you can't do this, you cannot win. You cannot only defend. Only [José] Mourinho can do this,' he laughs, with a nod of respect to the Portuguese coach who has something of a different outlook on the game to himself. 'He organises defences very well, and that's why he gets good results.' The acknowledgement of someone who appears a polar opposite is interesting, and it is a route into the rarely celebrated pragmatic side of Lucescu.

As we know, the coach indulged himself with his first Brazilian purchase shortly after arriving in Donetsk in 2004; Matuzalém, the inspiration he wanted for his midfield, from his old home of Brescia. Elano, an industrious and versatile attacking midfielder, followed early in the following year, 2005. Before the arrival of this pair, Shakhtar had won one

Ukrainian Premier League title in their history. With them, they won two in two seasons. Elano was more of a practical signing, one could argue; dynamic and with an impressive workrate which made an eventual move to England seem natural enough, and the £8 million that Shakhtar collected from Manchester City for him in August 2007 seemed like a good amount of money for the club at the time. It signposted the way to even bigger player development projects and even bigger profits, further down the road.

They were not the first, though. Brandão was atypical among Shakhtar's Brazilians in a couple of ways; he was a rangy target man of a centre-forward, not noted for a silky technique, and he pre-dated Lucescu, arriving in 2002. He was, however, a crucial component of the Romanian's team, providing a focal point for smaller, more gifted players to flock around, and was a mainstay until he left for Marseille in January 2009, after six-and-a-half years of service.

Brandão was key. Fantasy football was good for business and for appearances but, in order to win, an edge was needed as well. There was also the question of applying Brazilian magic to a UPL context, which would take time and education, even for the most apparently team-focussed. 'When I arrived at Shakhtar,' Fernandinho said to me in another interview for UEFA Champions League Weekly, this time in 2019, 'you had to respect the positioning more, in the training sessions and in the games. And the coach always asked us to stay in the positions that we'd been designated.'

Arriving in late summer 2007, just after his nineteenth birthday and with Shakhtar's 'Brazilification' much further down the line, Willian had a similar learning curve – and perhaps, as a more naturally attacking player than Fernandinho, a steeper one. 'Lucescu was a good coach for us, you know,' he says. 'He always tried to explain why. Sometimes the Brazilian players, when we come from Brazil to play in Europe, it's very different. The football is very different. You have to learn more tactically. He tried to help and explain some things [about what was needed] without the ball, and also when we have the ball. He was so important for the Brazilian players that played there at that time.'

Lucescu respected versatility, but he was too canny for the cliché of improvised, carnival football. 'I played a lot as a *volante* [literally *steering wheel* in Brazilian Portuguese, a midfielder who sits in front of the defence and drives the team],' remembered Fernandinho, 'or on the right or left of the midfield three. Sometimes I was even used as a right-winger, sometimes as a left-winger, and even at times more centrally, as almost a number ten. I'd played there many times in Brazil, so it was easy to adapt to the daily routine and the style of play as well. I fitted together well with my teammates, which was one of the most important things.'

He appreciated the opportunity to be put through his paces by Lucescu. If the end product was to entertain, the coach was determined that his players with the ability to do that would earn the right to do so. 'I learned a lot of things,' Fernandinho detailed. 'Defensive positioning, how to close the spaces in the middle of the pitch, to synchronise with the other players – especially when we were defending. This helped us to move together and I think this also allowed me to help the other

Brazilians that arrived at Shakhtar after, and that was the way in which they acclimatised really.'

Clearly it was self-perpetuating; once some Brazilians came, it was easier to get others to follow suit. Initially, though, getting over the perceived obscurity of the Ukrainian Premier League and Shakhtar's modest international renown required some creativity. Enter Lucescu's old ally Franck Henouda, who was teeing up players for Shakhtar in what was becoming a very lucrative pipeline from Brazil for him. 'I filmed the training ground, which was exceptional,' he told *So Foot* in 2020. 'I went and took photos of the Donbas Palace [hotel] and the square next to it, as well as some of the best restaurants. I could show them that they would be training in a magnificent place, and living in a small city where their family would be well looked after and content.' Naturally, there was also a financial incentive, helped by Ukraine having a markedly lower top rate of tax than, for example, France or Spain. 'We worked on a financial plan with Lucescu and the president after,' Henouda said. 'A fixed amount and big bonuses.'

Getting the introduction right was imperative. 'When foreign players arrived,' says Sergei Palkin, 'they often didn't know much about Ukraine or about Donetsk. So it was important for them to understand what sort of city they're in. When we brought them to our training ground or our stadium, they were [asking] "Where do I sign?" because they understand we're involved in football deeply, professionally. They understood that this is a huge project.' That, for example, was what Willian said attracted him, despite a good offer from then-French champions (and Champions League perennials)

Lyon. 'Actually, I didn't have so many offers, you know, from other clubs. I just had [that] one from France. I just decided to go to Shakhtar because of the project, at that time there [were already] some Brazilian players there.'

Willian got the full charm offensive as well, seeing the facilities and getting to know the surrounds over an extended period. 'I went there for three days before I signed the contract,' he says, 'to see the facilities and to see everything – the city, and to know more about the club. And then I decided to sign with them because I saw that could be a good option for me.' Palkin had always felt confident. 'We created really good conditions for them in Donetsk. They had great houses, played in a great stadium, we had a nice hotel here where we stayed from time to time. We had a very good training ground. In Donetsk we created almost a football city. Everything was tailored around having good players, a good club and good results.'

As well as having the trump card of Lucescu providing the cultural as well as the technical bridge from Brazil to Ukraine, the club built around their new colony off the pitch. Palkin talks of building 'a whole department' of the club around the Brazilians, with an infrastructure incorporating a team of interpreters and Portuguese-speaking helpers to find apartments and houses for the players, all squarely aimed at making sure they adapted quickly. Before player liaisons became best practice across European football – and certainly before they became well-funded and anything more than an afterthought – Shakhtar were making sure that every single detail that might occupy a player's mind off the pitch was being sorted out with the ultimate care and thought. The players would help each other on the field by being there for each other, but also by sharing a *lingua franca* both in terms of spoken word and by way of football upbringing and common references.

They needed to thrive socially as well though, when Lucescu wasn't there to talk them through everything. The football, as always, was the easy bit – and Shakhtar were aware of this. 'When the training sessions finish, everyone goes home,' Palkin says, 'and they all stayed at home. Some of the families went around to each other's houses every day, almost. They had a real community. So for us it was very important to help them adapt to the country, to the city. We provided everything for them to do this. So they arrived, any off-pitch problems [they might have] we take on and so they just concentrate on what's happening on the pitch.'

The recognition that the best method of the Brazilians getting support was through each other was imperative. '[Even then] we had eight Brazilian players there,' Willian counts up. 'And this was so important for me, to adapt well and to be able to play and also be able to live my life outside the club. That helps a lot in both situations – on the pitch and off the pitch.' When he arrived, Donetsk was an industrial, working-class city with limited options. It wasn't Kyiv. The Brazilian players favoured going around to each other's houses and apartments, cooking, Skyping friends back home – in the days before you could easily play video games online and remotely – and watching Brazilian TV on satellite dishes the club helped to install.

'We did a lot of barbecues when we had a day off,' recalls Willian, 'because Donetsk, it's a small city and we didn't have a lot of things to do in the city. You had some options of restaurants and one shopping mall but there weren't so many things to do in the city. So we decided to do barbecue or dinner or lunch. Any kind of things to be together.' Marlos appreciated it too. 'Without a doubt,' he told me in 2015, 'they all helped me to adapt. It also helps us to have a great atmosphere [at the club], an atmosphere where everybody talks to everybody, where we can joke with each other – and where we can eat things that we like.' By this point, the club chefs had learned how to make *feijoada*, a stew of meat and black beans popular in Brazil.

After Shakhtar sold the club to the Brazilians, it was the Brazilians' job to sell the club to us, the rest of the world. Such was the verve, individually and collectively, of this series of beguiling Shakhtar teams that it is easy to get sucked into the romantic vision of it, especially when you list the players. Douglas Costa. Willian. Alex Teixeira. Fernandinho. Taison. Yet Lucescu made the magic happen by instilling discipline, communicated to the players in an approachable manner in their own language.

It was an impressive partnership. And it did not go unnoticed at home. 'When you're talking to someone in Brazil,' Palkin says proudly, 'everybody knows us. Some people talked about us like we're the second national team of Brazil,' he grins. It only snowballed with the UEFA Cup triumph, then with the strides Shakhtar made in the Champions League. With Lucescu happy to reprise his own youthful adventures around Brazil, the club went on tour there for a series of friendlies in the mid-season break in 2014–15, riffing on their establishment among the expanded European elite with an extensively Brazilian cast. They were well-attended games, in front of crowds of 30–40,000. 'It was unbelievable,' Palkin marvels. 'And it showed huge respect to our club.'

In January 2015, some six months after the World Cup in Brazil, Shakhtar played at Brasilia's Mané Garrincha stadium – which had hosted Argentina's quarter-final win over Belgium and Brazil's third-place playoff with the Netherlands – against one of the country's most famous names. 'We played with Flamengo in front of a full stadium,' states Palkin. 'It was our winter period, but summer [and pre-season] in Brazil. They came to see Shakhtar because Shakhtar was a big brand.' This was a huge boost to morale to a club and players, at the time, displaced by the war in Donbas, and only very slowly getting used to their new circumstances, like kids in a divorce. After months of playing in front of paltry crowds in Lviv, to play and receive the recognition of a full stadium meant a lot.

Eventually, that golden generation of Shakhtar Brazilians had almost pushed the brand too well. They may have helped to define the differences between Shakhtar and Dynamo, but they also became known across the continent – and at that point, it began to be increasingly difficult to hold onto them. Fernandinho, the father figure of the dressing room who knitted it all together, went in summer 2013. 'He spoke very good Russian,' Palkin observes. 'He's a very clever guy. In my twenty years at the club, he's one of the cleverest guys I've known. That's why he went to Manchester City and that's why he stayed many years there. It's not just the legs that are important, but the brain as well.'

Why, though, did they stay quite so long? 'No, they didn't stay a lot,' Srna half-bluffs. 'Not compared with me.' He lets a wry smile linger for a second. He is right of course. Compared to Srna, nobody stayed *that* long. 'They liked playing for our club,' offers Palkin, 'because they understood that our club is like a trampoline to top European clubs. Manchester City etc. So they understood that.' Brazilian talents who went straight from South America to the biggest European clubs risked getting lost in the system, behind experienced and expensive superstars. Here, they could participate in mapping their own futures. 'You need something in between,' says Srna. 'Something in between is Benfica, is Shakhtar, is Porto. That's what you need from being a talent to going to a big club.' Joe Palmer concurs. 'We were,' he says, 'the perfect springboard.'

'Shakhtar is family,' Srna says. 'It's not a business club. It's a huge family. You enter once and it's difficult to go out.' When you think of those especially long tenures of Fernandinho and Brandão, that rings true. For Willian, at the club for five-and-a-half years, the family comparison had another side. He had to convince the 'parents' to let him spread his wings and go out into the big wide world. 'To be honest with you,' he tells me, 'I stayed because I had no other option. Not because there weren't other clubs. I had so many offers, but it was difficult to negotiate with Shakhtar. I had an offer from Benfica, had offers three times from Chelsea, from Tottenham, a lot of clubs. But for two years I was speaking to them [Shakhtar] to try to convince them that I want to leave. I always told them that my time is done here, [that] I want to leave. I started to get offers in 2011.' It was a grind, a contest of attrition to finally get what he wanted. 'From January 2011 until January 2013,' he details, deliberately. 'Over two years I was always speaking to [Shakhtar]. My agent was always trying to speak with them. I had a dream. I wanted to step up my career and to play in a different club. So it's supposed to be three years, but for two years I was [negotiating] and it's become five.' He allows himself a wry laugh, knowing the happy ending.

That 2012–13 Champions League campaign, incorporating five wins out of six in the group stage, including victory over holders Chelsea, left Shakhtar with a dilemma. They looked almost unplayable, perhaps the best version of Shakhtar yet. Did they stick or twist? It must have been hard for Akhmetov and Lucescu to consider letting their players go. 'Yeah, I understand,' concedes Willian. 'I understand them. But when this kind of club, Chelsea . . . ' This was not a negligible growing pain for Shakhtar. If they had tended to everything in their kingdom, and provided the players with all they could want, their increasing projection – and the glamour the Brazilians gave them – couldn't remain a secret. They were not the only interested parties. Shakhtar and their players had the attention of the world's very best.

This was a considerable and perhaps unanticipated block to their inexorable upward trajectory. Akhmetov's plan covered every internal detail but they could not lie in isolation. 'I understand the owner of Shakhtar,' Willian sympathises. 'Everyone there didn't want to let me go. But I was a little bit sad, because when you see a club like Chelsea that wants you and it was my dream – and then they didn't let me go. But at the end of the day, I went to Chelsea.'

Palkin didn't see selling the cream of the crop – Willian fetched a colossal €35 million, going to Anzhi Makhachkala in Russia before ending up at Stamford Bridge six months later – as an impediment, but as an opportunity. 'It gave us an opportunity to invest into new players,' he says. 'When we sold Fernandinho and Willian, for example, we reinvested the money directly into new players. We understood that if we stopped, you quickly arrive at the point in five years when you don't have anybody. No results on the pitch and no possibility to make big transfers going forward.' Bernard arrived from Atlético Mineiro in August 2013 for €25 million, which represented a large part of the fee received for Fernandinho (he spent a week in Donetsk trying the city and club out, before agreeing to sign).

It suited Lucescu's plan of keeping the squad young and competitive, and continually developing. 'Every time I had some players waiting behind,' he says, 'and this became a philosophy of Shakhtar. To have each time a second line and a third line. Yes, the first line left. But the second line played immediately without taking on new players. And after, step by step, because young players go step by step, they eventually get to be starters in the team. After one year, one-and-a-half years, two years, we are planning for absolutely every step of their development. And then they go on to succeed.'

By Paulo Fonseca's time, it was a well-oiled machine. The club had become so used to integrating Brazilians that it did it without even thinking. 'I think it was relatively easy,' muses Fonseca, whose appointment was in itself a nod to the culture, bringing in a Portuguese-speaking coach. 'In relation to the

Brazilians I was very lucky with the players I had there at the time, and who were very important for the team, players like Marlos, Fred, Bernard, Taison, among others, but they were completely integrated in the club and with the Ukrainian players. It was easy. I didn't experience any difficulty at all with respect to this. Brazilian players usually adapt very well, and there were players, such as Marlos and Taison especially, who had been in Ukraine for a long time. They didn't come directly to Shakhtar. They had played previously for Metalist. So they were completely integrated and rooted in Ukraine. There was an excellent relationship between the Brazilian players and the Ukrainian players. I never felt there was any problem between them. Of course, the Brazilians tended to spend time around the Brazilians more, and the Ukrainians spent time around the Ukrainians, but it worked really well because the Brazilians were integrated, rooted, I never felt any type of difficulty.'

Fonseca worked so well that when he went to Roma in 2019 after an unprecedented period of success, he was replaced by his fellow Portuguese Luis Castro, who had briefly coached Porto and Vitória de Guimarães. 'In fact,' underlines Fonseca, 'this goes even further back. From the time when the club were in Donetsk, the president always signed Brazilian players, and always had success with this. This was simply a continuation. When a Brazilian player came to Shakhtar he knew he had a chance of his career taking off in Europe, and players like Bernard, who was highly sought after, ended up coming to Shakhtar because they knew they would have this context of having a lot of Brazilians and this would be positive and favourable for them. It's a cultural question. You had [Facundo] Ferreyra, who was Argentinian, but practically all the other foreign players were Brazilian. It was a club thing. It was the culture of the club. They always signed Brazilians. When I was there they signed more Brazilians, and always successfully.'

Despite their social preferences, the Brazilians never existed in a bubble at Shakhtar. Even if Lucescu himself presented it as Ukrainian defence/Brazilian midfield and attack, it was more nuanced than that. The Brazilian influence in the team didn't just add stardust and exoticism. It shaped the way the team played and it shaped the other players around them. 'The Brazilian players who stayed at Shakhtar are really talented,' enthuses Taras Stepanenko. 'All players with a high level, and all of those players that stayed at Shakhtar [for several years] could play for the biggest clubs in Europe. So of course I tried to see what they do and how they make decisions, and that's helped me a lot. They were more the technical part of the team and us, the Ukrainian players, who play more in the defensive [roles], we're more the strong part of the team. Always in Shakhtar it was about that balance, between the technical players and the defensive players.'

That evolution of Shakhtar grew the brand, as Palkin would say, and made them a possibility to a wider range of prospective signings too. Manor Solomon admits he knew little about Shakhtar before they made him, and his club Maccabi Petah Tikva, an offer in 2019. He was quickly sold, however, on the footballing vision created over the years. 'Once we had the offer and we started to search and to analyse the team and

Shakhtar,' he says, 'we saw there were many Brazilians, and that the team was a combination of Brazilians and Ukrainians. The style of play is very attractive. It's always offensive. The attacking players were always good with the ball, technical players, so we thought that I could fit in there.'

Shakhtar didn't just have more money than most of the other teams in the Ukrainian Premier League. They had totally different cultural reference points that were so entrenched in the club's modus operandi that they stretched beyond just the Brazilian players. 'There was a big difference between Shakhtar and the other teams,' Solomon notes, 'And obviously together with Dynamo Kyiv, they are the biggest clubs in the the country by far.' Furthermore, by Solomon's second season in Ukraine, after Castro won the UPL in his debut campaign, Lucescu took over at Dynamo, spreading the 'Brazilification'. 'We always felt that we dominated [matches],' says Solomon, 'and that we needed to win every game. Of course, most of the games were really difficult because most of the teams, they came to sit back and to counterattack. We had to find a way to break it. It wasn't always so easy. Though it was different when we played in the Champions League.'

In a continuation of the original idea that Lucescu convinced Akhmetov was the way, the team got younger – partly because of sales, partly because of less revenue post-2014 – but partly because that's what was always supposed to happen. 'I think in short,' examines Solomon, 'when I arrived, some of the old generation were playing. Players that were the leaders like Taison, Marlos, Júnior Moraes, Stepanenko and Alan Patrick. They were older than me and older than some of the other Brazilians.' That senior committee was different to previous swathes of Brazilians at Shakhtar. There were those who had come, conquered and been sold to the elite level. This group were good players, but not quite that. Moraes and Marlos, who inherited the captain's armbands, even became Ukraine internationals after receiving passports. 'Recently Alan Patrick called me,' Henouda said in 2020, 'because a club in the UAE wanted to sign him even though he had two years of his contract left. You know what he said to me. "Franck, I'm a starter, I play in European competition every year, my wife is happy here, my kids are going to the international school [in Kyiv] . . . these guys really need to be paying me an extraordinary amount of money if they want me to give all this up." Like Dentinho, Taison or Marlos, he's one of those who are going to finish their career here.'

Things changed, however – and have since been accelerated by the war. 'Over the years,' Solomon continues, 'Shakhtar started to make the team younger. And as players like me arrived and like Marcos Antônio, Vitão . . . a lot of younger players arrived and there was a process. In the beginning, most of the Shakhtar team was more adult, more mature. And then during the years it came to be like more and more young.'

That vibrancy was on full display in those astonishing Champions League wins against Real Madrid in 2020 under Castro's leadership. 'Obviously we were playing against the best club, the biggest club in the world at the time,' he says excitedly. 'They had a great team with [Zinedine] Zidane on the touchline and so we knew we were facing a really strong opponent, but we knew that we could take something from this game.' That is putting it mildly. Playing at Estádio Alfredo di Stéfano at El Real's Valdebebas training centre, while works on the Bernabéu took place in the absence of fans, this young Shakhtar side gave a masterclass. They were 3–0 up before half-time.

'We analysed Madrid and we knew that if we would sit back more,' reasons Solomon, 'if we gave them the ball so we could move into good counter-attacks when we had the ball, we knew what to do with it because we had a lot of good players.' He and Tetê looked like the best of them. The pair combined brilliantly. Tetê had opened the scoring just before the half-hour, after a rampaging run from left-back Viktor Korniyenko made it all the way to the cusp of the Madrid penalty box. His penultimate touch, as he ran into the centre, seemed to be too heavy, but he made clear to the onrushing Marcelo that the ball was going to be his. He stretched out his right foot, slid the ball to Tetê and the winger swept the ball low into the right-hand corner of Thibaut Courtois's goal. It was almost the perfect illustration of what Lucescu had described all those years back, the cliché perpetuated until the point that it came to life. Tough Ukrainian defence morphing into insouciant and alluring Brazilian attack.

Four minutes later and Shakhtar caught El Real with another sucker punch. Tetê slalomed around half-challenges from his illustrious compatriots Marcelo and Casemiro. Again the left foot sprang into action, this time with a much more forceful shot that stung Courtois's hands, and which the Belgian couldn't hold. Raphaël Varane, trying to get the rebound away from the lurking Dentinho, prodded the ball into his own net. It seemed the smiling striker had the nerve to claim it as his own, but Shakhtar had every right to celebrate. There was more to come. Solomon's goal just before half-time, which turned out to be the winner after a couple of second-half goals from the home side ensured a nervy finish, was peak Shakhtar. A fast break and Tetê rolling a backheel into a central space for Solomon, who held off two defenders to finish with aplomb. 'So the first win in Madrid was amazing for us and – honestly – we didn't believe that we could win there.' When Luka Modrić and Vinicius Júnior scored twice in five second-half minutes (the second when the young Brazilian substitute mugged skipper Marlos, dithering on the ball, and fired home with his first touches) nerves jangled. When Federico Valverde's shot deflected past Anatoliy Trubin in stoppage time, hearts sank. However, Vinícius (Júnior) was standing a way offside, right in front of Trubin. Referee Srdjan Jovanović went to examine the VAR monitor then turned his back on it, drew the little TV screen with his index fingers, and disallowed the goal. Breathe out. Shakhtar were taking home a famous win. 'But after the game,' exhales Solomon, 'it was an incredible feeling.'

Here, in the top tier of European football under the steward-ship of Castro, they were almost in their ultimate manifestation of Shakhtarness, which Akhmetov had dreamed of two decades before. The characteristics of the team were in perfect synergy. Ukrainian wit, Brazilian hustle, with a young Israeli sprinkling the high art on top. Accordingly, they approached the return at Olimpiyskiy six weeks later with even greater swagger and belief. 'And then in the second game we already believed that if we beat them away,' he says, 'we could win also at home. And that's what happened.' The belief was apparent in the opener, smartly finished by Dentinho after some defensive dithering by the Spanish giants. Solomon's clincher in Kyiv was even better than his gem in Madrid. Bringing the ball from halfway in a counterattack, and with Viktor Kovalenko and Mykola Matviyenko making split runs to take the defenders away in either direction, the Israel midfielder cut inside to thrash a shot past Courtois from the edge of the area. 'I think it was a similar game to the first one, I scored in both games and they were, I think, the most important goals in my career.'

'I couldn't open my phone after that,' he grins, 'because of all the journalists [from home], all the people, friends and media people. Everybody tried to reach me and to interview me. Now I'm in the Premier League, if I score they try to reach me from everywhere. So obviously when I was younger and I was playing and scoring in Madrid, it was even bigger and it was an amazing feeling that I will always remember. And yeah, the feedback from back home was huge.' It had been thrilling, though Castro's Shakhtar were callow enough that despite those two jaw-dropping results, they were edged out of a qualifying spot for the last 16 after losing heavily to Borussia Mönchengladbach – twice. It put Solomon and his teammates on the radar, anyway. Even if the move ended up being more abrupt than anyone had planned, Shakhtar's ability to act as a springboard to the big leagues did work for him, just as it had for previous generations.

The connection remains. Palkin mentions Willian staying in touch. 'I met Willian in London a few weeks ago,' he smiles, 'and he still spoke Russian to me; he remembered everything.' The warmth is reciprocated. 'I think it's a special club,' says the winger. 'A club that has good people around, people that always want to work, always to want to do better and better. There are also a lot of humble people there, you know? I had a great time there. I won a lot of trophies there. And I'm always grateful to them that I played there five years.' And he did, after all, get his dream move in the end.

Even now, a whole decade on from leaving Shakhtar for the English Premier League where his fame hit another level, and back in Brazil at Paraná where it all started in his footballing twilight years, Fernandinho remains the star pupil. 'It's a club that opened the doors to Europe to me,' he told me in 2019. 'I was a young player who arrived full of dreams, and full of willing to do well. They gave me all the support I needed to succeed in those eight years and I felt the love of the fans, of all the players, of all the people who worked at the club. I'm still constantly in contact with them. Everything that happened for me at Shakhtar made me grow. I learned a lot. I'll be eternally grateful to the club, and I'll always be a supporter [of the club]. My story at Shakhtar was a beautiful one. Eight years of success, and of winning. It's a club that will be etched on my heart for the rest of my life.'

It works both ways. Even with the Brazilian contingent dispersed, at least for now, their influence on Shakhtar remains; the successes, the standards and the style. They helped to create a reputation and an aesthetic. The best version of a team can become the embodiment of a club and those versions of Shakhtar live on, across the continent and the world. That is as indelible as the mark that Fernandinho says the club made on him.

5

Building Donbass

'You can add it to the list of stadiums that call themselves Jewel in the Park. That was the idea, that there was this almost spaceship arriving into Donetsk – and it very much met the aspirations of the ownership of the club. And we're proud that what we drew in 2004 is what got built and opened in 2009, and is what was used in 2012 for the Euros.'

Chris Dite, architect for Arup, the designers of Donbass Arena,
Donetsk, April 2023

Chelsea were the European champions but here, on *their* turf, they were not the stars. The 50,000-plus locals wedged into the stands told them so as they bellowed, not just pushing the visitors back but forcing their own team forward, with Shakhtar opening at speed with bristling, suffocating intensity, as powerless in their own way to resist the force of will tumbling from the stands as Chelsea were. The people of Donetsk had their Colosseum and the normal protagonists were just prone vessels on their sea. Their message was clear, and they wanted everyone to know. This is our team, our club and our city.

It was, Darijo Srna had said to me, 'some sort of destiny that we would go from the Olimpiyskiy with the UEFA Cup to the new stadium.' The atmosphere on the night of 7 May 2009 at the old stadium had been wild, intoxicating, all-consuming as Shakhtar edged out Dynamo Kyiv for a place in the Istanbul final, but now it was time to go. As Srna says, the moment was symbolic as if, having wrested the right from Dynamo to represent Ukraine on the biggest stage, Shakhtar now needed somewhere else to grow, and to become even bigger.

Srna also told me how they had looked over the way in the closing weeks of that season as they played, and won, in the shadow of the new place. It was all set to take the club to the next level. They were indicating clearly where they were going with their actions on and off the pitch. The former, by joining Dynamo in being a European title winner from Ukraine.

The latter? This was the moment where if anyone had doubts over the ambition of Rinat Akhmetov, they would disappear. 'We played that first game against Karpaty Lviv, 4–0, I think,' says Srna. 'Andrei?' He asks press officer Andrei Babeshko across the table. 'Obolon [Kyiv],' comes the instant reply. 'Are you sure? I think it was Karpaty.' Babeshko quickly confirms, politely looking at his phone to check but already knowing the answer.

The first game at Donbass Arena was Shakhtar 4–Obolon Kyiv 0, on 27 September 2009. 'It was a dream,' says Srna, ever so slightly leaning back in his chair to bask in the memory. 'It's one of the best stadiums in the world. What can I say?' By then, the gala opening night, with Beyoncé making her first-ever appearance in Ukraine, had wowed the region and the country. Taras Stepanenko, at this point still playing for Metalurh Zaporizhzhia, admired it from afar. 'I saw the celebration on TV,' he remembers, 'and it was unbelievable.'

The scale of it all was, as he said, unbelievable. For this to come not just to Ukraine, but to Donbas, was mind-blowing. 'This was like the next level,' says Andrew Todos. 'Shakhtar were saying, "Listen, we've got a state-of-the-art stadium where the likes of Beyoncé are coming in to perform there. We want to become the new Eastern European powerhouse." And the renovations around the city in preparation for Euro 2012 were happening as well. Euro 2012 was massive for Donetsk. They obviously had loads of games [five] and they had the semi-final as well.' If there were no goals in that semi-final between Spain and Portugal it was still a thriller, with Cristiano Ronaldo almost toppling the reigning champions before the Spanish edged a penalty shootout, on the way to retaining their trophy in Kyiv. Poland and Ukraine may have been sharing hosting responsibilities but the star stadia of the tournament, between this and the rebuilt Olimpiyskiy in the Ukrainian capital, were not in doubt. The semi at Donbass was an elite level match for an elite level arena.

The point that it was something not just for Shakhtar but for Donetsk, for Donbas and for Ukraine, is crucial. 'They rebuilt the airport [into something] state-of-the-art,' Todos continues, 'lots of other infrastructure and prior to that, Donetsk was just like any old sort of grey Soviet city. That was the general consensus from outside. And the fact of the matter is that before 2014, Donetsk Oblast, the city and surrounding area, was the most heavily populated area of Ukraine [4.4 million, equating to around 10 per cent of the population, by

2013]. It was really heavily, densely populated. So they had a massive fanbase. Everyone just loved Shakhtar, probably more than the Ukraine national team, because they represented this region.'

It was pretty much as Akhmetov had dreamed it. Mircea Lucescu already knew the scale of Akhmetov's ambition; on those nights after matches where the two men talked for hours and everything besides, the president didn't take long to fully outline his vision for a new home that would lift the club towards the European elite. 'He said to me that he wants to build a myth, a legend,' Lucescu remembers. 'I said, "Mr President, if you want to be in Europe, we have to have a good stadium," because the stadium we played in [Olimpiyskiy] wasn't of a good enough level. He asked me, "How many spectators will we have?" I said, "Maximum of 30,000." He said, "I'm going to make a stadium for 55,000." He was right, because after it was full, totally full for Champions League. The people started to smile so much. He organised the team and the club so well. He gave the club a different perspective and, step by step, we started to be at a level as a club and as a team to [become] very professional, and also start to get good results. And I convinced him – I told him, "If you want to get good results, we need to bring spectators."'

This was where Lucescu and Akhmetov found their synergy. They knew from their shared vision of the game that exciting football which captured the imagination would be key, not just to scratching their own personal itches, but to attracting fans, to making Shakhtar must-see. If the dream of Akhmetov was vivid, making it flesh was going to be a more convoluted process. When people look back at the building of Donbass Arena it's often said that it was completed ahead of schedule, and then the opening delayed to coincide with Miners' Day. That may be factually correct but doesn't acknowledge how long it took in terms of imagination, planning and – of course – a few setbacks en route.

'It took almost five years,' says Sergei Palkin. 'The first step, we started to talk about it. Secondly, we got the architects, who were working on the design for six months. After that, we went through all the variants. We spent almost a year to come up with the detailed design. When we were building there was the economic crisis in 2008, and everything stopped in construction – but we renegotiated our contract with the Turkish construction company [ENKA] and restarted work. It was,' he says with a small sigh, 'long.'

The job of bringing Akhmetov's idea to life fell to Arup, a firm of architects specialising in sports stadia with offices in thirty-four countries worldwide. 'I was a jobbing architect in London,' remembers associate director Chris Dite, whose work on Donbass was his first major project with the company. 'An opportunity came up to work as a contractor, to help get the drawings out, get the design finished to work with on my first ever job.' Even coming into the project fresh, it was quickly apparent to him that the Shakhtar president was clear on what he wanted. 'The reason that [the] Shakhtar [project] existed for us,' he says, 'was because of the work we'd done on Allianz Arena and Beijing [the Bird's Nest, for the 2008 Olympics] and yes, Manchester City.

'Essentially we were brought in when the new ownership came in, when the glory years arrived as it were.' Dite and his colleagues, working under project lead Jay Parrish, knew they shouldered a considerable burden of responsibility because, just as Srna and his teammates knew where they were heading, the Arup team had the opposite experience. They could look across the way and see precisely where Shakhtar had come from.

'They were in the old Olympic stadium,' Dite says, 'just on the other side of the road. It was very eastern European, a very Eastern Bloc, cookie cutter kind of Olympic Stadium. They had a few security issues in there with their previous leadership so when the new ownership came in, they wanted to create something new, and a new hub for Eastern European football. The target was to challenge Dynamo and to be the home of, and create this new space for, Ukrainian football. And for a very working class town on a site which, on the surface, already looks incredible, fantastic. It's in the park.'

That, perhaps, was the genius of Akhmetov's vision. It was not that he was conceiving, financing and building an incredible modern stadium in his home city. It was that he was placing that as the centrepiece of something bigger, something that would put Donetsk on a pedestal and show it off to the world. The city that arriving players had tolerated would become a place that future talent attracted to the club could love, without losing any of its history or heritage. Those players had always loved the club's environment and the care and consideration they had received. Now they could appreciate the city and the region too. 'When we had the grand opening of the stadium, it was like the Olympic games,' Palkin almost gushes, something he is not prone to doing. 'We invited Beyoncé and it was like . . . when we launched the stadium, we changed our vision of our city and of our country. The centre of civilisation,' he laughs, 'moved from Kyiv to Donetsk.'

Representing the difference between the two cities was important, though. Staying faithful to the original idea was key to the magic of Donbass Arena. There were many moments when it could have been blown off course in a location, and a city, with more than its share of natural challenges. Even imagined in a picturesque park setting, the project was defined by what Donetsk was. The site was underpinned by a series of coal mines. 'So it's a nightmare to build,' details Dite, 'and a nightmare to design because of all the engineering that needs to go in.' Arup were able to provide the engineering as well as the architecture, but had to present four different scenarios to the club to legislate for all the potential issues. The 2008 global financial crisis threatened to heavily impact the final product too. Anka, the Turkish construction company engaged to realise the design, were especially affected. 'They tried to change everything to make it cheaper to build and we were retained by Shakhtar to try and protect what we've drawn,' Dite says, 'and we were pretty proud of what was done.'

The idea of magpie-ing from continental and even global football culture, compiling a greatest hits set in creating a new stadium is relatively new in modern stadium culture; it's something that Tottenham Hotspur openly did for their bar-raising new stadium, which opened in April 2019. Christopher Lee of stadium designers Populous told *GQ* in

January 2017, for example, that they had modelled the single tier south stand on the vast *Südtribune* terrace behind the goal at Borussia Dortmund's Signal Iduna Park. When you look at the Tottenham stadium from the train line heading north from London's Liverpool Street, it has a similar docked spaceship feel to the Donbass Arena.

This, however, was in the mid-2000s in Ukraine. Taking such a cosmopolitan approach to the project as a whole was refreshing. If the bowl was 'very similar' to previous builds Arup had done, according to Dite, the overall feel was something quite different. 'Even if you look at the corporate boxes,' details Palkin, 'you can see we travelled the world, going around the best stadiums, and taking the ideas of what they did. If you look inside the stadium, it's a bowl, and we gave the architects a task of 54,000 spectators, but for everybody to have a very good view of the pitch. We had this computer calculating over one week, simulating the bowl.'

The attention to detail got more acute as it progressed and Shakhtar's board knew they were looking at something special. Yet it was intricate and layered, for a number of reasons. Akhmetov was hardly penny-pinching here. It was a vast commitment, and he was staking a lot of his – and Shakhtar's – reputation on it. It was huge for Ukraine, not just for Ukrainian football, or Ukrainian sport. 'It was a project of $400 million,' Palkin says bluntly. 'At the time in the whole country, not just talking about sport construction, there was nothing in our country built of that level. It was magnificent.' It was also something that was consuming, you feel. 'It became part of you,' confesses Palkin, 'something really big in your life. It was very important. When we built the new stadium, it was a miracle.'

It fused two things for Palkin. Shakhtar, which he has been publicly associated with for as long as we care to remember. The other part is his previous life as a finance director. 'Before Shakhtar,' he says, 'I was working for PricewaterhouseCoopers. My friend Maksym Tymchenko was working for SCM, the president's holding company, and one day he called me and said there was a chance for me to go and work at a football club. But at the time I was finance director of two major production plants.' Palkin wasn't really looking for another job, but Tymchenko – who now runs DTEK, the energy company garnering relatively big headlines as they work to repair much of the critical infrastructure destroyed by Russian attacks – was persuasive. 'He said to me there's the possibility to build something big for the future,' Palkin says with a barely discernible smile. 'They just needed help organising their finance department.'

For their part, Shakhtar were at a crossroads. This was 2003, so they were just beginning to establish themselves as a top club in Ukraine, but far from being European big fish. At the time the Ukrainian Premier League was only twelve years old. It, and Shakhtar, needed to professionalise and modernise. 'UEFA had introduced Financial Fair Play [FFP],' says Palkin, 'and all clubs needed to comply. So my one condition of [taking the post] was to prepare for FFP, organise all these financial organisational issues, like finding a way to get the National Bank of Ukraine to deal with transfer fees better. They didn't really know what it was about at the time.'

It was not a quick handover. In fact, it ended up not being a handover at all. 'I did this for a year-and-a-half,' he says, 'and we had agreed that at the end of this, I would move to become the financial director of SCM. But what happened during this time was that the vice-president of the club proposed me as club CEO for an interim period, for three months. After years just working with figures and calculations, I was tired and wanted some more human relations in my work,' he laughs. 'I said, "Let's give it a try." And now it's almost twenty years.'

His story at the club has parallels to that of Srna. 'Me and Darijo arrived in the same year,' he offers. 'Him as a player, me as a director. He is a legend of our club, but he also understands how everything works inside our club. He is very close to our president. Our president is very closely involved with all strategic processes of our club. For me it's very important to have someone on the sports side who can speak the same language as the president and give a true reflection of what's going on.'

As we talk of Akhmetov's continuing desire to be constantly involved and Shakhtar's relationship with the Brazilian transfer market, Palkin's phone rings. He apologises and starts talking to the president, one of a few calls per day he fields from Akhmetov for updates and general discussion. He comes back a few minutes later, galvanised and full of life.

Akhmetov later calls Srna when we're talking in the lobby of the Cullinan. As part of the circle of trust for many years, the Croatian is also in conversation with his president at least once a day. Srna particularly appreciates his human qualities in the context of the moment. 'When I first met him he received us, strangers, like Ukrainians,' he testifies. 'From the first day, he opened his doors to all of us, and that's so important. I'm so happy to have the possibility to work with him and to learn from him.' He is also aware that working with Akhmetov is an opportunity to constantly progress. Srna is confident in his ability to carry out his role of sporting director, but he is also aware that he is still developing.

'I learned [from working with Akhmetov],' he says, 'how to analyse situations in life. It's not necessary to analyse when something bad happens. You have to analyse when something good happens, and then analyse how to be better. When you lose the game, it's easy to make the analysis. But when you win, you need to learn how to be better.'

That was Akhmetov's and Shakhtar's challenge post-2009. Successful, trophy winners, now in receipt of their dream home and doing it all in style, playing sensational football. So where next? 'We had in our minds to get to a minimum of Champions League semi-finals,' Palkin admits. 'The president started to invest in top players who could make the difference, for example Bernard, who cost almost $30 million and was already a star back home in Brazil. The president built this kind of football empire and we wanted to make a jump. To show the whole world what Donetsk was, what Ukraine was. If you look at what our mission statement was, it was to be a world ambassador of football and to connect Ukraine with the world.'

That naked ambition is clear, but hasn't spilled over into recklessness. Akhmetov is used to big challenges and has the determination to chip away at them systematically. Just like with the drawbacks which could have scuppered Donbass, but didn't. The challenges in terms of topography were not insignificant to industry experts, but Shakhtar were ready to dig in, metaphorically and literally. There were more than physical barriers to surmount, though.

'But I think the most interesting thing,' suggests Dite, 'was that the aspiration of the owner was something that the city had never seen.' This, however, was different. This was something so grand, so ostentatious, placed in a traditionally working-class city never known for its peacocking. But Akhmetov knew it was meeting a need that not everybody knew existed, as the phenomenal response to the arena's opening proved. 'It was bringing something that looked like the future into a place that never had really the aspiration for that,' Dite continues. 'There was an aspiration to move them into the elite of world football.'

From the outside, it might have seemed fanciful, too much, a vanity project. 'When I was starting to work on it in 2005,' says Dite, 'I'd tell my friends what I'm working on. They were like, "Where the hell is that?" But I think [Shakhtar] became a name that you expected to see in the Champions League. They were in Europe every year and I think the stadium played a part in that.' It changed it all – projection outwards and expectation internally. You had a soaring Shakhtar and an opportunity to bring in the whole of Europe during Euro 2012. 'It was this beacon of development and investment and hope in the region,' Dite underlines, 'and you just feel it's incredible. You're incredibly proud.'

Now it just needed its match of reference, to underline

Shakhtar's elevated status. It found it in October 2012, when reigning European champions Chelsea came to town for a Champions League group stage tie. The visitors had not lost a European tie under Roberto Di Matteo. The club legend had taken over from André Villas-Boas the previous March and orchestrated a comeback against Napoli in the last 16, in one of the most astonishing European ties ever witnessed at Stamford Bridge, on the way to winning the trophy in Munich. That unbeaten run was about to be ripped up in irreverent fashion.

With the stands full and noisy, a confident Shakhtar – who had not lost for eleven months – clawed into Chelsea from the beginning. The Lucescu template was all there. The eastern European back four, with Srna captaining on the right. Tomáš Hübschman's presence in front of the defence (in what has now become the Stepanenko spot) allowed Fernandinho off the leash to go full box-to-box, an opportunity he would end up grabbing with both hands. When he joined the attack he would make almost a front five with Alex Teixeira, Willian, Henrikh Mkhitaryan and Luiz Adriano.

That night, it sometimes felt as if there were more Shakhtar attackers than that. In fact, there were only two in the Chelsea penalty area when the home side took the lead, Luiz Adriano hustling a bevy of confused defenders and teeing up Teixeira to guide a composed finish into the far corner, just three minutes in. The scream of recognition from the stands almost took the space-age ring of a roof off.

It was relentless. Shakhtar had a staggering seventeen shots on target that night against (at least on paper) the best in Europe. For Willian, his typically effervescent performance had a motivation beyond the roar of the Donbass crowd. 'It was my dream to play for Chelsea,' he admits. 'To play in the Premier League and to play for Chelsea. I remember it was December 2011 – Chelsea made an offer for me. So December and January, I was speaking to [Shakhtar], and they said "no". And then in 2012, in the summer Chelsea came again and Shakhtar said "no."' Despite winning the Champions League, Chelsea were due a rebuild. At twenty-four and the image of a buzzing, forward-thinking team, Willian was an attractive prospect. The way he played against his suitors did little to dampen their ardour.

'We had a great game against Chelsea,' he reflects. Twice, in fact. 'At home we won and at the Bridge we almost drew the game – we lost at the end [via a Victor Moses header in the fourth minute of stoppage time] – but they were two great games. I played really well in these games.' He was even better in the return, bagging two clinical strikes which should have brought Shakhtar a point back from London.

In Donetsk two weeks previously, Chelsea had not got off so lightly. A Fernandinho burst had created and finished the second goal, charging from midfield, exchanging passes with Adriano and then firing into the corner of Petr Čech's net. It was a glorious goal, Shakhtar's football at its finest, a calling card written in quilled ink on gold leaf. And the roar that greeted it, piercing through the ears, moving down and rattling the jawbone, said it all: 'We are unstoppable.' Oscar may have grabbed a late consolation goal, but it really did flatter Chelsea, as Shakhtar went to the top of the group – on the way to eventually helping to dump the holders out at the group stage. This was the kind of night that Akhmetov and Lucescu had dreamed of, and it was a statement, on and off the pitch. A full stadium, partisan and thrilled by a young, ambitious, confident and enterprising team. The result was good. The manner, however, was impeccable. This was what they wanted all along and what many never dared dream of.

For all his myriad achievements at the club, Paulo Fonseca never quite got to experience a night like this. It wasn't as if, though, the club veterans never talked about Donbass Arena. 'Yes, [they did] a hell of a lot!' smiles Fonseca. 'Actually, everyone who worked at the club, from the kit man to the medical staff to Palkin, they were all from Donetsk, and I soon realised that all those people were hurting a lot due to the fact the team couldn't play in the Donbass Arena.' At the beginning, Fonseca might have had a passing thought that to experience such elite facilities would have added to his experience at the helm of the club. But that sense of longing, the feeling of loss, made him understand that the stadium was more than an impressive base. It was a symbol of change, and a feeling of having put home on the map, showing the drive and the steps forward of Donbas and its people. Having numerous locals at the club, and feeling their sense of something having gone missing in their lives, told Fonseca what it was really all about. 'People from Donetsk adored Shakhtar and they all went to the stadium,' he continues, 'and everybody spoke a lot about this, about how they missed it and how it was a pity they could not play in front of their fans.'

Even before the invasion of February 2022, getting back there had seemed like a long shot – even if you must believe. 'It's a bit heartbreaking,' laments Dite, 'to see lumps of the facade falling off. And yes, it's heartbreaking to see people using it for target practice. We'd love to be able to be part of a story of it coming back to life at some point in the future. But right now that's in the too difficult box.'

It's extraordinary that, after all the planning, the imagination, the desire and the love that went into building Donbass Arena, Shakhtar spent longer prepping it than they did actually playing in it. When they moved out of the city in 2014, the club had played in it for less than five years. It's incredibly sad.

'It was a good, healthy chunk of money that was invested to do it,' confirms Dite. He is, however, gently optimistic for the future, whenever that may be. 'All I know is that, for all of the damage that is done, a lot of the damage has been reasonably superficial to facades and stuff like that. And yes, deep down we're hoping that there's an opportunity at some point in the future, and that the concrete frame will survive as much as it can do. There will be an opportunity when the time is right to help the football club, either [to] rebuild what they have, or to take [another] look at how Shakhtar Donetsk [is] in 2024. We would look forward to any opportunity to get involved and help them to do it again.' Dite and his colleagues specialise in making dreams reality.

In the meantime, the nightmare continues. It's not really in the smashed panel windows and damaged canopies that have peppered news reports and social media, the superficial and the fixable. It's knowing that, rather than hosting Champions

League high points, the stadium has been used to store Russian-purchased rocket launchers. That's the crux, that the stadium in many ways looks like what was left behind. A big banner of Taison, the winger who was a hero of the club's glorious past over an eight-year period but left in 2021, looms down over a large banner on the outside of the stadium, as if things had never taken a left turn. That suspension of disbelief, rather than mere neglect, is reflected in the current governance of the stadium. Pro-Russian media announced in May 2018 the restoration of the turf at Donbass Arena. One wonders quite what for, with no football out there and precious little economy. In a macabre twist, the occupiers, under the Donetsk People's Republic (DPR) banner, have made it known that the stadium has been under their jurisdiction since 2017. They have also let it be known through local media that they have reopened the club museum. Not just stealing the venue, but stealing the club's history.

This is symptomatic, sadly, of the Russian kleptocracy which has blighted the progress of Shakhtar and Ukraine since 2014, and continues to do so.

6

Euromaidan and the fall of Donetsk

To understand the present, you have to have at least a grasp on the past. In 2013 I thought I knew Kyiv. I knew my way around, the monuments, the people, good places to eat and a good chunk of the history. Then, in November of that year, we visited friends living in the city as one of them celebrated a birthday. As we took an excursion out of the centre in a minibus on Saturday 22 November, my nose was pressed to the window. There were thousands and thousands of people on the streets, to the extent that you couldn't see an inch of pavement. It was a sight you couldn't tear your eyes from. Later, on the streets of central Kyiv, their mood was unmistakeable. They spoke from the heart, without bluster but with firmness and conviction. Those gathered thousands had all been heading in the direction of the city centre. Or more specifically, to Maidan Nezalezhnosti – Independence Square.

I already knew Kyiv as a magnificent city that had endured its share of tragedy. It was in the Ukrainian capital in September 1941 that one of the worst atrocities of the Second World War took place. Over the space of two days, thirty-four thousand Ukrainian Jews had their possessions taken from them by the occupying Nazis, before being marched to the ravine of Babi Yar, where they were shot dead. Babi Yar has since become a sacred memorial site.

Ahead of Ukraine jointly hosting Euro 2012 with Poland, Kyiv struggled to keep pace with the necessary preparations under the chaotic stewardship of mayor Leonid Chernovetskyi. Then-UEFA president Michel Platini threatened explicitly in spring 2010 to take it away from the country if Kyiv didn't get its house in order. 'We cannot waste any more time,' he said, adding that, 'if there is no Kyiv, there is no Ukraine.' In the scramble to increase accommodation capacity for visitors – there were 17,000 hotel rooms in the city, which amounted to less than a third of the capacity of the Olimpiyskiy, which was being built at the time – the city's council had approved an application to build a hotel at Babi Yar. For Kyiv's Jewish community of 110,000 – the biggest Jewish population in Europe outside of London, Paris and Moscow – it was a grave insult.

It was a sensitive subject for more than one reason. Not only was it considered sacred, but Ukrainian Jews being deprioritised stung them considerably. While Kyiv was still in the Soviet Union when the first memorial at the site was installed in 1976, there was no mention that the massacre had been of specifically Jewish victims. The casualties were simply referred to as 'Soviet'. The Jewish community had waited a long, painful period for recognition, and here city administrators were running roughshod over their history again.

The feeling this time, however, was that the authorities' lack of acknowledgment of citizens' feelings was altogether more nefarious. When Ukrainian president Viktor Yanukovych made an about-turn and refused to sign a projected association agreement with the European Union, favouring closer ties with Russia, the tradition of standing up for justice came to the fore again. Yanukovych's move felt deeply anti-democratic. The Rada, Ukraine's parliament, had approved signing the agreement in February that year by an overwhelming majority, with 312 of 349 sitting MPs voting in favour.

On 21 November, Euromaidan began. The sheer scale of it was breathtaking. Having not been there for 2004's Orange Revolution, it had been difficult to appreciate the full extent of a relatively newly independent country's thirst for justice and self-determination. 'It was always apolitical,' insists Paul Niland, a businessman and writer, and the founder of Lifeline Ukraine, a suicide prevention and mental health helpline. Euromaidan may have started as a reaction to a particular event but it quickly became Maidan, simply named after the epicentre of the protests. It was a cry for democracy, a tipping point where the people made it clear that corruption, and collusion with Russia, was unacceptable. That connotation lingered from the events of 2004, when widespread protests called out the then-would-be President Yanukovych for being at the centre of large-scale electoral fraud. So the protests targeted a culture, even if they were prompted by a specific event.

'From the very beginning the people of Maidan . . . there were politicians who were on the stage who were making speeches and so on,' Niland says, 'but it was like an unwritten rule that that political banners or flags of certain parties were not welcome on Maidan. It was, from the very beginning, a people's movement.' One of the more arresting moments in the 2015 documentary *Winter On Fire: Ukraine's Fight For Freedom* – at least from a western perspective – is that of the internationally respected Vitali Klitschko, an MP at the time who would soon become Mayor of Kyiv, being booed by the crowd for relaying his negotiations with the ruling powers.

'Maidan lasted ninety-three days and I was there for eighty-nine of them,' Niland tells me. 'But the day that I knew this was a revolution and we were going to be successful is also linked to that thirtieth of November and then the first of December.' This was when the Berkut – special police units – attacked the protestors with sticks and tear gas in an attempt to make them disperse. The counterattack the following day saw the protesters occupy City Hall and the Trade Union Building. Rather than ending the movement, the aggressors only succeeded in entrenching their positions. 'It just became like a little mini-city after a few weeks,' says Pete Josse, a British resident living in the capital at the time. 'So when the temperatures dropped in December, January, that's when it really started getting pretty serious.'

A major turning point was 16 January 2014, when the Rada passed a group of ten laws restricting free speech and free assembly, or anti-protest laws as they were (reasonably) perceived. One gave authorities the power to define protests as 'extremist activity', while another granted the Berkut immunity from prosecution for attacks on protestors. In a shambolic procedure, the vote in the chamber had been taken hurriedly with an unscientific (and very approximately counted) show of hands. On 19 January, the next weekly Sunday meetings held among gathered protestors in Maidan, opposition politicians suggested the introduction of the laws underlined that Maidan was getting the upper hand on Yanukovych. That Sunday was, according to Niland, 'one of the key days marking [Maidan] out as a non-political movement.'

For the Josse family, however, the shift transported a surreal situation into a more concerning one. They had moved to Kyiv less than a year before and were raising two young children in a city centre apartment. When the protestors originally set up their barricades to make camp at Maidan, the protest had been as peaceful as the people were determined. Pete Josse shows me a picture on his wall at home of the two boys, wrapped up in snow suits, woolly hats and scarves, stood smiling in front of the barricades of stacked wooden pallets. Yet as time crept on, this local backdrop showed the potential to turn. Every morning Josse would deliver his eldest son, who was five, onto the charter bus to his school, which went from the bottom of their street – 'one hundred metres from Maidan' – and collect him from the same spot at the end of the day. 'I remember one day we went down to pick him up from the little bus stop, and some guy with a gun in his holster turned around to us and said, "No, you should not be on the streets with your children. You should go home, take your kids off the streets. It's dangerous." So that was a moment where we thought, hang on a minute. This isn't just something to watch and observe.'

It marked a gear change in the prevailing mood. The protest was serious and heartfelt, but had been good-natured. A cottage industry in novelty items mocking Yanukovych, and Russia, had sprung up around Maidan. Makeshift stalls at the side of the road in the city centre sold Soviet army hats alongside toilet rolls with Vladimir Putin's face on. I remember my friend posted me a *'Putin Huylo'* ('Putin's a dickhead') T-shirt at Christmas. Yet outbreaks of violence were becoming increasingly frequent, with skirmishes on the edges of the Maidan camp. A short walk away is one of Ukrainian football's landmarks – the Valeriy Lobanovskyi Stadium, where Dynamo used to play. Protestors gathered there in a standoff with the Berkut for a few nights in January. On the way home from drinks with friends one night, Josse went to take a look and was confronted by a developing scene, with protestors and authorities on opposite sides of a row of burning tyres in front of the stadium.

As time went on, this was one of the saddest indicators of what was happening to this elegant city – the damage to its landmarks. 'Lobanovskyi's statue was covered in dust and flames,' Josse remembers, 'and the whole road was covered in burning tyres.' On reflection, he later thought that going to check out the protest at such close quarters 'was a stupid thing to do,' but it would have been unnatural to ignore such a fast-changing situation – and the escalation of matters, then and in the future, was difficult to predict. Every day saw a different nuance or twist to an already volatile status quo. As matters escalated, various countries decided they needed to get their citizens out. UK government advice didn't follow suit. 'We never got evacuated,' Josse says. 'Some embassies got their people out. Some nights were particularly hectic and when you're in an apartment two blocks away, it's very real.'

The most real was on 20 February. If the protestors were incensed with Yanukovych for the Berkut's tactics, a whole other level of atrocity was about to be embarked upon. Joelene, Pete Josse's wife and a Foreign Office official in Kyiv, walked to work as she always did. 'She used to walk across Maidan to the office,' Josse explains, 'and report en route about what the situation was every morning. This one morning she was walking across, and she called me [at] ten to nine to say that it was pretty quiet. There were [plumes] of smoke – all the camps are pretty smoky. It's fairly quiet. And she went to work. I was on Twitter and suddenly see all this stuff about shots being fired in Maidan. I called Joelene to say, "Let me know you're all right. Get out of there."'

He speaks without melodrama which, conversely, makes the retelling even more frightening. 'There's no phone at all,' he says. 'I can't get hold of her. I'm frantically calling her, "Where the hell are you?" So that was a really weird moment. She'd gone to the office. They'd all gone into a security meeting in the morning. It was all very quiet. [She didn't] pick up my messages until she came out of that meeting. And it was me that told everybody in the office what was going on in terms of all of the shots fired by these snipers. And I think over seventy people died that day. So that was a pretty raw moment to think about. [She] easily could have just walked into a load of gunfire that morning and she wouldn't have even known about it.' It had been the city's darkest day for decades.

The intensity of it all had become too much. 'I think just after that was when we came home,' he says. 'Me and the boys came home for a week just to get out of there because, after that moment, there's too much going on. Lots of violence, lots of killings. We said, "We'll get out for at least a week and see what happens." And almost as soon as we left, in fact, Yanukovych fled.'

The situation around Maidan had been changing so quickly that traditional news couldn't keep up. At that point, Twitter was a lifeline to the Josses – as well as to their work colleagues. 'I was following certain people who were on the ground,' he says, 'and you'd hear it straight away, way before it was on TV. There was still a little cloud of confusion because everyone's thinking, What's going on? If you're listening to journalists and whoever else is on the ground reporting exactly what's happening exactly when it's happening, then it's much better than waiting for a news report.' The confusion of rapidly unfolding events mixed with vastly different versions of the truth according to government mouthpieces and protestors left a lot to diffuse. 'It was an information war,' as Pete Josse says.

And it continues to be an information war, on all fronts. The link between the protests and football in Kyiv was clear, and the involvement of Ukrainian football's ultra culture in Maidan dispelled a lot of myths. Groups from Dynamo in particular were an active and prominent part of the Maidan protests, which largely coincided with the long winter break from

Ukrainian Premier League action. 'This reflects a recurring theme of major street demonstrations in eastern Europe over the past couple of decades,' wrote Jonathan Wilson in the *Guardian* in March 2014. 'The ultra groups are largely made up of young, fit men who are organised and practised in fighting with and evading police – they are useful people to have on your side.' It was not limited just to the capital, but was reflected in similar uprisings through the country. 'In Dnipropetrovsk on 26 January,' wrote *Radio Free Europe*'s Daisy Sindelar in January 2014, 'hundreds of Dnipro ultras backed an unexpectedly large crowd of pro-Maidan demonstrators as they attempted to storm the regional administration building.'

Josse had invited some friends over from the UK to watch Dynamo, who he regularly went to see at Olimpiyskiy, play Shakhtar in March. Instead, after Russia's invasion of Crimea, the match – as with the whole Ukrainian Premier League restart – was postponed amid rising tension. There were positives to come out of this, with Dynamo's ultras and their Shakhtar counterparts who had already booked their trips to Kyiv playing a match at Olimpiyskiy in place of the first team one. A sizeable crowd attended and the stadium even opened its concession stands for the afternoon. At full-time, Sergei Pavlichenko, a Dynamo ultra imprisoned under the Yanukovych regime and subsequently released after the president was deposed, gave a speech to which the gathered crowd followed his prompts. The two groups of supporters from either side of the country chanted the now-familiar *Slava Ukraïni!* (glory to Ukraine) to each other. While he was incarcerated, ultras across the continent from Romania to Portugal, and even Russia, had chanted and displayed banners in support of Pavlichenko.

It suggested in emphatic terms that more held Ukraine together than tore it apart. Donbas is nothing if not complex, as pointed out by Indiana University's professor of history Hiroaki Kuromiya in a 2015 lecture titled 'The Enigma of the Donbas: How to understand its past and its future', given at the Donkult cultural forum in Lviv. So assumptions were always ill-judged. 'Dismissing the Donbas as a trouble-maker,' Kuromiya wrote, 'is avoiding the political problem of Ukrainian nation-building.' Something that is complex and takes effort to understand can still be worth understanding, and many Ukrainians were (and are) willing to try.

'They [Kyiv and Donetsk] are a long way apart,' Josse acknowledges, 'but what I noticed really is that a lot of people felt interlinked. This is another of those Russian propaganda things where they talk about how, oh, it's the people in the east just speak Russian and they're all Russophiles. They don't care about the West and Ukraine and all that. But it's actually completely different. I found that in most families that we knew in Ukraine, everyone had a little bit of Russian in their families, whether it was mum that was Russian or dad was from Ukraine.' Closing that geographical gap, demolishing presupposition and building understanding that more unites Ukrainians than divides them would become crucial, and would be the source of the country's strength in years to come. In his subsequent work as an independent election observer in Kherson, Josse's own feelings that the truth was far more nuanced than the clichés were reinforced.

Joelene Josse said the difference on the streets became noticeable as 2014 progressed. 'When we first arrived there,' she says, 'there wasn't this massive differentiation between Ukrainian and Russian. Everyone was like arms open wide, and Russian and Ukrainian were interchangeable. Then over time, as Maidan grew before Crimea was annexed, and before everything really started properly kicking off in Donbas, you saw this evolution of people, starting to wear more and more national dress, and more people not speaking Russian in the streets, because they were mainly Ukrainians. And then it morphed into this situation where you wouldn't go down to Besarabsky market and speak Russian anymore. Everyone was speaking Ukrainian.'

After Crimea fell, tensions rose in Donbas. Nothing was isolated. In the Shakhtar offices, there was concern for Joe Palmer about what was happening in Kyiv, but it felt far removed from where he was. On his doorstep, the tide was incremental. Pro-Russian protestors moved from talk to action, and took over the regional administration building, directly opposite where Palmer lived. 'They barricaded themselves in,' he recounted. 'There was a wall of tyres around it and they'd set booby traps. There were guys patrolling [the perimeter] carrying baseball bats with nails through them.' Even then, however, it was self-contained – in a sense, like Maidan. There was no, as Palmer put it, 'outreach of violence.'

There was largely calm in the Shakhtar squad. Partly, perhaps, because of the distance and partly because footballers get very good at compartmentalising, with the need for short spells of intense focus. Even so, life felt normal. 'It started in the winter in Kyiv,' remembers Taras Stepanenko, 'and then some things were happening in Donetsk too, with troops taking over the regional government. For normal people like me . . . I just had training, my usual life. I read some things in the news, and then my mum called me [from Zaporizhzhia] and asked, "Taras, what happened?" And I told her, 'All good." I was still walking with my family in the centre of the city, with no problem.'

That sense of 'keep calm and carry on' spread, says Palmer – which might well have been for the best. 'So while you felt it was shocking . . . most Ukrainians were quite desensitised to it,' he says, 'which put me at ease anyway.' Being part of Shakhtar, as well, created the feeling of having an extra layer of protection. 'Because of Akhmetov's power, we knew what was going on [to an extent] and there was security all around the stadium,' he points out. 'I never felt particularly threatened. There were moments coming up to May where you could feel the tension, but you still felt there could be a resolution.'

While the mood around the city was phlegmatic, there was a sense among the foreigners in Donetsk that they might need to communicate more with one another. Their community was not as numerous as the expat equivalent in Kyiv, for example. 'We were having quite a lot of meetings with the other expats,' Palmer details. 'So there were people from Germany, France, Holland, and thankfully one of the Swiss guys that was running the Donbas Palace hotel in Donetsk, he was receiving information every day from Swiss intelligence explaining what was happening, what he shouldn't do and where he shouldn't go. We were monitoring that and we started to meet more regularly, and [we were] texting and updating each other every day with the latest. Funnily enough I knew the British Ambassador in Kyiv at the time and the only thing I received from him was an invitation to an Ambassador's reception dinner in Kyiv, which I thought was very British! Even though it was the time of almost-war here, it was, 'Come for dinner, everything will be fine. Cup of tea?''

Polite discussion was only ever going to go so far. There was a crunch moment approaching. 'When it got towards twenty-fifth May and the elections were due, we sat down and we were saying to ourselves, "It's going to kick off." Whoever gets in power, the rebels are not going to accept [them].' By this point, even the Stepanenkos were erring on the side of caution. 'When I left for the national team and my wife stayed in Donetsk,' he says, 'around the end of May, I could see some bad things were starting to happen. So I said to my wife to take my son, take some things and go to Zaporizhzhia.' Palmer also hurriedly made plans to leave. 'I made the decision to pack up as much as I could and fly out on the Saturday. The elections took place on the Sunday and on the Monday, it kicked off.'

That is something of an understatement. On the morning of Monday 26 May, purported pro-Russian rebels took over Donetsk International Airport. As government forces responded, the First Battle of Donetsk Airport began. The images of what happened next hit home all over the world. The combat was swift and brutal, lasting less than two days, and plumes of thick black smoke streamed skywards. Heavily armed troops on both sides exchanged fire and Ukrainian air strikes were launched to dislodge the invaders. Palmer was getting scores of text messages from friends and acquaintances checking he got out. Friends from Donetsk sent messages telling him what was happening back there, which looked like 'scenes out of a zombie movie' – abandoned cars and emergency vehicles, and bodies in the street. 'You just thought,' he asks with enduring incredulity, 'What's happened here? How did it escalate that quickly?'

It was to be the last time he was there, in a city that had given him so much and had a bright future, he thought. With the post-Euro developments – Donbass Arena, the airport, regeneration – also came the opening of an international school, a sign that Donetsk was opening up to the world. No more. The eventual destruction of the airport had been particularly symbolic: seeing a new, ultra-modern sign of Donetsk's progress and future reduced to rubble. Not to mention the city's will to connect with the rest of the world, bringing people in and out. It was now a closed society. 'It was horrific,' Palmer sighs, 'but thankfully all the people I was close to got out. It was only in the months after that you thought this could be tricky, and we had no idea when we were going to be able to come back. If indeed ever.'

The low-key exit of Yanukovych from the country on 22 February 2014, eventually to a safe haven in Russia, felt like it should have been the start of some sort of stability. Yet he continued to poke and prod from the sidelines, famously in his 28 February address from Rostov-on-Don. The use of Putin-esque language to frame his argument is now, looking back, even more noticeable. 'Power was taken by nationalists, fascists, youngsters who are the absolute minority of Ukraine. This is the result of the irresponsible policies of the West, which was supporting the Maidan.' Yanukovych spoke in Russian, not Ukrainian.

The question that was posed, post-Orange Revolution of 2004, post-Euromaidan in 2013 and post-war starting in Donbas in 2014, was 'How well did the different parts of Ukraine know each other?'

'There was Russia's disinformation machine,' Joelene Josse underlines, 'pumping out stories that were just not true, but what you also saw with all the disinformation at the time was that the Western media were also getting it wrong. There were a lot of news stories that were just inaccurate both coming out of Russia Today [RT], but then also being perpetuated by the Western media in terms of that neo-Nazi story.'

Ukraine had already protested misunderstanding in the past, reacting with anger to the BBC documentary *Euro 2012: Stadiums of Hate*, which aired in May 2012, a few weeks before the championships were scheduled to start. The BBC strongly defended it, and the Ukrainian foreign ministry spokesman, Oleg Voloyshn, who called the programme 'a direct assault' on the tournament's organisation, seemed to be contesting the framing of the film rather than its facts.

Speaking to Paul Niland, I say to him, makes me go back and examine my own use of language. I rewatch the opening of the 2015 film *Shakhtar Donetsk: A club in exile*, which I co-wrote and presented for the *Guardian*. I'm standing outside Arena Lviv on a Shakhtar matchnight. 'Donetsk has been under the control of pro-Russian forces since last summer,' is my opening line. It is striking how insidious some of our misrepresentations, hung around repetition, actually are.

Niland speaks eloquently about how wearing the constant Russian gaslighting is. He needed to take a break from social media, he says, having been a target for Russian trolls, possibly from the Internet Research Agency, the troll farm operating from Saint Petersburg. 'At the time that was compounded as well by the notion of what then unfolded in the Donbas,' he explains, 'not even the whole of the Donbas but parts of it was somehow a separatist movement. It wasn't – it was a Russian movement, a Russian operation from the very beginning.'

Based in Kyiv for more than twenty years, Niland has bridged that gap between west and east himself, with Lifeline Ukraine fulfilling a need that became especially prominent following the outbreak of war. 'The first reason why we came together,' he details, 'is that we needed to provide a suicide prevention support structure for veterans who'd been fighting in the Donbas since 2014. You know, in the UK it's the same when you've got people who've returned from serving in Iraq and in Afghanistan. You have to provide that support structure to them. When I looked at how to approach this and I studied the American model, the Veterans Affairs Office, a peer-to-peer support structure is the optimum way of providing support. I went out to recruit a bunch of veterans and work alongside them every single day.'

Helping to facilitate that sort of support gave Niland greater insight not only into the issues surrounding the experience of war – coping not just with immediate threat but living with trauma on a daily basis – but also an understanding of how different post-2014 experiences were for people in different parts of Ukraine. 'While we've been living with war since

2014,' he recognises, 'Crimea was relatively bloodless. But the Donbas war was not. It was also distant. But then on the twenty-fourth of February of last year, when the full-scale invasion happened and when Kyiv itself was under attack . . . I thought I knew war because I studied a lot and had to understand why it is that veterans particularly have issues with PTSD, and processing their experiences on the frontlines. When the all-out invasion began I realised that, actually, I really didn't know very much.'

'Today's Ukraine is a young nation and its nation and state-building process is not an easy or short process,' wrote Kuromiya. 'Yet one has to see that there is no fundamental contradiction among democracy, conflict, freedom, and nation and state-building. If anything, Ukraine's tradition of freedom and democracy, however messy it may be, should be an advantage rather than a disadvantage in comparison with Russia's tradition of autocracy. Ukraine seems far ahead of Russia in this critical respect.' Despite Russia's long-term efforts to divide and conquer, nine years and counting of war have brought Ukrainians closer together.

Chapter 7

Far From Home

'I'm not sure if war changes us. I think we will be able to understand that after the war ends. It's just that the war puts us in different conditions. Different conditions of existence. The conditions in which you have to choose to either remain human or turn into an animal, a terrorist, a marauder, a rapist. The war is a choice. And it's a difficult choice, because hatred towards your enemies overwhelms you daily. Hatred towards enemies who took away the life one had before. But you have to suppress your hatred. To know that it's the enemy, yet [to] fight by the rules. As in, staying human. And that is a hard choice.'

Volodymyr Zelenskiy, from *My Next Guest with David Letterman and Volodymyr Zelenskiy* Netflix Special, 12 December 2022

It had been the jewel, as we've heard. The symbol of a new Donbas, a prosperous Donbas. Now it had become something else. A symptom of war, of fear, of desperation and of nothingness. A void. Where before there was life, hope and optimism, there now would need to be a grim determination to hold on and to grasp sustenance where you could. Queues of civilians collected food parcels from the Donbass Arena, filing past tonnes of supplies piled high next to images of players lifting trophies and scoring goals on the internal stadium

Shakhtar's Brazilians were a key part of their years of success, even after the departure from Donetsk. Here Taison lifts the 2018 Ukrainian Cup after victory over Dynamo Kyiv in the final. Left to right: Ismaily, Dodô, Taison, Dentinho, Olarenwaju Kayode, Fred, Marlos.
© *FC Shakhtar Donetsk and Michael Maslovskiy)*

Perhaps the most important player to wear the Shakhtar shirt, Darijo Srna has served as player, assistant coach and now sporting director since arriving from Hajduk Split in 2003. Here he celebrates a goal with Douglas Costa (back to camera) and now-captain Taras Stepanenko. (© *FC Shakhtar Donetsk and Michael Maslovskiy*)

Club CEO Sergei Palkin marks 20 years at Shakhtar in 2023, and has been a driving force and eloquent spokesman since they have been forced on the road. He is pictured here outside Donbass Arena in 2009. (© *FC Shakhtar Donetsk and Michael Maslovskiy*)

Owner Rinat Akhmetov (left) was delighted to stave off competition from big European clubs to sign coach Roberto De Zerbi, whose daring philosophy was going to take Shakhtar to the next level in Europe. Here Akhmetov greets De Zerbi on the coach's first day in Kyiv. *(© FC Shakhtar Donetsk and Michael Maslovskiy)*

After victory over Manchester City in Kharkiv saw Shakhtar through to the Champions League last 16 in 2017, Fonseca was forced to make good on a bet with team manager Vitaliy Khlyvniuk and dress as Zorro in the post-match press conference. 'Vitaly said: "Hey coach, let's make a bet. If, tomorrow, we beat Manchester City, will you go the press conference dressed up as Zorro?" I replied: "If we beat City I'll do anything!"'
(© FC Shakhtar Donetsk and Michael Maslovskiy)

The Donbass Arena was the pride and joy of Shakhtar, its staff and its players. After war broke out in Donbas and the club left in May 2014, the unused stadium suffered damage, symbolic of the conflict and the club's predicament. (© *FC Shakhtar Donetsk and Michael Maslovskiy*)

Mircea Lucescu guided Shakhtar to triumphs beyond the wildest dreams of most during the majority of his 12 years in charge. This is where everything began to change, in a 2014 press conference with his assistant Alexandru Spiridon (right) and CEO Sergei Palkin (left), as the club make a statement on the outbreak of war in Donbas.
(© FC Shakhtar Donetsk and Michael Maslovskiy)

Academy product Mykhailo Mudryk was Shakhtar's star in their Champions League run in 2022–23, and his €100 million sale to Chelsea in January 2023 gave the club some much-needed liquidity. Here he is beating Celtic's Josip Juranović and scoring Shakhtar's equaliser against the Scottish champions in Warsaw, 14th September 2022.
(© FC Shakhtar Donetsk and Michael Maslovskiy)

With Ukrainian clubs required to play their UEFA club competition matches outside the country after the full-scale Russian invasion, Legia Warsaw's Stadion Wojska Polskiego became Shakhtar's safe European home. This is the crowd choreography, symbolising the unity between Poland and Ukraine, before kick-off of the match against Real Madrid on 11th October 2022. (© *FC Shakhtar Donetsk and Michael Maslovskiy*)

From 2014, president Rinat Akhmetov has driven and bankrolled extensive humanitarian efforts for the disadvantaged and displaced in Donbas and beyond. After the 2022 invasion, Shakhtar helped put up refugees in Arena Lviv, and here defender Valeriy Bondar visits residents at a shelter in Warsaw while on Champions League duty in the Polish capital. (© *FC Shakhtar Donetsk and Michael Maslovskiy*)

The Donbass Arena not only brought a world-class stadium to Donetsk but regenerated and modernised a whole part of this traditionally industrial, working-class city.
(© *Courtesy of Arup and J Parrish*)

Shakhtar's Champions League home fixtures took on another dimension after their move to Donbass Arena, a fervent, 52,000-capacity wall of noise. In its first season hosting Champions League matches, the Ukrainian champions beat Arsenal, Braga, Partizan and Roma here. (© Courtesy of Arup and J Parrish)

walls. It felt as if Shakhtar were still there, even though the team no longer were.

There would be no more full stands at the Donbass Arena, no more joy, no more communion of football supporters and epicentre of regional pride. It became, however, a lifeline of a different sort. Shakhtar and their staff may have suffered considerable trauma in being forced from their homes and their place of work on a frantic timetable. Yet they, arguably, were among the luckier ones.

Many were left stranded in Donetsk and the surrounding region as the lifeblood drained from it, with businesses and shops closing left and right. The elderly, the infirm and those with family tying them to the region were stuck and facing no future. 'After the invasion in 2014 started, the Donbas region,' says Sergei Palkin, 'from an economic point of view, became very poor. People lost work . . . it was catastrophic. People had nothing to eat. We organised big numbers of trucks, moving to the Ukrainian border, moving to Donetsk, and in Donbass Arena we had this logistical hub. All these trucks arrived and we distributed food all over Donetsk and all over the region. President Akhmetov, he helped a lot.' Even though it was far from easy, the club were maintaining strong links with their native region. Over eight million aid packages were handed out in the two years after the hub was set up in August 2014, just under three months after Shakhtar left the city.

'Then in a moment,' sighs Palkin, 'it just stopped. The Donetsk authorities, this fake republic, they stopped accepting these trucks with food, with everything.' Akhmetov's efforts to help had hit a major roadblock. There had been few suggestions that the owner's intervention was political, but it was no longer welcomed by the DPR, the unrecognised republic covering the city and Russian-occupied areas of Donetsk Oblast. The DPR was keen to make it known that the Donbass Arena was theirs. Later, in May 2018, pro-Russian media reported that the damaged pitch had been restored while other parts of the infrastructure in the now-idle stadium were under repair. With the DPR having already announced that the arena was now under their jurisdiction in early 2017, the theft was complete.

Even before this – ever since, in fact, the move out of Donetsk in 2014 – the club had been busy working out the best way to carry on, all while coming to terms with what they'd lost. Nine years on, Srna admits he still thinks about what used to be home, back when he was still a player, all the time. 'Of course. I still have my room in our camp there. I have my things there . . . ' He takes a breath. 'It's painful to think about that, really painful. Because one day we had everything and then . . . '

Everyone you speak to has a slightly different take on leaving Donetsk. Not in terms of what it meant, but how it felt at the time. There was not the short, sharp shock of the early morning bombing of 24 February 2022, but the feeling of something creeping up – and advice that it would be best to leave, and not to hang around and think on it. 'It was not quite war when I left,' Srna tries to explain, 'but some kind of strange atmosphere. Really strange. It was something in the air.'

By the time the business end of the season was approaching, the goalposts were shifting. 'We played our last game of the season against Zorya somewhere near Kyiv,' Srna recounts. Footballers are often sketchier on the details than fans and journalists. Their lives are a string of training sessions, hotels, gyms, gaming battles, calls home, matches, flights and coach trips. It all blends into one. Given the context here, the blur of a club shifting, it's amazing Srna remembers it as clearly as he does.

Shakhtar's notional visit to Zorya was their penultimate game of the season. It was in Cherkasy, two-and-a-half hours south of Kyiv. It was Zorya's home game, as they were in the same boat as Shakhtar, displaced, with the Football Federation of Ukraine deciding that no matches should take place in Kharkiv, Luhansk or Donetsk. With tensions rising in the east, the FFU decreed in early May that all UPL matches would be played behind closed doors for safety reasons. The political situation was already fraying the edges of the season, with both Sevastopol and Tavriya Simferopol thrown out of the league after Russia annexed Crimea in spring (with both clubs subsequently disbanding). The league lost another team mid-season after Arsenal Kyiv's financial collapse. Real life was heavily conditioning the sporting competition.

Having opened the season in mid-July 2013 with a 2–0 win over Hoverla Uzhhorod, in front of a crowd of over 36,000 at the Donbass, Shakhtar would end it ten months later with the same result but as lonely champions, with Luiz Adriano's brace taking care of Volyn Lutsk in front of just 2,300 people at Stadion Tsentralnyi in Cherkasy – their second successive game there. Most of Shakhtar's players and staff had only left Donetsk for the last time a few days before that final match.

It had been abrupt. They were living in a whirlwind.

'I went on the sixteenth of May and left everything in my house,' confirms Srna. 'Three cars, all my watches, my clothes, the children's clothes, my wife's clothes. Everything. I left it there and never went back.' Never? 'Never.' Does he know if the house is still standing? 'Yes. It's still there. I have information that someone, some Russian soldiers, they entered my house.' He pauses, and briefly raises his eyebrows and offers a wan half-smile. 'My ex-house.' It is far from the first time that Srna has gone over this, but it is not something you ever really come to terms with. The sense of violation of a private space is still there. Yet he and his teammates were forced to leave it all behind, to move on, to compartmentalise and to continue, as footballers do. Onto the next game.

After the move, Shakhtar were playing games initially in . . . 'Everywhere,' Srna cuts in, drily. But despite the club's world shaking on its axis, Akhmetov was determined to try and make it as business as usual as humanly possible. 'The president didn't change anything,' he insists. 'He continued to pay the salaries, the bonuses. In that aspect, the motivation was the same. But it was more difficult to win the championship without fans. You need time. In the first two years we lost everything, but step by step you start to live with that and you start to get used to the situation.'

The situation required tact and care. 'You can't be ready for something like this,' is how Yuri Sviridov puts the moving process. 'It wasn't organised in one go.' In a sense, that blunted the impact of the upheaval, with the end of the season allowing a sort of soft departure from the city. Many of the players went off on holiday and simply didn't come back to Donetsk. The staff's departure was more gradual. 'Every player, every director, every person moved from Donetsk at that time,' Sviridov recounts, 'but over May, June, July. Personally, I left on the fifth of July.' He takes a second to absorb his goodbye to his home city. Palkin also left Donetsk that month. When the club reconvened, first in Switzerland for a pre-season training camp and then gradually in Kyiv, there was much to organise. 'I remember we had to start in July, almost from the very beginning.'

It was different for many non-Ukrainians. Upstairs in the club's offices one of them, Joe Palmer, had fled in what felt like the nick of time. He was still attempting to carry on the strategic and commercial side of the recalibrating club's operation, but it was complicated. The aim had been to use the move to the Donbass Arena and on-field triumphs to push the club's profile up to the next level. In an instant, the target had become to simply be able to keep going.

'I was still working for them because we were just getting to work on a big internationalisation project,' he details, 'a strategy that would look at how we could expand our universe because obviously the Ukrainian league was quite limited in terms of commercial opportunities.' With the domestic ceiling, it made sense to lean into one of the main characteristics that Shakhtar was becoming known for further afield – the Brazilians. Building on that glamour and exoticism could make the club far more easily exportable, perhaps more so than any Ukrainian club had ever been. Palmer felt that the Brazilian market was a natural fit, the feeling was mutual, and he worked on developing partnerships with TV companies and sponsors, and he was already looking at rolling out merchandising. In the short term, then, leaving Ukraine and working outside it had little immediate impact for Palmer, as his focus was settling squarely on international development. 'I would fly out to Kyiv every now and again,' he adds, 'but I was very focussed on these pre-season tours to the US and Brazil to see how we could continue to develop.'

The immediate struggle for Shakhtar was to make sure the Brazilians stayed. Even those who were fairly sanguine about the situation had relatives who were not so relaxed, being bombarded back home with television images of violence and chaos. 'We had to explain that we were well,' midfielder Marlos told me during the 2015 recording of *Shakhtar Donetsk: A Club in Exile*, 'that we weren't having any difficulties, and we tried to explain this to our relatives. But they didn't really get it, because in Brazil they were only hearing bad news.' It was a little different for Marlos. He was acclimatised to Ukraine, having arrived from two years at Metalist, but he also signed for the club once the move was underway. 'For me, I didn't experience any sort of difficulty,' he said. 'Shakhtar always made it totally smooth for us. They always left us calm and feeling good, so we could just get on with playing football.'

For those already there, going through the move had been significantly more unsettling. By early July it felt like a relative calm might have fallen over Shakhtar's newly forming daily routine. The squad were pre-season training in Switzerland, preparing for the Super Cup against Dynamo later in the month. They had a plan. 'We were supposed to play our home matches in Kharkiv,' says Sviridov. 'I know even some players had already rented houses there at that moment. Then on July seventeenth, the tragedy happened. MH-17.'

MH-17 was the Malaysia Airlines flight between Amsterdam and Kuala Lumpur that was shot down by a surface-to-air missile near Hrabove, a small village in Donetsk Oblast midway between Luhansk and Donetsk. All 298 passengers and crew were killed. The Ministry of Justice in the Netherlands and its Joint Investigation Team would later find that the Buk missile system used to fire at the aircraft was moved from Russia to Ukraine on the day of the attack, and back to Russia on the following day.

Kharkiv had been the next-best; it wasn't Donetsk, but it was only 300km north of it. Now the proximity to home which recommended it spawned the thought that it was too close to the violence and imbalance that was forcing the club out, and made it untenable for a number of the squad. 'There were five or six players who refused to go back to Ukraine,' Sviridov says sombrely. 'There was a huge crisis for us because we could have lost them all.' Another plan would have to be hatched, and quickly. 'Then the decision was made to play our home matches in Lviv.' The western city's proximity to the Polish border, and the club's willingness to react quickly to concerns, brought an equilibrium to the mood. 'And it worked out,' Sviridov says. 'The players step by step, one by one, they came back and we managed to stay together as a team.'

The club's move still wasn't quite complete. There were still club staff at Donbass Arena working at the humanitarian hub. 'Some people moved to Kyiv,' continues Sviridov, 'some to other cities, and we were scattered, literally scattered around the country. There wasn't a [bespoke] solution [or an agreed policy] at that moment.' Shakhtar's board wanted the hundreds of employees affected by the move to find what they were comfortable with. Eventually, says Sviridov, the move to Kyiv almost naturally occurred, with the club's key figures all gathering there.

With the club's existence becoming more hand-to-mouth, Palmer started to feel that he might be surplus to the club's very particular requirements. 'By the time it got to 2015 you had the feeling that this was going to go on for some time,' he lamented, 'and I got to the point where I felt I couldn't give them anymore. It was very tough for them.' While he was far away his colleagues were working in the Opera and Kyiv, where many of them were also living. At the same time, the club as a whole was coming to terms with being on unfamiliar territory in the capital and in Lviv, where they played their matches. 'We'd done our research on where our hotspots were, and this definitely wasn't one of them,' as Palmer says. It was not ideal, but it was practical. It was also, however, a long way from the vision that Palmer had pursued, and he felt less needed, leading to his leaving the club. 'They just needed to concentrate on the football and just getting games played,' he told me.

Meanwhile it wasn't just the first team that needed to regroup. The club was a complicated, layered business with hundreds of employees and a long list of considerations and obligations that stretched way beyond what the senior squad needed. Dealing with that was Miguel Cardoso, Shakhtar's under-21 head coach and youth academy coordinator from 2013, the year before leaving Donetsk. The two jobs had probably been too much for one person, but Lucescu had personally requested he take the dual role, 'because the under-21s were connected to the first team, but all the academy was all separate,' he tells me. 'So it was like two different arms of the organisation. We changed these dynamics.'

The plan was to extrapolate the Romanian's style of play – Akhmetov-endorsed, of course – throughout all the age groups. 'So it was my job to listen and work with Lucescu and his staff,' Cardoso says, 'and to be able to adapt and create some specific programmes that could lead us well, as close as possible to the idea of the game of the first team. Lucescu was coach of Shakhtar for twelve years, so there was some identity in the club, connected and built up with the beliefs, the wills and the likes of the president [as well].'

Cardoso had already accrued a good deal of experience in top-level football as assistant to Domingos Paciência at Académica, Sporting and Braga – they reached a Europa League final together in 2011 at the latter. Yet Shakhtar's head of scouting, Luis Gonçalves, a good friend of his, saw him in more of a lead role. 'He was always challenging me,' Cardoso laughs. 'Something like, "One day you'll have to take your life in your hands." And he did it. So basically, he one day invited me to go to his home and he put me on a Skype with Sergei Palkin. So my first contact with Shakhtar was like a blind date because I went to Luis's house without knowing that I was going to have a chat with the CEO of the club. And basically he threw the situation at me.' The next thing Cardoso knew he was invited to spend some days in Donetsk, and he was dining in Cavallino Bianco, the chic Italian restaurant neighbouring the Donetsk Art Museum, with Palkin and Lucescu.

The coach had the feeling that Cardoso had done his homework. He already knew the Shakhtar team in detail having been on the Braga bench with Paciência when they faced the Ukrainians in the Champions League in autumn 2010. 'So there was a very good connection, empathy between the parties, you know?' he says. 'And during this lunch, there was a moment when Lucescu winked to Sergei. He left because he had a training session, we finished lunch, and Sergei took me to his office in Donbass Arena. And immediately he told me, '"Miguel, I would like you to come to work with us."'

It is a very Shakhtar story, about the connection between people, with the details being worked out afterwards. That trust and responsibility endured. In May 2014, Cardoso planned a short trip home, and got the sense from Palkin that something big was in the air. 'I left Donetsk and Sergei told me, "you won't come back.' And I told him, "I will." I left from Donetsk airport and one week later, it was bombed.' Yet as the club replanned its immediate future, Palkin had an even bigger task to demand of Cardoso.

While the Shakhtar first team, and the Ukrainian Premier League at large, had conceived an improvised finish to 2013–14, the under-19 and under-21 seasons had just stopped. There needed to be a plan to resume for the following campaign and it was far from straightforward. 'The city was already taken by the separatists,' Cardoso says. 'I went to Kyiv and

I discussed the situation with Sergei. He asked me, "Miguel, are you capable of going back to Donetsk?"' The club's under-19 and under-21 teams were still in Donetsk, ready to begin their season. Cardoso quickly agreed to a task that he knew was big, but didn't realise quite what an undertaking he had committed to until he was on the road. 'I flew to Kharkiv,' he details, 'and went from Kharkiv in a minivan together with my translator and the driver. I went to Donetsk and crossed fourteen checkpoints. Fourteen. So I crossed the frontline of the war and I arrived in a ghost city, because Donetsk was a ghost city at that moment. No one on the streets. No fucking one. And for two weeks I coached under-19 teams in the morning, under-21s in the afternoon inside Shakhtar's academy training ground.'

It was an incredible effort from Cardoso and his staff, all of whom were Ukrainian. 'I had not been allowed to bring technical staff with me,' he explains. His job had another aspect – developing coaches. The situation, however, was unsustainable. 'During these two weeks, I received many phone calls from the consul of Portugal in Kyiv,' he says. 'At that moment, I could hear the bombing, the shelling in the night. It was already clearly war. And after ten days, I had to leave Donetsk because my consul told me, "Miguel, we will inform the Portuguese government that we're not going to take responsibility for you anymore." So I called Sergei Palkin and told him, "Sergei, I received this phone call, and I need to leave the city."' Palkin asked Cardoso to sit tight while he made plans. 'So the next day he called me and a convoy was organised with two or three buses [carrying] all the players from under-19s and under-21s, me and my Ukrainian staff, the medical staff. We had police ahead and behind us. And we travelled around the frontline. We entered Russia. We came back into Ukraine. And we went to a city called Poltava.'

Out of concrete grew roses, as Cardoso is understandably keen to underline. If the first team struggled to adapt, the age group teams were doing Shakhtar proud. 'Let me point out one thing,' he insists, 'because this is historical. The year we were in Poltava was the year when the under-19 team went to the final of the [UEFA] Youth League. So the most difficult year of the club was the year the biggest sporting achievement of the academy happened.' In April 2015, approaching a year since the withdrawal from Donetsk, Shakhtar reached what was essentially an age-group Champions League final.

It is astonishing. Shakhtar's youngsters had not lost a single one of their nine games on the way to the final against Chelsea, in which they were just edged out 3–2 by a very good side. There were a clutch of recognisable names in the Chelsea line-up, such as Ruben Loftus-Cheek and Andreas Christensen, now of Barcelona. Tammy Abraham of Roma and England came on as a late substitute. Six of the eleven that started for Chelsea in Nyon on that sunny April afternoon are now regularly playing in Europe's top leagues, including England, Italy and Spain. A couple of modern-day Shakhtar regulars played that day too – Mykola Matvienko and Oleksandr Zubkov, who was one of the leading assist-makers in the competition. Andriy Boryachuk and Viktor Kovalenko, now at Spezia in Italy, also played. (Kovalenko came on and scored the goal of the game, even if it turned out only to be a consolation.)

The benefits for the club were already clear, but quite how Cardoso put up with the demands on him is a mystery. 'Later on, we were able to start the training sessions from the under-12s to the under-17s.' Those younger boys worked at a training camp in Shchaslyve, a village in the direction of Kyiv's Boryspil airport, to the city's south-east, where Shakhtar had begun to set up camp. 'During that season, I had to divide my job between coaching the under-21s in Poltava and travelling to Kyiv to coordinate the other groups,' says Cardoso. 'So in summer conditions, I was driving by car at least 400 kilometres every week. Two days in Kyiv, five days in Poltava. And in winter [I went] by train, travelling with the soldiers, travelling with the spirit of the war. Because this road, Kyiv-Poltava-Kharkiv-Donetsk, is the road that takes people from Kyiv to Donetsk.' It was the journey that reminded Cardoso of what the club had lost, and how precarious it all was. 'Ukraine is very big,' he underlines, 'and when you live in Kyiv and there's the war in Donetsk, despite you're living every day with the war you [don't have to] deal with the war. Poltava was a calm city. There you could not feel it. But when travelling from Kyiv to Poltava, you felt the war. Every day you could feel the war on people's faces.'

It was most difficult for him and his family immediately after he returned to Donetsk. 'Because in that moment,' he says, 'I was giving interviews on a regular basis, almost every day for the Portuguese TV. So they [his family] were aware of the situation. It was on the TV everywhere. Everywhere and in the Portuguese channels and, of course, I had a lot of demands in terms of speaking with people.' He managed to retain a calm. 'I never really felt under threat despite the fact I could hear the bombing, despite every day in the evening I had visits from journalists.' He eventually moved to stay in the same accommodation as those journalists, showing him that compartmentalising sport and real life wasn't really an option. Speaking daily to war reporters, camera operators and photographers deeply affected Cardoso, seeing their indefatigability in the face of extreme difficulty, and their commitment to sending daily reports back to their networks. On a human level, he tells me, 'it was an extraordinary experience.' It also gave him the necessary level of perspective to allay the fears of his family back home, though he frequently passed the message that his posting there was temporary, not permanent. 'They also knew,' he says, 'that Shakhtar would protect me. We knew that we were not targets because we believe that Shakhtar was respected.'

Even if Cardoso dealt with the situation with his degree of sang-froid, something had to give. The plan had never been for the situation to last for that long, with Cardoso and his staff propping it all up. 'During this season, I discussed it a lot of times – that we could not work this way because we could not have everybody separated.' With Lucescu, Palkin and Cardoso all pulling in the same direction, eventually the whole academy ended up relocating to Shchaslyve. 'When we left in 2014,' Palkin says, 'we started to rent and renovate pitches. We had five pitches and a small stadium for 2,000 spectators.' A development project that would normally take several years to plan and build was pulled together in just over twelve months. 'The club took control of a full hotel,'

Cardoso says, drawing the parallel to the first-team setup at Hotel Opera. 'They took control of the free pitches, so after one year, we could be all together again.'

'I was in this situation for one whole year,' he reflects, his lively voice taking on an uncommon hint of tiredness. The model for the age-group teams was shifting to ape that for the first team, and the effort of Cardoso in maintaining three teams in Poltava and five others in Kyiv was done. 'It was an unbelievable effort,' he says proudly. 'Financial, organisational, technical and in terms of human beings and human relations. An unbelievable effort that everybody made to survive.'

It was all kept afloat by Shakhtar's reputation, built over the years. Without the confidence of the scholars' parents, none of it would have worked. 'For us it was good that before we even left Donetsk, we had Brand Shakhtar,' Palkin points out. 'It doesn't matter where you move. I mean if you got to see our camp in Donetsk, it's top. All the parents who bring their children, they want to stay, it's so nice. Now we cannot show them this. But we have this brand. And for this brand people come, bring their children, and want to collaborate with us. For example [Mykhailo] Mudryk. He joined our academy in 2016, when we were already staying near Kyiv. Now we have a squad of guys; part of them from Donetsk and another group that arrived from 2014 and in around 2019, they arrive into the first team.'

The work of Cardoso, and the vision and commitment of the club, is standing Shakhtar in good stead now. Without these years of graft and preparation, it is certain that they wouldn't have been able to negotiate the sporting side of things after

24 February 2022 as well as they have been able to. Between 2014 and 2016, though, it was tough to acclimatise to life together in Hotel Opera – palatial as it might have been – and the endless string of flights. The fog of ennui that hung over the club in the first couple of years after leaving Donetsk was unmistakeable.

'It's been a difficult year,' Marlos told me in May 2015, 'in terms of not having the warmth of our fans close to us. We've played all our games away from home. It was maybe something that made a difference in the Champions League too, when you see what we did against Bayern [a 0–0 draw in Lviv, before the German champions won the return 7–0 in Munich after Oleksandr Kucher's third-minute red card]. It was a game that, if we'd played it in Donetsk, we could have got an even better result.' This was no idle speculation. Arena Lviv was full to its just-under 35,000-capacity that night. Those in the stands weren't exactly pushing Shakhtar on to victory. 'The people who were at the game were more for Bayern than supporting Shakhtar,' Marlos added,

Playing in the Champions League should have been a fillip in that first season away, 2014–15, a legacy of their times of plenty, linking back to the imperious, unfettered-with-worry Shakhtar of before. Instead, it was another battle of attrition for the team and the rotating cast of unsympathetic fans that they played in front of pretty much every week.

Speaking directly after the Ukrainian Cup semi-final second leg against Dnipro in Lviv later that week, Srna was more blunt. 'It's not easy. You've seen,' he nodded his head back from the media zone towards the stands. 'We've been here one year.

We bring them Champions League and they support against us. Also when we play Dynamo Kyiv, they are supporting Dynamo Kyiv and not us. But this is the period of our lives [that we are going through now]. We must be professional, we must play for our club and for our fans and we are confident that everything will be OK.'

For Taras Stepanenko, only twenty-five back then but already the team's defensive midfield fulcrum, it was maybe even tougher than it was for Srna. Like his teammates, his life had been turned upside down, but for him there was the extra layer of being rejected by his countrymen. Many Ukrainians simply didn't understand why Shakhtar moved out, he tells me, with no acknowledgement of exactly what they had been through. They had left everything behind, but in western Ukraine, many wondered why. 'To be honest it was really difficult at first,' he tells me, 'not only because you left your stadium, your city, and your training base, but because of the attitude of a lot of people in Kyiv and Lviv. At that time, there was like a line between east and west Ukraine.' When he arrived in Kyiv, he and his teammates were frequently asked why they didn't stay in Donetsk. Ultras from other clubs challenged Stepanenko in person and on social media. Many of them that had backed the Orange Revolution and supported the Maidan movement saw him – and by implication Shakhtar – as ideologically opposed to them. 'It was a misunderstanding,' he says.

The hangover of the Soviet Union, and the perception in much of western Ukraine that Donbas was culturally as well as geographically close with Russia, stuck to Shakhtar. 'I think it took them a long time to come to terms with the fact that, well, they felt really unwanted everywhere else,' says Andrew Todos, 'and I feel that like a lot of Donetsk residents that used to live in Donetsk and moved to Kyiv . . . for example, in Ukraine, number plates are done by area. So if people saw that they had Donetsk number plates they were shunned by some people and all that kind of stuff. That was more the minority generally speaking, but it was just all very new and people still had their guard up because they didn't really trust people from Donetsk because of all the links that [are perceived with Russia].'

On the sporting side there were also wounds which needed clotting. The drip, drip, drip of talent, seeping away. Douglas Costa left for Bayern and Luiz Adriano joined AC Milan on consecutive days in July 2015. In February 2016, Alex Teixeira joined Chinese Super League club Jiangsu Suning for €50 million. This was the third time in ten days that China's transfer record had been broken, following the moves of Ramires from Chelsea to Jiangsu Suning, for a reported €28.4 million, and of Jackson Martínez from Atlético Madrid to Guangzhou Evergrande for €42 million. Martínez's move from Spain was confirmed just two days before Teixeira took the plunge. It was a record which would be surpassed twice in the following twelve months.

It underlined just how the club's dreams of reaching the elite were slipping away – though Chinese football's spending spree was not unhelpful. This new centre of financial power allowed Shakhtar to extract more than maximum value for Teixeira at a point when losses were mounting and revenues were, at least semi-permanently, down. Jiangsu's mind-boggling offer had outflanked a rival bid from Liverpool, who were eager to offer their new coach, Jürgen Klopp, some reinforcements of choice. Leaning too hard against that glass ceiling, just getting too big, too good, as Lucescu previously described, had made these moments inevitable. Replacing the talent, however, would be harder than before.

Shakhtar also needed something to shake that feeling that little was going right, on or off the pitch, despite their best efforts. That they let the UPL slip in 2015 had perhaps not been unexpected in the circumstances. When they faced Dynamo Kyiv in the 2015 Ukrainian Cup final, however, after edging Dnipro in that semi-final in Lviv, they were set to take at least some consolation from a tough season. It went to a penalty shootout after 120 goalless minutes at Olimpiyskiy. Shakhtar scored their first three, while Dynamo, who by this point had already been crowned champions, missed two of their first three. Shakhtar had one hand on the trophy. Subsequently Taison, Yaroslav Rakitskyi and Oleksandr Gladkiy all missed, and Dynamo had the double. It was agonising.

In the following season, 2015–16, Shakhtar reached the Europa League semi-finals, dropping down from a Champions League group containing Real Madrid and Paris Saint-Germain. They swept aside Schalke, Anderlecht and Braga with ease. In the last four they gave a good account of themselves against eventual winners Sevilla, going in level at half-time in the second leg in Andalucía after a brisk 2–2 draw in Lviv. It took all that Unai Emery's team had – and a fantastic swerving shot from range from a Sevilla Brazilian, right-back Mariano – to finally move Shakhtar from their path. In the

Estádio Ramón Sánchez Pizjuan that night, in the intense southern Spanish heat, the cacophonous crowd reminded Shakhtar of what they had lost in terms of the unconditional love of a local crowd, as well as the match itself and a chance at the ultimate prize. In the league, they eventually finished seven points behind Dynamo as their rivals retained their title. Lucescu, seemingly stuck for answers for once, moved on. The next move would be a crucial one.

It was about finding a way of winning, both post-Lucescu and – even more importantly – post-Donbass Arena. The hope within the club had always been that the absence from Donetsk was (and is) temporary. On the one hand keeping that optimism alive is crucial for morale, for sanity, but the people around the club have learned to treat it like it is a permanency in order to concentrate on the task in hand. If hope is important to be able to carry on, so is practicality. Hope must be taken from diligence, and from the club's own spirit of invention.

The courtship of Paulo Fonseca was not as prolonged as Akhmetov's chase of Lucescu all those years before, but it was slow and stealthy. 'I was at Braga when I received the first contact [in early 2016], through the agent who still today collaborates with the club and is a good friend of Sergei Palkin – Amadeu Paixão – who asked me if I was interested in meeting with them. I confess that, at the time, I knew very little about Ukraine, but I knew Shakhtar from the European competitions and I knew they always had a very good team with lots of high-quality Brazilian players.'

Like Palmer had been, on closer examination Fonseca was taken aback by just how big the operation was. 'I dug a little deeper and I realised that Shakhtar was a club of huge dimensions. Before the end of the season I had a first meeting with the club, which went well. The president of the club and the CEO wanted to make a change. Lucescu had been there for around twelve years, and there was a desire to change. Near the end of the season, we reached an agreement. They were very keen for me to go there, and I didn't think twice. I wanted to work abroad, so I accepted the job and went to Shakhtar.'

It was Cardoso who had established contact initially via his Braga connection, and it developed from there. It was a new start on the pitch but also a break from the old Shakhtar; no clinging on to false hope but dealing with reality. 'Let's not think this is temporary and we'll go back and everything will be like before,' is how Cardoso was framing it, 'but [let's accept] this is our reality. We'll live like this. And the fact that Fonseca had nothing to do with the previous Shakhtar because the only Portuguese guy that ever lived in Donetsk was myself.'

That part of Shakhtar, knew Cardoso, was being left behind. If the dream of going home was still alive, everyone understood what the present entailed. The players began to buy houses and apartments of their own in Kyiv, and mostly felt more settled as a result. The club were also putting down roots, and Fonseca bringing a new energy, and fresh perspective, helped with that. Together with his compatriot Cardoso they transformed the gym and fitness area at Sviatoshyn, and made it really theirs. They were starting anew. 'Acceptance was probably the starting point,' agrees Cardoso, 'of a new mindset.'

This is said, on all our parts, with the benefit of hindsight. It was a tough start for Fonseca. Shakhtar lost the Super Cup to Dynamo Kyiv the week before the UPL season began, and went out of the Champions League in the third qualifying round to Young Boys, the Swiss Super League runners-up with a fraction of Shakhtar's means. Both matches were lost on penalties. European football meant everything, as Fonseca quickly came to realise. 'It was difficult because we were always travelling,' he says, 'and it was difficult because Shakhtar had practically no fans in Lviv. We played in a stadium with very few spectators; we didn't feel the love of the fans. It was very difficult to motivate the players for some games when you practically had no crowd. In the European competitions it was different. The stadium had more people in it, as Shakhtar fans came from different parts of the country to watch the European games, but at the start it was tough.'

With the shadow of the Young Boys defeat hanging over him, Fonseca almost didn't make it that far. Allied to Akhmetov's constant desire for the aesthetically pleasing, the culture change was complicated, and Palkin admits they considered pulling the plug on the new era quite early on. 'When he arrived, he played a different scheme [to before],' he reasons. 'We were used to 4-2-3-1, and we had the players for this type of game. He started to play 4-4-2. But we lost to Young Boys, we started the championship very badly, and it was a moment where the club could have made a decision to stop this [Fonseca's tenure]. We spoke to Darijo, the president, and we said 'ok, let's be patient.' Let's give him the next three games. It was Karpaty, who were quite strong at the time, Dynamo Kyiv . . . they were not easy games. And this was the moment where everything changed. We're playing at Karpaty, and we're down 2–0. I was watching at home thinking, it's finished. But in the second half it went 1–2, 2–2, 3–2 . . . and after that, he won everything in Ukraine. Three championships in a row, cups, we started to do well in the Champions League. Sometimes it's difficult to be patient when fans [are] killing you, journalists [are] killing you. But being patient is the most important tool.'

It's remarkable to think that those three league and cup doubles in three seasons might never had materialised had Shakhtar continued to slump that afternoon against Karpaty in Arena Lviv, their de facto home of the time – in August. How did Fonseca ride it out? 'Well, first of all,' says Cardoso, 'he's undoubtedly a very good coach. Secondly, because the club was patient enough to understand that in football you don't grow something that is different in days. It's very easy or it's more easy to substitute a coach that doesn't have a heritage. And from Lucescu there was a heritage.'

Fonseca himself acknowledges that. 'I realised from the start it wouldn't be easy,' he admits. 'Lucescu had been there for twelve years, he'd won what he'd won. It was a very big challenge. Some players were there who had practically only ever worked with Lucescu.' He did, though, feel intensely motivated by the opportunity to pull Shakhtar out of their post-move slump. 'The chance to play European competitions was motivating,' he says. 'But it was also a club that, since it had moved to Kyiv, since it had left Donetsk, had not been winning. In the previous two years it hadn't won [the title]. So there was this huge challenge to work to make Shakhtar champions again. This was a big motivation for me.'

He had the advantage of a *lingua franca* with the team's Brazilians, but he was presiding over a major change of tack on the pitch, even if continuing to evolve off it was perhaps more demonstrably necessary. 'My way of thinking about football was completely different to Lucescu's,' he emphasises. 'And I also believed bringing new ideas to these players, who practically only knew Lucescu's way, could also work out. Then I also realised that Ukrainian players are extremely disciplined, very hard-working, and with an immense desire to learn, and bringing new ideas to these players could also be highly positive. That's how I looked at it. Understanding that it would be tough, but at the same time it was a tremendous challenge and extremely motivating. Of course, I knew it was a huge responsibility replacing Lucescu.'

The players certainly were open to it. Stepanenko admits it was a considerable adjustment, but it also changed the direction of his career and development. 'He's from a new generation of coaches with a different view of football,' he describes. 'He [Fonseca] taught me a lot tactically and technically, because he insisted on really small things and these small things helped me to change the style of my own play. He insisted on me changing the position of my body when I received the ball, the point at which I should play the ball. He wanted me to play more vertical football, and to play more between the lines. At that point we had some really good players like Marlos, Taison, Bernard, who could receive the ball in these small spaces and play with one or two touches so quickly that opponents couldn't react to their movements. I think about it still every time I train.'

With a stimulated squad and a style to please the president, Fonseca's star was on the way up. After the hard times, the new coach's ability to bring a little joy to the way Shakhtar did things, as well as a fresh vein of silverware, was important. The win over Premier League giants Manchester City in Kharkiv in December 2017 provided a bit of both, the smiles and the glory. It was a Herculean effort, handing Pep Guardiola's team their first defeat in twenty-nine games. Bernard's opener, cutting inside Danilo and curling a delicious shot around Ederson after a Marlos dribble, was described by Guardiola as 'magnificent'. The second was also a rekindling of classic Shakhtar Champions League nights, with Marlos sweeping a handsome crossfield pass into the corridor of uncertainty behind City's defence. The goalkeeper, Ederson, came, Ismaily got there first, rounded him and slotted home.

The fullish stands in Kharkiv responded lustily – another aspect that made the occasion reminiscent of old times. They had all the encouragement they needed, as it could have been more before half-time. Taison, shaking off an early knock to play a real captain's role, went close with a shot that skimmed the City crossbar and landed in the full frost behind the goal. Sergio Agüero pulled one back for the visitors from the penalty spot, but it was deep into stoppage time, and Shakhtar had made it. A 2–1 victory took them into the Champions League last 16, a triumph for their prestige and finances alike. Srna stood high in the directors' box, pumping the air with both fists. Afterwards, though, it was the team's tactician that stole the show at the press conference.

'A journalist who works for the club asked me, when I was a child, who I dressed up as on Halloween,' grins Fonseca. 'I was always crazy about horses when I was a kid, and because it was an easy mask to make, I said that when I was a kid, I dressed up as Zorro. That was the end of it. When I left the press conference, Vitaliy [Khlyvniuk], who worked with me at Roma, but has now gone back to Shakhtar, my [team manager] who was always with me, said, "Hey coach, let's make a bet. If tomorrow we beat Manchester City will you go the press conference dressed up as Zorro?" I replied, "I'm up for that no problem. If we beat City I'll do anything!"'

In the euphoria of such a statement win, this all slipped Fonseca's mind – but not those of his staff. 'When I got to the press conference room, Yuri [Sviridov, the club's director of communications], Vitaliy and Andrei [Babeshko, press officer), appeared with the Zorro outfit,' he smiles. 'I was so happy we had made the last 16 of the Champions League, I didn't think twice. I put on the Zorro mask and went to the press conference. Some people may think it was a marketing strategy or something but it was nothing of the sort. It was just a joke that ended up having a big impact, given that it isn't a usual situation in football. I think sometimes in football people take things too seriously, and having these light moments is also positive. Of course, I was heavily criticised too, but it was simply a joke that worked well.'

What wasn't a joke was that Fonseca guided his players to three league titles, three Ukrainian cups and even a Super Cup in just three seasons at Shakhtar. After the struggles of the first two years, it was life-affirming. The stability of the club and its management was vindicated, and on the field Fonseca had shown Shakhtar how to succeed post-Donetsk. Even now, it means so much to him.

'I'll never forget the first title we won,' he says of their 2017 UPL win, clinched with four games to go by a 3–2 victory over Zorya in Kharkiv, 'because we won the championship without a home. Since Shakhtar had left Donetsk it had not won the league, in the two previous years, and winning the title with no home meant an enormous amount for the people who worked at the club, for the president – it was fantastic. Winning in these difficult circumstances was fantastic and something I will never forget, above all seeing the joy of those people, how important it was in that difficult time. They had to uproot themselves from home and base themselves in the city of their main rival [Kyiv], and winning was fantastic.'

Kharkiv had been Fonseca's preferred venue for home matches, just as it had been for Lucescu (there was something they did have in common), who had made clear his opinion that the hostility in Lviv was acutely damaging to his players. Starting to move towards a fuller ground, even if it wasn't quite packed or really home, was progress. 'It was better playing in Kharkiv,' he says, 'because we felt the support of our fans, although it was still tough, because we still didn't have a home.' The extra travelling was just a drop in the ocean. Fonseca describes it as constant and, doing a mental tally as we go, estimates that the team took around one hundred and twenty-five flights per year. It became normal, though.

Finding routine, even one far from the ideal, had been the key. 'We've lived here since 2015,' says Stepanenko of Kyiv.

'Two of my sons were born in Kyiv. I love the city now. It has really good people. Time changes attitudes and it changes your perspective on life and your thoughts about the situation, and how you see situations from the past.' That initial distance has dissipated over time. 'When we moved to Kyiv in 2014, during the first year we had about 100 flights. So we had too much time staying in Lviv, and it was really difficult for the players because every time you stay in the hotel before and after the game.'

Stepanenko is a thoughtful speaker, careful with his words. A considerer and an avid reader, far from the clichés assumed of super-rich modern footballers. He has thought a lot about the mental health impact of the last nine years on his teammates past and present, and particularly about how hard it was at the beginning, oscillating between shock and denial, and the sheer despair of the constant feeling of being on a conveyer belt.

'Some players had depression, some players couldn't see their families,' he confirms. 'It was really difficult.' If Stepanenko liked Fonseca for his football brain, he loved him for his human side. 'After Fonseca came to Shakhtar it changed a little bit,' he remembers, 'because most of the time we stayed in Kyiv and travelled just before the game to Kharkiv. When we started to play in Olimpiyskiy for me it was more easy, and for the rest of the guys, because – and I thought about it a lot – after the game it's taking you four hours less. After the game in Kharkiv and Lviv you took a shower, you went to the airport, fly to Kyiv and go home. So minimum four hours is taken away from your rest. When you're in Kyiv, you play the game and you're home in half an hour. For me it's much better.'

172

If there's now greater warmth between Shakhtar and the people of Kyiv, did that have an effect on their Champions League home games in the capital, which continued to throw up reminders of how exciting Shakhtar can be – even after Fonseca's departure in 2019? 'Of course it's not the atmosphere that it was in Donetsk,' he feels obliged to say, 'when 50,000 people always came to the matches. The size of the crowd depends on who you're playing. If it's Real Madrid it's full, and if you're playing the fourth-placed team in the Bundesliga – Wolfsburg, or Borussia Mönchengladbach – it's maybe 20,000. It's always a good atmosphere but we can't compare it with the Donbass Arena.' Palkin will never rid his mind of that contrast either.

'When you are losing your home it's difficult,' he says matter-of-factly in the lobby of a hotel in Antalya. 'We are already without our home for nine years now. For example, yesterday we went to see some Turkish championship, Antalyaspor were playing. And you see the stadium, fans. It's different feelings. Everything's different. We left Donetsk and we moved to play in Lviv. After that we moved to play in Kharkiv. After that, we moved to Kyiv. Yes, people come to see us. Not the same number like in Donetsk. But in Lviv, Kharkiv, Kyiv it's average, or maximum, 11,000. It's a completely different story. We have a home match, but it's not a home match. Why do you have a home match? It's for the fans to support you, to be like your twelfth player on the pitch. But we don't have this advantage.'

That glosses over some of the difficulties from the outside, at least. 'With Fonseca we got through the group stage of the

Champions League, we got to the semi-finals of the Europa League, but if these clubs [we beat] arrived to our [training] camp in Kyiv and they see what conditions we have, they would say, "are you kidding or what?" We have one pitch and a changing room that's sixty or seventy years old.' He puffs his cheeks out.

It's always one step forward and two steps back, whatever the investment or preparation. 'We took Fonseca, he got amazing results, we sold Fred and other players,' Srna says. 'And we came back to, let's say, more or less a normal life in Kyiv. We bought apartments, set up a small [training] camp. Today, we don't even have that. At the start [in 2014] I wanted to help to keep the team together. It was a huge [learning] experience for all of us. We said, "it can't be worse than this." Now,' he says in 2023, lightly pursing his lips, 'it's worse.'

8

It's Happening Again

'I can tell you that if we had a reaction like now in 2014 about Crimea, about Donbas, it would never happen. Putin would understand that it's not possible. That we need to negotiate. That the whole democratic bloc will support us. It never happened. Putin is the kind of person, for you to understand, that if he makes one step and there is no reaction, he will make the second step. So now, why does the whole of Europe support Ukraine? Because they understand. If they invade Ukraine, next it will be Poland. Putin understands just power. When you're weak, he destroys you. So if the world reacts in 2014 like now, I tell you – there would be no war.'

Sergei Palkin, Shakhtar CEO, 6 February 2023

A year, it turns out, is a long, long time. Two trips to the same place, symptomatic of a long-term routine but, in this case, underlining the contrast between what one had and what one had lost. When Shakhtar were fulfilling their traditional mid-season training camp in Antalya in January and February 2022, there were worried whispers of war. Little did those players and staff know how quickly it would all decant and that when they were back in Turkey for the same reason twelve months on, what was previously a seasonal chore would be the closest to a stable base that they had experienced for some time.

It wasn't just Shakhtar, either now or ever. Ukrainian clubs flock to Antalya at this time of year, like well-heeled New Yorkers summering in The Hamptons. There's generally good weather – far warmer than Ukraine in February, obviously, but considerably more temperate than the 50°C that Antalya regularly hits at the height of summer. There are also comfortable hotels and resorts, facilities including excellent small-scale stadiums and bespoke pitches, and everything is provided at good value prices, particularly given the tumbling Turkish Lira of recent years. The distance from Kyiv to Antalya is half that to Marbella, for example, if we're comparing potential warm weather camp venues.

They all go. In January and February of 2023 Shakhtar are present, further back from the summer tourist strip of Lara Beach, in the palatial grounds and manicured full-sized pitches of Belek. Dynamo Kyiv are situated a little closer to Antalya city, training at Mardan Sports Complex (the host venue for the 2008 UEFA European Under-17 Championship) but only fifteen minutes' drive away. When I check in to my own hotel in Belek, not far from the Shakhtar camp, I find a host of Veres players (placed ninth in the UPL at the winter break) flocked around the pool table in the lobby. When you go down to the basement fitness centre, there is a photocopied sign emblazoned with the club crest blue-tacked to the reception window, informing you of the hours of the day when it is blocked off for the squad.

The Antalya trips are not only best practice among

Ukrainian clubs. They are something to feel part of in these extraordinary times, a chance for players and pressed-for-time executives to see some familiar faces. It is safe territory as well, and a magnet for some low-key shows of support. Oleksandr Usyk, the Ukrainian heavyweight boxing champion, turned out for FC Polissya in the Winter Cup in 2022, in what was widely described as his 'professional' debut – really, his debut with a professional team – against Veres whilst warming up for a rematch against Anthony Joshua, on the cusp of the breakout of war. In 2023 there were rumours that he would play again, though he limited himself to watching one of his childhood favourites, Dynamo's friendlies, against North Macedonian side FK Sileks, instead. At the other end of the scale it gave teams like Dynamo the opportunity to invite refugee children to come and see their games and meet players.

The 2023 atmosphere differed hugely from the mood in 2022. Even if Ukraine is now at war, the feeling in Turkey was of a calm that was conspicuous by its absence the year before. The mid-winter training camp, a familiar fixture in the calendar and an unrushed experience, is a juxtaposition to the perpetual motion in which Ukrainian football exists in the modern world. 'In Turkey [in 2022] there was a very tense atmosphere,' remembers De Zerbi, 'because Brazilian players were very worried, we as coaches were very worried. It was the same for the Ukrainian players, as their families were in Ukraine.' These camps are intended to cut teams off from the concerns of the outside world, to achieve perfect concentration on preparation for the restart. In 2022, it was anything but. Concerns were accentuated, and anxieties heightened.

'I remember in that period we were having highs and lows in training sessions due to this situation,' De Zerbi says, 'because the heads of the players were not fully focused on the pitch. Of course [they were] following what the media were reporting, like Russian forces massively assembled next to the Ukrainian border, or the Russian army getting ready for the invasion. That's why the feeling that a conflict could start was something we already had in Turkey.'

Once Shakhtar returned to Ukraine there was an almost eerie sense of clarity for the Italian and his staff, thinking, correctly, that the die had already been cast. They arrived back from Turkey on Saturday, the players had a day off to recover and see their families on Sunday, before going back to training in Sviatoshyn on Monday. On Monday evening, De Zerbi and his staff watched Putin give a press conference on television. He had referenced Soviet history on several occasions. 'Let's start with the fact that modern Ukraine was entirely created by Russia,' he had begun. 'More precisely, by the Bolshevik, communist Russia.' Watching on, the feeling among De Zerbi and his team was unanimous: Putin planned to invade. Yet a strange calm descended on the squad. 'I remember that Monday, Tuesday and Wednesday we did outstanding training sessions in Kyiv,' he recalls. 'It was probably the best way to finish. Then, on Thursday morning, Russia invaded Ukraine and from that moment everything has changed.'

Most immediately it changed Shakhtar's, and Ukraine's world, but it changed the world at large too. This hit differently.

Some argued that the way people in the UK felt about Ukraine and the plight of Ukrainians was dictated by skin tone. Their suffering was easier to relate to because they were, quite simply, whiter than those put through the unimaginable and the unbearable in countries like Syria and Yemen. Maybe, for some, that was true. For me, it was personal. I had a sense of home, of belonging in Kyiv. I visited many times since first going in 2009. I have marvelled at the architecture, the history, the greenness, the river, the people and – of course – the football. Imagining those beautiful monuments to history damaged and decaying – Independence Square, City Hall, the famous bench in front of the Valeriy Lobanovskyi Stadium. Knowing all along that they're just things, replaceable, not like the people. But knowing that those desecrated highlights of history represent what has happened to those people, to their city, to their country, to their lives.

For those players, staff and the people who could escape, there was the question of what to do next. For many of those overseas players, it was immediately apparent that they wouldn't be coming back. Some of them, like Ismaily, had been through it twice. The long-serving left-back arrived at Shakhtar in February 2013 and was part of the group leaving Donetsk little more than a year later. Unlike previous clutches of Shakhtar Brazilians who stayed for some time, like Fernandinho or Willian, he had little opportunity to feel a real sense of Shakhtar belonging in Donetsk, in their city, in their region. His was a career of endless flights and hotels. Ismaily would also be one of the last to leave, joining his old coach Fonseca at Lille in August 2022.

179

Others barely had time to get their feet under the table. David Neres was part of Ajax's eye-catching side which made a magnificent run to the Champions League semi-finals, in which he had scored important goals against Real Madrid and Juventus in the knockout rounds. He had been at Shakhtar for little more than a month when the invasion happened. The Ukrainians had paid a fee potentially rising to €17 million for the winger, a sure sign that, despite the years of flux, they could still attract prime Brazilian talent and that Akhmetov was still prepared to invest good sums of his money in it. Neres, at twenty-four, was a fine player with considerable upside. He represented ambition and a bright future. But he never pulled on the orange and black jersey in a competitive fixture. By June, he had signed for Benfica.

As De Zerbi said to me before, everything he had built, all his plans, fell apart like a newspaper in a rainstorm. This squad had been built to his specification whether it be Marlon, the centre-back who played such a part in mapping out the coach's vision of the game from defence in his Sassuolo team, or Neres, a player representing an extra level of talent which De Zerbi would have struggled to attract to a middling Serie A side, without an increased salary or the carrot of European football. 'To talk about Shakhtar is painful from a working point of view,' De Zerbi told me, 'because it was my creation, something that I wanted so much and that I spent a lot of energy to improve. I decided to accept a big challenge to change country, and my creation has been snatched from my hands.' This was supposed to be his step up to the big stage and where – like Lucescu before him – the visionary coach had his own private kingdom in which to create his version of perfection.

When De Zerbi arrived at Kyiv's airport mid-morning on 25 May 2021 to acquaint himself with the club, its personnel and its facilities for the first time, he was met by a small club committee. It was led by Srna, engaging with his new coach in excellent Italian (a legacy of that year in Sardinia in the twilight of his playing career), showing him around HQ at the Opera and introducing him to Akhmetov at SCM's offices. The owner posed gleefully with his new signing, the two men clutching either side of a Shakhtar jersey with 'De Zerbi' printed across the back. Akhmetov's satisfaction at getting such a bright young coach on board – with all the inherent possibilities of freshening Shakhtar's playing style – was clearly evident.

Later in the visit, Srna also talked De Zerbi through their plans to develop and improve the Sviatoshyn training ground, the club's working base since 2014, situated around twenty kilometres to the west of Kyiv's city centre. This recognised De Zerbi's keen eye for detail and predilection for meticulous preparation. Despite their years of flux, Shakhtar remained a big draw, innovative and ambitious, with the thinkers who had the capacity to connect with coaching talent, as well as playing talent.

The early signs had been that it was coming together. Like Fonseca, De Zerbi had been thrown straight in at the deep end, with vital matches en route to qualifying for the Champions League group stage to contend with. Luis Castro's team had enjoyed some glorious moments in the competition in the previous campaign, but the Portuguese coach's team letting their Ukrainian Premier League title slip meant that De Zerbi would have to go around the houses to get back there.

'We played very well in the four games in the Champions League playoffs,' he remembers, and he's right on at least three of them, as they (eventually) breezed past Belgian champions Genk and won a challenging away game in Monaco for the first leg of the final playoff round. The return in Kharkiv, against the team that finished third in France's Ligue 1, was a different story. 'Monaco is a very strong team,' emphasises De Zerbi. 'In fact, of that Monaco now one player plays in Real Madrid [Aurélien Tchouaméni] and a couple of days ago another one [Benoît Badiashile] has been transferred to Chelsea.' Monaco came out of the blocks fast, and scored twice before half-time. Shakhtar just had to hold on and, even after Marlos got the goal to force extra time, they were on the back foot. 'Honestly,' confesses De Zerbi, 'we have been a bit lucky in the home game.'

He can say that again. Pyatov rolled back the years with a string of great saves, including one plunging to his left to deny Kevin Volland a goal in the added minutes at the end of normal time which would have sent the Principality club through. Eventually it was Mykhailo Mudryk, thrown on to relieve exhausted legs in the team, who made one of those now-familiar bursts down the left deep into extra time. Mudryk was trying to find Alan Patrick at the opening of the penalty area, and saw his easy pass blocked by the visitors' captain Ruben Aguilar – but the block spun up in the air and it looped over Alexander Nübel and into the Monaco net. 'It's like winning the lottery,' yelled an exhilarated Paul Dempsey, the match commentator for BT Sport. 'Your number just came up.' Shakhtar, at the end of an incandescent night in Kharkiv, were through to the group stage. The new regime had, at least, had the rub of the green that Fonseca and his staff had not had on arrival five years before.

The first big domestic test was in the Ukrainian Super Cup against Dynamo Kyiv at Olimpiyskiy, in September 2021. It was a showpiece Shakhtar had lost thirteen months before to the same opponents at the same venue, albeit in front of empty stands. Not only was it the new regime's first crack at silverware but it was an opportunity at an immediate riposte, having lost the title to Dynamo in the final flickers of Castro's reign. Shakhtar needed more than a result. They needed a statement, having gone out so ostentatiously to make one in luring De Zerbi in the first place. 'I had been working a lot on creating order on the pitch,' the coach relays, 'to keep an organisation with ball possession but also without the ball, because I don't like when players just run around on the pitch but I like when the positions on the pitch are occupied properly.'

It wasn't just about the tactics, though. The mindset had to be about more than just zonal marking, counter-pressing and half-spaces. Shakhtar had been chastened and were, lest we forget, no longer champions. 'I had also been working on the mentality,' De Zerbi says. 'The season before I came, Shakhtar finished in second place, eleven points below Dynamo, but we were Shakhtar and we had to win. So I was pushing hard to win every game by 4–0, 5–0 because when you think that is never enough, it helps to improve our mentality.'

In the Ukrainian Super Cup, Shakhtar and De Zerbi laid down a marker from the off, buzzing with intensity. As Denys Boyko received the ball at his feet in his six-yard box in the opening minutes, he seemed to have plenty of time. But all of a sudden, he was pinned by Alan Patrick, the forward charging down the goalkeeper's clearance which, fortunately for the latter, spun off to the side rather than into his goal. For the opening goal, Marlon's dribble forward from the back opened the space on the right for Dodô to swiftly change feet and to ferry the ball in, with Lassina Traoré applying a headed finish. Vladyslav Supryaha had clattered a shot against the post before Traoré's opener, and Dynamo certainly kept Pyatov honest, particularly in the first half. That openness, of course, was all part of it. Shakhtar were already De Zerbi all over; positive, energetic, daring and a little bit reckless.

It started to flow. Stepanenko smacked a lightly deflected shot against the post from range as they began to tighten their grip, and Traoré added another after a flowing move. Pedrinho turned and floated a pass over the head of Dynamo right-back Tomasz Kędziora, with Ismaily charging past him on the express line. He fizzed across the face of goal, with Traoré gleefully tapping in at the back post. De Zerbi bounced up the touchline, exhilarated and wild-eyed. It was all clicking and, after a disappointing fallow domestic season, Shakhtar were well and truly clearing their throats.

The third goal summed it all up. Dynamo captain Serhiy Sydorchuk collected the ball in a central position some thirty yards from the Shakhtar goal. Maycon was straight on him, almost in his shirt, robbing him and poking the ball on to

Alan Patrick. The latter sped off over the halfway line, pulled the ball on to his right foot and smashed an imperious shot into the top corner of Boyko's goal. The time from Maycon dispossessing Sydorchuk to the net rippling was just eleven seconds. When, some ten minutes further on, another silky move on the right was abruptly ended by Oleksandr Syrota's brutal scything down of Dodô, it was abundantly plain that Shakhtar's style had really got under Dynamo's skin. For the coach, it was an early vindication. In rolling over the old enemy with such authority, De Zerbi had also become the first Italian to win the Ukrainian Super Cup.

It felt like an achievement. If Shakhtar were officially at home at Olimpiyskiy, it remained Dynamo's turf. As players and staff celebrated joyously in the corner with a smallish band of orange-clad supporters at full-time, it was underlined that despite their reinforcement, and despite taking root in the capital, Shakhtar were still outnumbered. 'Kyiv's an amazing city,' reflects De Zerbi, 'but [we're] not with our fans [there].' The vast majority of the 27,553 crowd were, naturally enough, supporting the men from the capital. It may have become habitual in one sense but Shakhtar were still dancing to their own song in the lion's den. On the following day, 23 September, the club's principal shirt sponsor, Parimatch, celebrated by sending a Shakhtar shirt into space attached to a specially made balloon. It felt like the beginning of a new chapter of club history being written.

It was harder in the Champions League proper, admittedly. If the playoff round had been an adventure, it was easy to wonder if the exertions – emotional and physical – prevented

Shakhtar playing with some of the abandon they had done in the previous season's group stage under Castro. Their coach, as well, was taking the helm of a European campaign for the first time. 'The Champions League is like the league, the Premier League is like Serie A – it's always football,' De Zerbi argues. It wasn't just the coach who was learning, though. The years of gently downsizing meant talented, callow players were finding their way. 'The average age of my Shakhtar in Champions League was 21.2 years old, one of the youngest teams [in it].' Naturally, De Zerbi coached his team to express themselves, rather than to keep it tight. 'I prepared my team based on the quality [they have], trying to put in the first eleven as many quality players as possible, and I was working on enjoying [ourselves] and always playing good football.'

It was a noble sentiment. The reality was tougher, particularly after an opening match in Moldova – or Transnistria, as the city of Tiraspol self-identifies – at Sheriff, in which they went down 2–0. It was a result which looked more forgivable after Yuriy Vernydub's team followed it up with a stunning win over Real Madrid at the Bernabéu in their next match. There was merit in Shakhtar's campaign after that – 'a not very lucky match against Inter at home we deserved to win but at the end we drew, [and similar] against Real Madrid,' as De Zerbi puts it – but little reward. 'We finished in fourth place in the table,' he reflects, 'but I think we deserved more.' Vernydub, a Ukrainian in his mid-fifties from the western city of Zhytomyr, would later quit Sheriff and Transnistria to return home and join the army directly after his team's elimination on penalties to Portuguese side Braga in the Europa League last 32, before later becoming coach of UPL side Kryvbas Kryvyi Rih.

That sense of unfulfilled potential was something for De Zerbi, and Shakhtar, to get used to. His players were responding. 'He changed a lot,' remembers Manor Solomon, 'and obviously when he came straight away we saw a great manager with strong ideas. He liked to press all the time. He likes to have the ball all the time. The formation was a bit different and we needed to adapt to it. I think Roberto is a top, top manager. We see it now in Brighton and I'm sure that if he stayed in Shakhtar he would have done some great things there.'

His team were two points clear of Dynamo when the winter break kicked in; their last match was a 2–1 win at Oleksandriya on 11 December 2021. From there, the UPL table would be frozen forever. Shakhtar collected the Champions League place for the UPL's first place when summer 2022 came around, but no championship title was awarded. Fonseca and even Castro had been given time by the club. Time, one sensed, was something the club were particularly keen on giving him (and one felt they probably would have done even if the early impressions hadn't been so bright). The real world, however, had different ideas.

'This Shakhtar was a fantastic team,' he says ruefully. Even with his landing at Brighton, in a fulfilling post in the world's most lucrative league, with the opportunity to both build a dynasty on his own terms and to win respect as a smart, progressive coach in a competition watched all over the planet, there is a sense of regret, of the unfinished. It is clearly still on De Zerbi's mind a lot.

'I think that my team could have been winning a lot but also becoming a legend for the way they were playing, for the huge talent of the players, and for the way we could have played in Champions League. The feeling of having a great team . . . ' It is something he clearly struggles to find the words for, even in his native Italian. It was something he touched in Kyiv, but didn't really have time to get familiar with and develop.

'Unfortunately I had it only for a moment,' he muses, 'because while I was the trainer I didn't have much time to realise how strong that team was – I was working so hard to improve the team day by day. Today, when I think about that Shakhtar, I feel very sad, because it could have been the nicest thing that I could have had in all my career.'

And just like that, it was gone. From building an ideal, a mission, to being hit hard with real life events, events of the worst kind. Now it was departure, departure, departure, until there was almost nothing left. And when Júnior Moraes went, a Brazilian-born player who wasn't going to run for the hills at the first sign of trouble, whose level of integration into the country and culture was such that he had accepted Ukrainian citizenship and gone on to play for the national team eleven times, it truly meant something. Moraes joined Corinthians on 16 March, taking him back to São Paulo, the principal city of the state in which it all started for him; a sure sign that if he – this most intrepid and adaptable of players and men, the one who nipped out of the Opera for nappies with everybody huddled inside hoping for salvation – needed safe haven in familiar ground from his youth, then so would the rest. There was, as they all knew deep down, to be no quick resolution. For now, at least, the multinational dream was over.

In truth, that ideal had been on the wane for some time, as Shakhtar aimed to keep their very particular brand flickering in the years after the exit from Donetsk. 'I'm afraid to say that Shakhtar lost popularity and relevance in all Brazilian social strata in the last decade,' says Frédéric Fausser, the Brazilian-based founder and CEO of Samba Digital, a football-focussed digital and e-marketing agency. After the UEFA Cup win of 2009, Shakhtar were still working out how best to finesse their appeal, and they were coming to terms with stepping up a level in terms of status in European football. The window to that was a smaller one that anybody expected, for obvious reasons. The next step had been to build the club's image beyond a sort of Champions League/Europa League finishing school for players of promise, to embrace those new horizons and to sell the club's story and character to the world. There were talks over a link-up between Shakhtar and TV Globo, Brazil's most powerful and far-reaching media platform, but that cooled after the move from Donetsk.

As it was, there were two stages of that potential appeal to the Brazilian market, according to Fausser. Firstly was the arrival of 'young, potential players,' as he puts it – the stars of the future. So Willian or Tetê moving to Shakhtar, both at the age of nineteen, albeit twelve years apart. The second part was 'when these players started to be [transferred] to the main football centres and European leagues. In this second stage, [Shakhtar's] popularity rose.' There is a difference, in other words, between the curiosity of a concentration of young

189

players from one country finding a place to call home so far away from their own. When it becomes clear that Shakhtar represented a route to the very top they're not just a curio, but a constituent part of a glorious dream. So the biggest brand ambassadors for the Shakhtar plan were 'Douglas Costa, Willian, Luiz Adriano and Fernandinho, in this order,' says Fausser, as they reached the biggest names in England, Germany and Italy by way of the Shakhtar Express.

The reframing of Shakhtar, by necessity rather than design, as a Ukrainian rather than a Brazilian-led cosmopolitan spread of talent, would close the current possibility of making that connection. Yet it turned out that in times of extreme need, beyond the boundaries of sport, the club were much better at diffusing their message globally than anyone had previously imagined, including, possibly, themselves.

For Shakhtar, it has been years of practice. Sharing their plight, their concerns, getting out a story considered niche in European terms but which set them apart from all their contemporaries in UEFA club competition. As their war became a full-scale nationwide invasion of Ukraine, everything they had talked about for eight years had a global audience receptive to it, ready to listen. And they had the skills to make their point. That can be extrapolated and it could be said that Ukrainian public figures in general, after all those years living in the shadow of Russia's intentions, have become used to expressing their concerns and issues with considerable adroitness. Since February 2022, President Zelenskiy's connection with the West has been something to behold. 'What Zelenskiy was doing was so natural,' reflects British journalist Adam Crafton.

'It's the kind of stuff that companies in the West would spend millions trying to get that authenticity.'

The next stage of that projection came with the Shakhtar Global Tour of Peace, running concurrently with Dynamo's own Tour for Peace in Ukraine. Football was always going to be visibility and connection, and they got it up and running with impressive speed. Starting out in Greece against Olympiacos at their Georgios Karaiskakis Stadium on 9 April, Shakhtar went on to play games in Turkey, Poland and Croatia; Dynamo also played in Germany, Switzerland, Romania and Estonia. In place of the normal players' names on the backs of the Shakhtar shirts, they commemorated the Ukrainian cities under Russian fire. Bucha. Chernihiv. Kharkiv. Mariupol. It was striking – as was the presence on the Shakhtar bench of De Zerbi. He was sticking around. He had really meant it.

Solomon, who had only played 108 minutes in friendlies for Israel since the final Champions League tie with Sheriff a week into December, would also plant his flag of support. 'I was happy to help and to be with them again,' he said, 'and I tried to be as fit as possible. I trained with my fitness coach and with my personal coach. So I worked really hard in this period of time, and it was also a time for me to be with my family and in terms of football to work on my weaknesses.' With less than two months having passed since the full invasion, Srna's job was to reassure where possible and try and mobilise the squad, even while uncertainty reigned. The Brazilians were out, of course, with the club's preferred agent Franck Henouda working on loan deals for many of them ahead of the Brazilian transfer deadline on 12 April. 'Srna called me and asked me to come,' remembers Solomon, '[telling] my manager that it will be important for the club that I come. It would help the team, and it would help Ukraine because all the money that they receive from the tour would be donated. So straight away I said, "Of course, I'm coming."' Getting out there was good for Shakhtar, and good for Solomon. 'I came a few days later and then I would say that the atmosphere there in Turkey was really nice. I can say that the Ukrainians, they were calm. And I was really happy to see them again.'

Ukraine's national team would go on to pick up the baton, playing May friendlies at Borussia Mönchengladbach, Empoli and Rijeka. In the circumstances, every blade of grass covered and every pass made felt like a minor miracle. Mudryk, representing the senior side for the first time, opened the scoring at Mönchengladbach, gliding past their vastly experienced goalkeeper Yann Sommer and rolling the ball into the net with the sort of apparently effortless grace that would come to characterise his golden autumn of 2022 for his club. As he jogged away with an earned, deserved, childlike joy on his face, the legend on his chest caught the eye. 'United for Ukraine,' it said, with the phrase surrounded by an outline of the country's border made up of the flags of the countries that supported them.

In the meantime, Russia's pariah status grew. Poland led the way, in football and outside it, in supporting Ukraine. Two days after the full-scale invasion, the president of the Polish Football Association (PZPN), Cezary Kulesza, announced that his country's national team would refuse to play their World Cup qualifying playoff with Russia, scheduled for the following month. 'This is the only right decision,' he wrote on Twitter, and was quickly backed by replies from captain Robert Lewandowski and Andrzej Duda, Poland's president. 'Russian footballers and fans are not responsible for this,' wrote Lewandowski, 'but we can't pretend that nothing is happening.' The measures touched other sports too, with the All England Lawn Tennis and Croquet Club (AELTC) announcing on 20 April 2022 that the Russian and Belarusian athletes would be excluded from that summer's Wimbledon tournament.

The International Olympic Committee (IOC), however, were looking for a way round the Russian and Belarusian athlete ban – perhaps having them compete as neutrals. In March 2023, laughably, IOC president Thomas Bach said governments contesting the idea of the athletes returning were behaving in a 'deplorable' way. The battle to make sport take a stand as one is clearly far from won, even if Mayor of Paris Anne Hidalgo voiced her opposition to such a scheme of neutrality ahead of the Paris 2024 Olympics.

Akhmetov didn't make his sport decisions around money – he never had and likely never would. 'He lost so much money,' says Srna, face aghast. 'First in Donbas, now in Mariupol.' Yet if the numbers would send a shiver down the spine of most, Akhmetov was not for turning. 'But when he calls he's still full of enthusiasm, full of happiness, full of confidence. He's always positive.'

Yet the approach would be different going forward. It had to be for both logistical and financial reasons. If Akhmetov, still Ukraine's richest man, was going to have to start watching the balance sheet, so would others. It was an even more acute version of the living on reduced means that followed since the move out in May 2014.

For many, it was still hard to think about playing competitively. Shakhtar's first regular venue for home matches after leaving Donetsk in 2014 had been the Arena Lviv. Now, in the west on the way to Poland, it had become a humanitarian centre providing emergency food and shelter for refugees, with mattresses placed on the floor of the executive areas in the main stand for people to sleep. After the overseas players were successfully evacuated, Palkin spent most days volunteering at the Arena.

With Ukraine, like Poland, involved in World Cup qualifying playoffs, it became clear that country would come before club in the return to action. Scotland, Ukraine's opponents, were patient, and happily postponed, but even with the game rescheduled to the middle distance, it seemed like a steep climb to get there. 'We don't know when the war is going to finish,' says Stepanenko, suggesting he and his countrymen couldn't simply wait indefinitely. 'At that time it was unbelievable,' he continues, 'because some players were staying in Ukraine, some were staying in Europe, and Ukraine as a [sporting] nation didn't know what to do, didn't know how to get a team together, how to organise a training camp, how to play the game against Scotland. It was a total mess. And of course the mood was very bad because every time you read the news, you don't think about football. You think about your people, you think about your country, you think about the war and it was difficult.'

Yet coming together again was a moment of epiphany. 'When I realised – and all the guys realised – that the only way to support your country was to be strong, and to play a good game against Scotland, to celebrate your country and to distract a little bit from the situation in Ukraine, to watch a bit of football and support your national team, we really got power from that. We got good emotion from this. We were really motivated.'

Every aspect of that game in Glasgow, on the first day of June 2022, was inspiring, the best of international football turned up to eleven. 'I had goose bumps,' says Stepanenko as he gently rubs his palm across his forearm, 'when I heard the anthem of Ukraine. I really couldn't hold my tears in. Some other guys in the team were crying. There were a lot of refugees who came to see us, and we realised how Great Britain helped a lot of Ukrainians. Scotland fans were great with us.' Ukraine's 3–1 win at Hampden Park will live long in the memory, even if it just paved the way for Andriy Yarmolenko's unfortunate own goal to eliminate them at the final hurdle, against Wales in Cardiff, four days later.

From the middle distance, everything about these five days of Ukraine coming back out to play felt near miraculous. When British and Scottish media talked of rearranging the playoff it seemed like an act of goodwill, or of defiance against those who assumed, foolishly, that Ukraine would eventually yield. That it was happening was extraordinary. That Ukraine summoned a performance of bravery, pride and defiance as they did simply beggared belief. It was magnificent.

The club game began to respond presently and correctly too. Holding wealthy Turkish club Fenerbahçe to a draw in their adopted home of Łódź already felt worthy from Dynamo Kyiv, in the Champions League's second qualifying round. As they travelled for the return leg to Şükrü Saracoğlu Stadium a few days before the end of July 2022, where they had hoped to lift the UEFA Cup thirteen years before and their rivals Shakhtar actually had, they finally faced their big challenge. Striding against a lack of fitness from extensive inactivity, versus the resource and expectation of a Fenerbahçe team now helmed by Copa Libertadores-winning coach Jorge Jesus, and facing some local baiting which stepped well beyond the boundaries of acceptability, with some ghouls chanting in support of Vladimir Putin (although some home fans later applauded the visitors).

Dynamo buried any anger and hit the home side where it hurt, with Oleksandr Karavayev's powerful back post finish winning the tie in extra time, marking another moment of glory for Lucescu in Kadiköy. Knocking out Austria's Sturm Graz in the next round represented another huge achievement. It guaranteed Dynamo a place in the Europa League come what may in the final playoff round. That, eventually, is what they got as they were comprehensively beaten to a place in the Champions League group stage by Benfica. For the final goal of the Portuguese club's 3–0 second leg win in Lisbon, Neres finally had the chance to play against Dynamo – netting a wonderfully casual curling left-footer – though not in the time and place that Shakhtar fans had hoped for earlier in the year.

At domestic level, the plan for resumption had changed and changed again. Former Shakhtar academy boss Patrick van Leeuwen agreed to return to Ukraine and join Zorya Luhansk as head coach in June 2022. When he took the job, he had been under the impression that when the Ukrainian Premier League resumed, it would be outside the borders of the country itself. The Ukrainian government decreed that was not the best option. The UPL would stay at home.

'That was decided so that there was some form of motivation towards all [the players'] fellow countrymen,' van Leeuwen told Omroep West in his native Netherlands, 'that something positive was happening in the country. It was a message not only for Ukrainians and the fans, but also for the outside world. That people and athletes, despite the war, could continue to develop through sport.' The parameters were quickly set. The games would be behind closed doors of course, and every stadium used would have to have a bomb shelter, with swift and orderly evacuation of players and staff when an air raid siren went off.

On 23 August, when Shakhtar nominally hosted Metalist 1925 at Olimpiyskiy for the start of the 2022–23 season, and the first Ukrainian Premier League action of any sort since mid-December 2021, the sense of ceremony was there, even if fans weren't. A recorded message from President Zelenskiy was played on the big screen before kick-off ('We are always ready to defend our blue and yellow flag,' he said). That was followed by the players emerging from the tunnel, each one wrapped in that very flag instead of a jogging top, a sight which would become familiar in the coming months.

There may have been no supporters in the stands but there were, however, media representatives from several different countries. This was despite the difficulty in getting there, the time taken, the risk perceived, with sports reporters pushed to the brink of a war zone, if perhaps not exactly to the frontline. Twitchy risk assessors at media outlets spent hours on the telephone to insurers and sent reporters out for crisis training before seeing them off on their journeys.

For Ukrainian reporters their content was more important than ever, as the conditions under which they had to produce it became more challenging. Interruption had become part of daily life – and not just in the stadiums – but the acknowledgement that they must continue was total. 'I can say that our job never finished, not for even for one day,' Iryna Koziupa, a writer for *Tribuna*, tells me. 'We worked under rocket attacks, under the air raids and [bringing] the news and our writing never stopped, even for one day – during all of this difficult year, even when there was big problems with electricity, and with the blackouts.'

Most journalists are familiar with flagging laptop and mobile batteries and finding acceptable internet connection in order to file reports. In wartime, those problems took on a different dimension. 'Me and my colleagues, try all possibilities to do our job,' Koziupa continues, 'to write an article, even if we had only three hours of electricity a day, trying all the time to find a restaurant or some place with electricity and internet to do our job.'

For Ukrainians, it wasn't a choice. The second day back in action – 24 August, Ukrainian Independence Day – confirmed this, with the game in Lviv between Rukh and Metalist becoming 'the never-ending match,' as Dima Rebrov described it on *Vavel*. Metalist's 2–1 win kicked off at 3pm local time and, after three separate interruptions for air sirens and accompanying retreats to the stadium's bomb shelter, it finally concluded nearly four and a half hours later, at 7.27 p.m.. 'The "never-ending" match,' wrote Rebrov, 'was a confirmation and, for some, somewhat of a reality check that football during this time remains a risk.'

So when a foreigner chooses to come back, and come back to this, you have to sit up and take notice. Even if there is a clear difference between being a journalist at the coalface and working in greater security at the country's premier club, it is noteworthy that Igor Jovićević chose to return. So we must ask why he did, after two years working in Ukraine, with his family back home in Zagreb. 'I went back to Croatia [after the full-scale invasion],' he relays, 'and I was there for four months. Helping the Ukrainian people, helping my team, helping my president . . . financially, with humanitarian [issues].' Few would have judged him for supporting the cause from afar and taking another – probably more lucrative – offer to continue his coaching career elsewhere. He was firm, though. 'I said that I didn't want to work in another place because it would be dishonest,' he argues. 'I had offers from Saudi Arabia, from [United Arab] Emirates, from other countries to work, but heart just said no. It's war. So my heart is there, with the Ukrainian people. I can't just go for the money. So I decided that if I go back [to work] it would be Dnipro, it would be Ukraine.'

Jovićević had assumed that he would be going back to Dnipro-1, after guiding them to an unexpected third place (at the point at which the UPL was interrupted in February 2022) and a Europa League qualifying spot. 'We're going forward at Dnipro,' he remembers. 'But then some days before pre-season Roberto De Zerbi left, and Shakhtar gave me a concrete offer to join the biggest club in Ukraine. It was a very tough moment for me. It was just motivated by sport.'

He does not exaggerate. Dnipro-1 was founded in 2015 but gradually absorbed the infrastructure of FC Dnipro, the 2015 Europa League finalists forced out of top level Ukrainian football in 2017 and out of business entirely in 2019. The new club was promoted to the top flight only in 2019, and was not expecting to fly so high so soon.

'In two years you'd made history with this club,' Jovićević says with a modest detachment. 'You took it not two steps forward, but ten steps [forward]. But to some offers in life, you just can't say no.' His president at Dnipro, Yuriy Bereza, didn't see it that way, and was incandescent when Jovićević made the choice to move on to Shakhtar. After that, he still had to explain to his family that he wished to carry on in Ukraine, even under these altered conditions, though he says, 'my family supported what I wanted inside,' and quickly agreed. Like Srna, he is Croatian, but is really an honorary Ukrainian. 'He played a lot of his career both as a player and then as manager in Karpaty Lviv,' points out Andrew Todos, 'so that I think national pride and patriotism sort of rubbed off on him when he was there. And he embodies that sort of idea now.'

It was also a chance that Jovićević felt he had to grasp because, frankly, he might not have been offered the job in many other contexts, despite his eye-catching work in Dnipro. He was the man for the situation forced on Shakhtar. 'You have someone who knows Ukraine,' says Iryna Koziupa, 'who speaks Ukrainian, and is very good with young players. But what we've also seen about him is that he's a really, really inspiring speaker.' He is perfect for these times, for his philosophy and for his ability to project Shakhtar's mission on the world stage.

Koziupa first spoke to Jovićević at length about a week after his appointment, in mid-July 2022, in Rotterdam, with Shakhtar in the Netherlands for a series of friendlies. 'It was my first travel from Ukraine after the invasion started,' she says. 'And at the time we're still thinking, is he the right man for the job? He was speaking Ukrainian. I knew him since he was a player in Ukraine, so he knows Ukraine very well. But it was still a big question. How will he deal with the team, with young Ukrainian players, totally different than the previous season? It was the first game. For the first game in Amsterdam he picked ten Ukrainian players and since then, everybody started to talk about how it's a new brand new Shakhtar with a Ukrainian face, and a Ukrainian-speaking coach. What I like about him is he's not afraid to experiment and to put young players on the field in the very important games. He's a really good motivator. You know they have this spirit of fight. They are fighters and it is probably because of him. He gives this push to the team, like fighting to the end.'

That is as on brand as Shakhtar would want. Palkin still reiterates tirelessly the message from the top, from Akhmetov. 'He said Ukraine can win this, even before all these army and war experts said that yes, Ukraine has a chance,' he says with real conviction. 'For us, it was very important. He gave us this energy, this belief, that we need to do our job. And our job will bring results for the future, and this will be useable in the future, because we will have peace and we will win.' People can get worn down by news of the war, desensitised to the horror. The drudge of the effects on the west – inflation, the cost of living, the rising price of electricity etc. – can become detached from one of the major factors causing it. So if there is ritual, ceremony, at moments like this, it is felt absolutely necessary to remind the world of the atrocities unfolding.

Because even on the Ukrainian side of it, in 2014, a semi-sense of routine was developing, albeit a more difficult, discombobulated one – but a routine of sorts nevertheless. Adrenaline doesn't last indefinitely. There are changes; sometimes big, sometimes little and sometimes way too much, just when they weren't expecting it. For Stepanenko it was his friend Serhiy Kryvtsov leaving, accepting a two-year deal to head to Major League Soccer (MLS) and join Inter Miami in January 2023. The pair had first met in Zaporizhzhia – the home of Europe's biggest nuclear power plant, and a particular target of Russian shelling – over fifteen years ago when making their way as young players at Metalurh Zaporizhzhia. After moving to Shakhtar in a joint transfer in May 2010, at twenty and nineteen years of age respectively, they had been friends and teammates ever since.

When the time came to say goodbye, it hurt. As Jovićević addressed his departing stars with the players stood in a semi-circle in the foyer of the Cullinan, with Kryvtsov dressed in his civilian clothes, you could see Andriy Pyatov welling up, underlining his coach's oratory skills. Stepanenko, stood opposite Jovićević, starts to softly weep. The two best friends share a strong, heartfelt hug before Kryvtsov pulls on the sides of his jacket and starts to move towards the reception doors. Stepanenko and Kryvtsov had been through it all together but here, they were simply best friends, preparing to say goodbye.

When I sit down with Stepanenko over tea in the basement café of the same hotel a few weeks later, I tell him that I want to start by asking him about that. 'Ah,' he replies, an incredibly intelligent, articulate man briefly reduced to the monosyllabic. It is hard to recount. 'I was really sad,' he nods, 'because we've been friends since Zaporizhzhia, even before Shakhtar. For thirteen-and-a-half years we were roommates, we were always together. So his leaving is a little bit stressful for me. We won a lot of trophies, we sometimes lost very important matches . . . it's just friendship for life. Our families are friends, our kids are friends, our wives are friends and now there's a big distance between all of us. My family is in Spain, his family is in Poland, now he's in the USA. It's life and sometimes you realise that things change all the time, and you just need to keep going. And you need to keep this strong connection with friends like him.' It's this candour, this humanity, which makes Stepanenko such a compelling leader.

Finding safety and comfort for players, staff, friends and family takes time. As when Miguel Cardoso was at the helm of the youth academy, a solution needed to be found for Shakhtar's scholars in February 2022. The academy moved temporarily to Croatia, where eighty-five scholars between the ages of ten and seventeen went to stay in Split in accommodation arranged by Srna. As well as a moral obligation to protect, there is the knowledge that, without the right leadership, the next generation could be lost. A generation that Shakhtar, again, will probably want to lean on quite hard.

Some will always go, feeling the need to start again, and they can't be criticised for that. Oleksandr Zinchenko, now of Ukraine and Arsenal, had been one of those Shakhtar scholars. Interviewed on a Channel 4 news broadcast on 26 March 2023, ahead of Ukraine's Euro 2024 qualifying opener with England at Wembley, he was asked about his eventual first steps into the professional game with Russian Premier League outfit Ufa, having taken the decision to leave the Shakhtar academy. Zinchenko has been a frequent and eloquent speaker for Ukrainian expats since the outbreak of full war, but he employed a careful sidestep on this occasion. 'I just want,' he told Krishnan Guru-Murthy, 'to forget that part of my life.'

Sometimes, there is no getting away from what you're facing. The curious juxtaposition of 2023's mid-season training camp in Antalya was evident every night. While there were Ukrainian footballers as far as the eye could see, in hotels there were also Russian holidaymakers everywhere in one of the few European countries that still opened its doors to them. It made for an uneasy atmosphere as some of those players and staff faced people whose countrymen were responsible for unleashing all kinds of misery on their country. Some of those tourists nevertheless swaggered about unapologetically, seemingly without a care in the world. There is something especially jarring about being flanked by a man wearing a T-shirt covered with the phrase Made In Russia, with a sketch of a bear next to it, at breakfast.

Sometimes, as well, the provocation is too much. Vzbirna ran a story about Shakhtar's Danylo Sikan hitting one Russian tourist who was a little too confrontational in the hotel; a story that the club didn't deny. Sometimes, the places which should feel the most like home just aren't anymore.

9

Welcome to Warsaw

It was one of those characteristic Toni Kroos crosses looping high, hanging ominously and as it held its trajectory up towards the blinding lights in the chilly October air, you just knew it spelled trouble. In our minds we told Shakhtar's brilliant young goalkeeper Anatoliy Trubin not to come, all the time knowing that he would. As Trubin sped from his line and jumped towards the ball he was on a collision course with Antonio Rüdiger, the Real Madrid centre-back who had appointed himself as a de facto centre-forward as they chased an equaliser with ever greater mania. The heads of Trubin and Rüdiger crunched together in mid-air but not before the defender nodded the ball goalwards. It hit the inside of the post, lurched across the line and finally, agonisingly for Shakhtar, it rolled into the net.

Several players in orange and black sank to the turf. They had given everything. Trubin and Rüdiger were there already, laying prostrate. Rüdiger left the field with a towel held on his bleeding head and later hurriedly exited the dressing room with twenty stitches in two neat parallel rows over his left eye, while Trubin posed for a picture with his bandaged head on Instagram the following day. Shakhtar had come so close to the most famous of all wins, less an exploit than a near miracle – far mightier than either of those two sensational group stage wins against Real Madrid under Luis Castro in 2020 – against the greatest of them all, the Champions League holders. But it's the moments like these, when a single, late dramatic action feels like it syphons the oxygen out of the stands with a single, sharp, collective involuntary breath that makes us feel, that creates attachment. This was the night on which Shakhtar and Warsaw moved from a handshake to an embrace.

That sense of place is what makes football clubs what they are, what grounds them, gives them their identities, their sense of pride, to unite and to represent a community. It's what made Shakhtar so proud of the awe-inspiring, futuristic-looking Donbass Arena, that 52,000-capacity spaceship. They already had the team back then – several slightly different but equally uber-talented, mesmeric versions of it – for some years, and now they had an arena. It was 'one of the best stadiums in the world,' as Sergei Palkin once described it to me with not even a hint of grandstanding. It was an arena to match the on-pitch majesty.

The Donbass had given Shakhtar wings, especially on those transcendent Champions League nights when they went

207

toe-to-toe with the continent's good and great, packed to the rafters and roaring them on. Donetsk, far from the elegance of Kyiv, was an unremarkable, post-industrial city. I once asked Fernandinho, as he prepared for Chelsea's visit to Shakhtar in that arresting Champions League match back in 2012, what he would advise visitors to do and see. He told me that he had no idea, as he never went out. The Donbass gave the city a landmark of some renown, a living, breathing, shouting and perspiring source of pride, and so much more. Those evenings, gala occasions on which the whole of Europe, and the world, saw how far this club had come on the back of the multi-billion investment of Akhmetov, the strategy of Palkin and the aesthetic vision of Lucescu, were so validating.

It was also why they left such an emptiness when they were no longer there. Shakhtar were forced out almost overnight in 2014, but the inertia of hotel life in Kyiv and playing at 'home' in Lviv and Kharkiv was almost made worse by the Champions League and European nights they hosted in the stadiums of others. What had once made the hairs on the back of the neck stand up was now like a high-spec exhibition match. It felt like a dinner party without a main dish, a *baile funk* block party with only bossa nova coming out of the speakers. Shakhtar found themselves housed in Poland for European games in 2022. Indefinitely on the road, in search of a home, as well as visibility.

The traditional closeness between Poland and Ukraine has shown its depth and sincerity since the full-scale Russian offensive. Over two million Ukrainians took refuge in Poland in the three weeks that followed the renewed invasion, according to UNHCR, the UN Refugee Agency, so it was always natural – and practical – that Ukrainian football would lean on its neighbours to get their football back on its feet. In mid-June, when Ukraine's national team fulfilled a brace of UEFA Nations League fixtures in Łódź, some 120 kilometres to the south-west of the capital Warsaw, it felt like a minor miracle. There had been games already – the fund-raising friendlies in Mönchengladbach, Empoli and Rijeka, and the real thing in Glasgow, the World Cup qualifying playoff in which Oleksandr Petrakov's team turned Scotland over on a visceral, emotional night. The World Cup dream may have been extinguished four days later in Cardiff, but being there was, in itself, nothing less than an absolute triumph.

After the second of those games in Łódź, against the Republic of Ireland in June, Ruslan Malinovskyi told me of the rush of playing for those Ukrainians who had crossed the border. 'I'm so proud of the team,' he said. 'We gave everything in these games. We played today for the whole country because we know a lot of people lost their house, lost their job, lost everything. We know with this we can help, and off the pitch we can help them. It's difficult to keep your emotion inside, even before the game and after the game, because they are supporting us so hard in these games and they come from all Poland. I think we had a great atmosphere in these two games.' He also made a point, before he made his way to the team bus, of using us to thank supporters from Glasgow, Cardiff and Dublin for the support they had shown the visiting Ukraine team, and their people. 'Their supporters were really lovely in these games. We felt a lot of love from them. This is football and everyone wants to win but when it's done and the result is on the table, when you feel the support it makes you feel proud.'

Going home, or not home, hosting matches representing your nation in a country not your own, had been a challenge. Yet it was galvanising and showed the resolve of this national team and the people it represents. The culture appeared instantly in Poland, a joint effort between the displaced and their hosts, waving blue and yellow flags from little memorabilia stores on wheels, applying face paint, gathering outside to play traditional Ukrainian music on the concourse outside the stadium and inside, singing songs in support of the nation's military engaged on the frontline. After the second of the two games in Łódź, a 1–1 draw with the Republic of Ireland, the players formed a circle in front of the junction of Widzewa's south and east stands, where the majority of the Ukrainian fans were gathered, and led a faux-Icelandic thunderclap, chanting the word in portions with increasing insistence and rhythm. Oo. Cry. Een. A. Oo. Cry. Een. A. Oo-cry-een-a. *Ucraïna*. A celebration of being there together. A celebration of simply being.

So when it came to the country's clubs taking their places in UEFA club competition, Poland offered a welcome home. Dynamo Kyiv used Łódź as their base through the Champions League qualifying rounds before moving to Kraków, in the south, for the UEFA Europa League group stage after dropping into the second-tier competition. For Shakhtar, it was off to the capital. On 15 July 2022 the club announced a lease agreement with Legia Warsaw, the 2021 Polish champions, to play at their

Stadion Wojska Polskiego, initially for the three Champions League games that they qualified for automatically as Ukrainian champions. 'I want to thank the management of Legia for the fact that the club has met our needs and provided their stadium,' said Palkin in a statement. 'We really hope for the support of Shakhtar and Legia fans, the Poles and Ukrainians currently residing in Warsaw and other cities.' They were also welcomed into the Legia training centre at Książenice, a village some twenty-five kilometres to the south-west of the city. Shakhtar branding was introduced in Champions League weeks – not just externally, with banners flying alongside club crests at the entrance to the complex, but inside, with the players having personalised lockers to make them feel at home.

Match night, of course, was something different. The hope was for what Malinovskyi defined as his own experience, but it was a step into the unknown for a club team that had been shunned before. When Shakhtar 'hosted' for the first time, welcoming Scottish champions Celtic on 14 September, the 30,000-capacity Wojska Polskiego was only fractionally short of sold out. It takes time, though, for a house to become a home. If Palkin had enthused about the 'excellent conditions' provided by Legia, it quickly became clear that 'the incredible atmosphere created by the fans in the stadium' might have to wait. The travelling Celtic fans were heavily in the minority, with the away section comprising 1,500 supporters. But they out-sang those in the home stands throughout. It was a solid home backing on paper, better than anything Shakhtar had received outside of a match with Dynamo Kyiv or in a match in European competition for years, and this outside their home nation. From the locals there was support, goodwill, empathy – but neither passion nor familiarity. At least not yet.

The contrast between the sentiments was clear as I stood outside the stadium waiting to catch a lift a home after the game had finished. There is a large bar embedded in the front of the stadium on Łazienkowska, wedged between the club shop and the ticket office. I peered through the window, attracted by whoops and hollers, imagining that something wild must be happening in the other Champions League games. Instead, there were several hundred Polish fans losing their minds in beery elation as their national team closed on a shock EuroBasket quarter-final win over superstar Luka Dončić's Slovenia. It was far louder than anything expelled from their lungs in the stands that night. A case study in curiosity versus genuine investment.

Not that Shakhtar were feeling sorry for themselves. The importance of the Ukrainian Premier League, certainly symbolically, to carry on in the face of everything, was lost on nobody. But on a sporting and sheer sensory level, this was several steps up. In front of a full stadium, rather than echoey, empty stands, it mattered little that the seats weren't full of dyed-in-the-wool hardcore fans. After the meat and potatoes of domestic action, this was the dessert. With a glass of Château Rieussec Sauternes to complement it.

The players deserved a sip of the good stuff. They finished that first game in Warsaw with four points in the bag already in a challenging-looking Champions League group that few expected them to get much change from. The opening match at RB Leipzig on 6 September set the tone. Defending deep from the off, Shakhtar got their touch of fortune when home goalkeeper Péter Gulácsi got in a tangle with the ball, unsure whether to dribble or pass, and presented it straight to Marian Shved, who rolled it into the open net.

When Mohamed Simakan fired high into the net after a flowing Leipzig move to equalise just before the hour, it had been coming, and it felt pivotal. It was – just not in the way we expected. We were straight up the other end with Mykhailo Mudryk stretching the play on the left. He slipped the ball into Shved. The striker's shot flicked off defender Willi Orbán and nestled in the opposite corner. Shakhtar were back in front. It had taken eighty seconds for the visitors to retake the lead.

It was now Mudryk's show. With Leipzig overcommitting too soon to chase a second equaliser, they were caught out. Heorhiy Sudakov broke on the right and quickly realised he and Mudryk were alone versus a solitary defender. He played the ball across field, knowing his friend's pace would get him there. It did, and his burgeoning talent allowed him to rifle into the bottom corner. Another sizzling Mudryk run down the left channel led Shakhtar on another speedy break, and his cross was snaffled by substitute Lassina Traoré, sparking euphoria on the touchline. Five shots, four goals. The perfect heist. It was beautiful.

Adam Crafton and his team, there to bring out the inspirational elements of Shakhtar's struggle in their series, couldn't have scripted a better start. 'I think they were shocked,' he says. 'Nobody really expected it. If you'd have watched the first half of that game, or until it was 1–0, you wouldn't have thought it would be that scoreline. It was just one of those freak games where a team sits back against a team that's out-of-form. They get a couple of goals on the counter-attack and a crazy thing happens.'

It gave Shakhtar an early foothold in the group that they couldn't have dared hope for, at the home of one of the Bundesliga's best squads. 'From then on,' Crafton notes, 'it basically meant they were going to be in it, [probably] right until the end. If you're getting four points from your first two games and you've got a team like Real Madrid in the group that's going to beat everyone else, then you've got half a chance. So I think it was a massive relief, but there was a story to it in terms of this very, very young team, with seven or eight of the starting line-up aged twenty-one or under and Ukrainian. I think it's only Lassina Traoré that was not from Ukraine, Lucas Taylor and a couple of Croatians – obviously the manager as well. But it was mostly just this group of players that have known each other for years, like kids on tour with a couple of old stagers.' It was, Jovićević tells me later, 'the happiest day of my life. Because the first time, you don't know how good you are. The day after that, at the hotel, we looked into each other's eyes and said to each other, "Wow, you are good." None of us had experience but we just said to ourselves, "Let's try. David can beat Goliath."'

Even with the uncertainty, or perhaps because of it, the players really felt the magic. The day before the Celtic game, I had asked Lucas Taylor – the sole Brazilian in a squad that habitually over the last decade had a dozen of them – what had made him come to a club in a country gripped by war, having spent the previous season in picturesque northern Greece at

PAOK. Stood on the edge of the pitch, he lightly shrugged as if the response was obvious. 'It's a huge club, famous in Brazil,' he said. 'And it was my dream to play in the Champions League.' Little else, it seemed, had entered his head when weighing it up, if indeed any pondering was necessary. The pull continued to be real. That European campaign would turn out to be even more of a lifeline for Shakhtar than anyone dared imagine.

It was the same for his coach Jovićević, the garrulous, engaging Croatian whose move to replace De Zerbi in July had caused a degree of consternation at his former club, but whose eyes shone when you talked to him about the uphill climb of pitting a diminished, restructuring team against the best the continent had to offer. 'These type of games are a challenge for me,' he smiled. 'When you see that you're in the comfort zone, you must change something, even if it's a risk. We are products of the risks we take in our lives.'

Though the step out of Ukrainian borders was from one perspective a necessary compromise ('to our great regret,' as Palkin put it) it was a relief too, an opportunity to breathe for players and staff. It was an opportunity on every level, in fact – to seize their deserved relevance, to grasp the news agenda, to remind people that the Shakhtar who had won four league titles, four cups and reached two European semi-finals since taking their leave from Donetsk were still alive and kicking, even after their latest, most drastic displacement. To put Ukraine front and centre as news cycles threatened to move on, with UEFA agreeing to give headline – and giant screen space – to Pitch In For Ukraine, the club's charity to take the humanitarian aid provided by owner Akhmetov for the last near-decade to the next level, as was desperately required. Nothing shouts from the rooftops quite like the Champions League.

And Shakhtar provoked a strong degree of local curiosity. Adam Pawlukiewicz, writing in *Przegląd Sportowy* on 24 February 2023 – the first anniversary of the full-scale invasion – compared Shakhtar's continued successes to the inertia of many of Poland's clubs. 'How is it,' asked Pawlukiewicz, 'that despite so many problems, the club from Donetsk is doing so well?' The desire to answer that question had reached a crescendo after the Leipzig win. A heavy defeat – which many expected – would have increased the exhibition feel of Celtic's visit. Instead, Warsaw welcomed a team that were a going concern and, just as importantly, ready to fight hard to keep their new audience, infused as they were with fresh belief.

The signs that the locals would warm to their house guests were plenty. Shakhtar are a big deal, designed to compete at the top level of football domestically and continentally, but they never act big time. They are not remote. They are human. Pawlukiewicz wrote of an issue with tickets when he and his three friends arrived for the Europa League tie with Rennes further down the line, after Christmas. 'It was easy enough to contact the club by email. Within ten minutes the matter was settled – in Polish.' Shakhtar were not just clinging on and asking to be led. They were defining the space and mapping the route. 'Many of the club's [Legia] employees are involved in organising the matches in Europe, and this is valuable experience for the future,' concluded Pawlukiewicz.

The Champions League speed dating, Warsaw edition, didn't start brilliantly for the men in orange. Celtic pinned them back from the off, just as Leipzig had done. This time, though, Shakhtar cracked. As the ten-minute mark rolled by, Reo Hatate broke from midfield and smuggled the ball across Shakhtar's six-yard box. Artem Bondarenko, sliding in to clear, inadvertently placed the ball past Trubin to give the visitors the lead. It was one-way traffic. Then enter Mudryk.

It was, again, the link with Sudakov, spotting his teammate's run and guiding an inviting pass inside Josip Juranović, the Celtic right-back, to find him in the channel. Once Mudryk was away, he would never be caught. Without even breaking stride he headed directly to the penalty area from his favourite spot, and smashed a left-foot drive high past Joe Hart into the net. Looking at the winger making great decisions with no hesitation at breakneck speed, it was clear he was a special talent. The sort of talent that conjures an equaliser from nowhere, against the run of play.

From a neutral point of view, Mudryk was thrilling to watch, one of those rare, undeniable talents. It wasn't just that, though. The youngster was particularly useful to this new, more reactive Shakhtar. It was a new team having to play a different way, because we're used to seeing Shakhtar dominate the ball. Now they were soaking up pressure and Mudryk was their out ball for those Champions League games.

According to Iryna Koziupa, Mudryk was also symbolic of something else – changing some long-held perceptions. 'It's not so much about the result on the field,' she says, 'but how people in Ukraine started to think about this Shakhtar this season. In previous years, it was always that Dynamo was always more popular. The question was, "Is it a Ukrainian team or is it a Brazilian team?" The Ukrainians were always in the shadows. We haven't had a Mudryk before. Even if the previous season he did all he could to get his chance, but it would be more difficult to show all his freedom on the field, if the Brazilians were still there.'

His goal stabilised Shakhtar and was good enough for a point, consolidating a fine start. They could even start dreaming of qualification, so convincing was their fortitude, as well as the results. 'It means so much,' Jovićević told me, daring to look to the possibility of a round of 16 spot before contextualising. 'We're not favourites in any of these games – Celtic are favourites, Leipzig are favourites, Real Madrid are favourites. We are not favourites. I know the Ukrainian people are proud of us. We play today for them. It's 40 million of them in our hearts. I want to thank the people in this stadium. We heard them [tonight]. And we are very proud.'

The following home game, against Real Madrid, was the big one. Shakhtar had suggested they could compete in the first game in the Spanish capital, withstanding pressure and only going down 2–1. Many of the visitors to Legia's lair that night were not, however, coming looking for a fair fight. There were strong suspicions among some of Shakhtar's staff that many locals had purchased the Champions League mini season tickets just to see the holders, and who would blame them? Checking into a hotel a short walk from the stadium on the afternoon of the game, I snaked through a lobby full of young Polish Real Madrid supporters, lads with dads, brought from the provinces to the capital to fulfil the dream of seeing Benzema, Vinícius and the rest at close quarters. Again, Shakhtar didn't mind. Being part of the show already meant so much.

It was, though, the moment when the relationship between the football fans of Warsaw and Shakhtar really started to click. A beautiful choreography before the game, a human mosaic composed of thousands of people with red, white, yellow and blue cards depicted the Ukrainian and Polish flags joined together across the length and breadth of the yawning stands, acknowledging and giving thanks for the unique friendship between the countries. If that touched from a distance, how the first chants of 'Shakhtar' tumbling down the south stand must have made the players' hearts swell.

Those players would have been forgiven for having their hearts and minds elsewhere. After the Monday bombings of Kyiv, Lviv, Khremenchuk, Kharkiv and beyond, many of them had spent the morning before the game anxiously scrolling through their phones, WhatsApping friends and relatives for news. 'I have to be honest,' confided their Burkinabè striker Traoré after the Real Madrid game, 'that yesterday was a really bad day for the players, and I felt sorry for them. We had to deal with it, and then prepare for the game. But it was so difficult for them yesterday and I felt sick about it.'

Crafton was with Shakhtar to give his listeners some behind-the-curtain insight but this, he admits, is a moment where he felt uncomfortable. 'I think that morning that bombs are falling is when you start to feel like you're intruding rather than reporting,' he says, 'even though [that's] actually not true

219

– because they're the most important moments to report in some ways, because they're the most powerful. I remember the impacts of the reporting around that game. Just the engagement on it was so much higher because all of a sudden everyone was looking at Ukraine again because it was being bombed again, whereas maybe the week before that people were paying less attention.'

As with 24 February, it was all about timing. Life was not quite normal, but a semblance of regularity was possible. But three days before the Real Madrid game, an explosion on the Crimean Bridge had been seen as a victory for Ukraine, and damaging to Russia. Retaliation was coming. 'Kyiv hadn't really been touched for four, five, six months,' Crafton remembers. 'And what had happened with the Crimean Bridge, the Ukrainians were pretty giddy about it. Whether it was Russian sabotage or the Ukrainians doing it, whatever had happened, Putin had taken a blow and they were excited about it. And I remember someone saying to me, "Something's going to happen. They're not just going to accept this."'

Crafton was in Warsaw and had been set to go to Kyiv. 'I was checking my Twitter feed and it was explosions in Kyiv,' he says. 'I was talking to our security team at the *New York Times*. I think my train was meant to be around half-ten, eleven a.m. from Warsaw into Kyiv. I was asking, "What do we do?" They then told me to wait for a little bit and then they'll call me back. [They then told me], "These explosions are literally by the train station for the train that you're coming in on," and it was in Shevchenko Park. I think that shocked everyone because that was like the war was very much back on your doorstep.'

For the club staff back in Ukraine, it certainly was. 'People going into the Shakhtar offices in Kyiv that morning could literally see explosions driving in,' Crafton continues, 'and had to go underground and subway stations and things like that. Because I then wasn't getting that train, I just went for breakfast with the Shakhtar team at their hotel. And it was the first time where I felt like I was just intruding. It had gone past the point of curiosity, into these guys really don't know if their families are safe. They're all there scrolling, scrolling, scrolling on their phones, doom-scrolling the news. I think one of the things was Stepanenko's family were meant to be traveling from one part of the country to the other that day, and he wasn't quite sure where they were. Others were just reading there's going to be more explosions and things like that. Some of them have vulnerable elderly relatives. Others have children. It was just horrible. I saw Jovićević that morning and he just thought, What am I meant to do?'

Once he had mentally regrouped, Jovićević was back on to that mantle of leader. 'He went to his press conference,' says Crafton, 'and it was probably one of his most powerful press conferences that day in terms of the way he spoke about what was happening and using the fact they're playing Real Madrid. The coverage that would come out of that would really amplify their message.'

'Everyone has a different personality,' Jovićević told the media. 'Most of us have families in Ukraine and we are worried about this situation. But still, the game won't be cancelled. We don't know what will happen in the next week. But we do know FC Oleksandriya aren't playing today. Of course they aren't. Who can think about football when there are more important things than football? But tomorrow we will not have to cancel the game. We must go out on the pitch. We have to go out there and show we fight for each other, and for the Ukrainian people.'

His sense of grasping the occasion, and being a leader of young men, always seemed to come very naturally to Jovic′evic′. Yet there was no aloofness there. Perhaps with one eye on that coverage, he invited the media into the Shakhtar family unit. 'He is very energetic,' observes Koziupa, 'and the staff of Shakhtar are pleased with the job he is doing, because he is very straightforward in speaking with everybody, always saying, "Hello, how are you?" He has always done that even with us journalists. A couple of words, a smile. I remember we didn't go to the press conference after the final game in the Champions League and he was really sad about that. He asked, "Why did you didn't come to the press conference?" It's not very often that you will hear the coach appreciate you [being] at the press conference and asking him a question.'

He certainly got his message across to his players. '[They] were definitely imbued with this sense of defiance,' agrees Crafton. 'I actually said to Stepanenko, "Are the players OK to play? I think most people would understand if you don't want to play that game." He looked at me as if I was mental. He said, "It's people going to war. We can go and play a football match. We have to go. This is our way of contributing. We're not in the country. We have it easy in some ways in this nice hotel in Warsaw." Which is fair enough, but also kind of mad. I remember seeing the goalkeeper coach [Curro Galán] with

Trubin. He was just going through these clips of Benzema and Vinicius and Modrić and Kroos. I'm [thinking] this twenty-one-year-old goalkeeper who's from Donetsk . . . he's looking at this like taking it all in. I think he made probably ten saves in that game, and then made a mistake for the goal.'

Crafton was also struck by the prevailing mood that night – the sense of genuine unity. It was the occasion but it was also a sense that Poland needed to be ready to stand beside Ukraine, more than ever. 'The geographical location,' argues Crafton, 'of Poland meant that, you know, it's like if your flat's on fire, the neighbour needs to help, because the fire is going to spread into your house. And I think that's probably the way that Poland and Polish people have seen this. So I think that was a really interesting element of all of it.' The game was combining with the mood in Warsaw, where residents took to the streets to protest outside the Russian embassy after the renewed bombings – 'and the Russian embassy in Warsaw is about a hundred yards from the hotel Shakhtar stay at,' Crafton underlines. The spirit of resistance was all coming together.

On matchday the mood among the Shakhtar delegation was understandably heavy. When the whistle went, a switch flipped. The emotion was high from the events of days that led up to it, from the stands, from the never-stronger sense of unity, and with the scale of the game. That last clause seemed to matter little. Shakhtar was not just dogged, but they were daring. Real Madrid appeared taken aback by just how brave their opponents were, and they struggled to create.

It wasn't just Mudryk taking the fight to El Real, even if

his dribble pointed the way to the shock opening goal. He slalomed inside, playing the ball into the corridor outside him into which Bohdan Mykhaylichenko was charging. The cross to the back post was good, Oleksandr Zubkov headed down and in, and Shakhtar had a lead that was improbable in every sense. The roar of celebration from the stand came from the heart as well as the lungs.

It could have been more. The moment, really, was Traoré's chance, after a glorious, flowing counter between Sudakov and Zubkov saw him arrive one-on-one with Andriy Lunin, Madrid's Ukrainian reserve goalkeeper. Lunin stopped the striker dribbling around him but the ball broke kindly for Traoré. He deftly tried to lift it over the defender on the line, which he did, but it kissed the top of the bar and went over. The crowd's collective hard sigh and hands-to-the-head showed just how fully they were implicated. The onlooking Jovićević put both palms to his mouth.

Traoré, at twenty-two, is an extraordinary young man, an Ajax academy product with a big future who chose not to follow most of the other overseas players out the door after the 2022 invasion, reasoning that 'they stuck with me when I was injured.' (He was just returning from an anterior cruciate ligament (ACL) tear, with the Real Madrid game his first start in over a year.) His performance, like his team's, was heroic against the holders, only denied a sensational victory against Carlo Ancelotti's megastars by that Rüdiger equaliser. Their bravery, their engagement and their ambition brought the crowd onto Shakhtar's side, changing them from sympathisers to supporters. The tigerish defensive effort in those closing stages of that second half would have been, in different circumstances, framed in military clichés – of battening down the hatches, of defenders and midfielders digging deep into the trenches in resistance. The real-life situation that Shakhtar find themselves in now, and that they have found themselves in too many times in the past eight years, reminds us of how absurd and overblown those footballing allegories are. 'We say thank you to them,' Traoré says of the locals after the game. 'They really pushed us and we showed more strength, more energy.' Those players had felt respect and recognition. Now they felt the growth of genuine affection. If there is now a strong bond between the people of Warsaw and Shakhtar then this was the day on which it was forged. This was the day when Warsaw turned itself from a house into a home.

Even those who had experienced it all with Shakhtar hadn't experienced this. 'For me,' says Palkin, 'over the last twenty years [at the club], it's the biggest surprise I've seen. In those twenty years it was the best football, for me. From the start of the season to the end of the year, we played very well in the Ukrainian championship and Champions League. I was proud of our guys and how they played because when you are playing Real Madrid . . . we lost half of the team, we lost all of the coaching staff. We lost almost everything. We started almost from zero. And I understand that they were fighting to the end.' Yet as we said, this wasn't just about effort. It was about the combination of implication and inspiration. Palkin has seen a lot of great football at Shakhtar. For him, this topped it all, and he dared to broach it with the club's chief aesthete. 'I discussed it with the president and I said that the football that we're playing now, it's amazing. How our boys are playing. And I'm not just talking about how we defend. Because against Real Madrid you have to defend. But we play football, really good football. Therefore for me this period of the story after we didn't play for half a year . . . this part of the story is unbelievable. I don't understand it. I think we'll continue this.'

The swift promotion of these young Ukrainians, and the ability to rise to it, would be laudable on its own. The flurry of news from home on that week made it even more so. 'We understand what's in their minds,' empathises Palkin. 'Every day you receive a lot of SMSes, you hear all this news, almost all negative news, and it's killing you.' He slaps his palm on his chest. 'We know when they go on the pitch to play it will be unbelievably difficult from a moral and mental point of view.'

On those Champions League nights, a short advertisement played on the stadium's big screen, promoting UEFA's campaign of the season, highlighting the harmfulness of online abuse of players. Inadvertently, it calls to mind what these young Shakhtar players have to deal with. Players suffering fans' criticism online is so insidious because it is inescapable, coming after you on your phone screen in the safety of your own home. It is the same for this young Shakhtar squad with news of the war. There is no getting away from the horror of what's happening.

Does Palkin worry about the stress placed on this digitally ever-present generation in wartime? 'We understood that almost all of them have relatives in Ukraine,' he says, 'in different places and different situations, and they worry about it. To be honest, when we started playing Champions League, and even when we started playing Ukrainian championship, I didn't expect too much. I just said "Guys, we need to play." Because our government give us permission to leave the country to play European [football]. And the whole country will watch the game. Whether they're on the frontline or at home. Everybody will be watching.' As we talk at a table in the café-bar of the Cullinan, where Shakhtar are staying in Turkey, London soul crooner Omar's blissed-out 1990 anthem 'There's Nothing Like This' softly coos in the background, unaware. It feels like a reminder, and a painful one, that elsewhere the world carries on, often without a care.

Sometimes, it needs to. The insouciance of youth is perhaps the only thing that could make Shakhtar function as they have this season, in Warsaw and – particularly – in that memorable visit of Real Madrid. 'I think there's a lot of testosterone around,' smiles Crafton. 'Yes, there's this defiance, but I think there's also this young bloke mentality of, "I'm going to fight for whatever I'm doing. I'm fighting for my country and for my family." I mean that in a positive way, and I think that that was a big part of it. I think [finding a] distraction was a big part of it [too]. I think quite a few of them, to be honest, if they weren't footballers, would just have been in the army.'

These players have grabbed a chance to share their feelings, and their very selves, as well as what they represent, with the world. 'I think they were kind of told, actually, this is quite a good opportunity for you to spread this message to a different audience,' Crafton says. 'To connect with different people.' They have done it remarkably well. 'You're ten seconds away from beating Real Madrid and you go to Leipzig and win that. That tells Ukraine's story of defiance, talent, spirit. And it's just a different way of doing it than if you've taken up weapons. But you're always using that platform with big international audiences.'

What might been seen as solitude, single-mindedness and an army-like life has actually afforded them some of life's simple pleasures that have been stripped from many of their compatriots. 'It was back at their hotel after the game,' remembers Crafton, 'and at about 1.30 a.m. you had Mudryk and his best mate, Sudakov. They went out of the hotel and they just went for a walk around Leipzig for about an hour or so. And when I came back, I asked, "What are you doing? Why are you going for a walk around Leipzig at half one in the morning?" They said firstly, "We just can't sleep because of the adrenaline after a game. But also it's really nice to just feel free to walk around the city. To breathe that air and just not feel like you're sort of escaping something. Just that freedom." And that was quite a powerful thing for young people to say at that time. So I think I there was an escapism to it all and also this sense of youthful adventure to it. You know, you're on a bus with your mates travelling around Europe and it's all a bit imperfect but you're kind of having quite a lot of fun with it at the same time.'

Even if we feel like we know our favourite footballers – and some of the ones we don't like so much – as they become omnipresent on our screens and timelines, we don't. We choose to focus on whichever apparent aspect of their character or demeanour suits our perception best. Now in Ukraine, it's different. There can be no more sitting on the fence. Political views, rarely seen as a defining feature of a footballer, now truly matter. Iryna Koziupa's readers want to know 'what's his position, how much he has Ukrainian views.'

Shakhtar have adapted to this, and their evolution has been very positively received. 'This season was totally different and Shakhtar became almost worldwide,' says Koziupa. 'Probably all Ukrainians were under the magic of this Ukrainian team because, as I said before, there are a lot of Ukrainian young players in the squad, speaking mostly Ukrainian in their interviews.'

That those new spokesmen for the club are candid and sensitive has not gone unnoticed, either. 'They say, "Thanks to the Ukrainian army we have an opportunity to play football. So we fight for them on the field." Their coach speaks Ukrainian,' Koziupa makes a point of saying. 'The bosses at Shakhtar made good decisions in difficult real-world situations. They deleted the Russian version of their website, which was a big step. They also did a lot of charity games with the good strong messages to the world about what's happening in Ukraine.'

Their status now is discernibly different, partly because of the dignity with which they've conducted themselves in these trickiest of circumstances. And, of course, because of the profile lent to them by the Champions League. 'They are something like a national team for the whole country,' Koziupa carries on. 'And now maybe for the first time in the history Shakhtar become this team of all Ukraine. It was always the team of Donbas, of one region, of one city. They always said we are the club from Donbas. We want to represent this part. But this year probably they represent all of Ukraine. And this is why I think this is their most biggest, their most precious win in that they become beloved by Ukrainians.'

The speed of the change has been rapid, but profound. '[Ukraine] is very proud,' Andrew Todos says. 'I think the fact of the matter is, is that I mean, Shakhtar are now called Shakhtar. They're no longer really called Shakhtar Donetsk. And yes, the club has got very close connections and ties with everyone who works there and all that kind of stuff. But I feel that it's become more of this national club that people take pride in.'

Bringing in the right coach for now has been a huge part of that. Jovićević has something of the feel of Luiz Felipe Scolari coaching Portugal, a rabble-rouser who pulls off the remarkable trick of persuading members of his adopted country to get waving their real – or metaphorical – flags. Shakhtar know how to pivot and are doing it more skilfully than ever.

'They've adapted,' continues Todos. 'And I feel that they've probably been doing that quite well since they left Donetsk, because they've had to. It's sort of like adapt to survive. Obviously the fact that they have got funding and all that kind of stuff, the fact that they've been able to continue and not die or fizzle out. For example, Dynamo Kyiv look incredibly deflated as a team, even in terms of the inspiration that they've got, the motivation in just this past year. Whereas Shakhtar have been able to keep that momentum going since 2014 and over the past year when shit properly hit the fan for them.'

No club is an island, though, and for all the good work Shakhtar have done at every level, their union with Warsaw has lifted them up just that bit higher. 'Poland is the first country that met our people,' emphasises Taras Stepanenko, 'our refugees from Ukraine and helped a lot. Of course you know a big amount of Ukrainians are living in Warsaw. When we played against teams in the group stages of Champions League, a lot of Ukrainians came to see us in these matches, gave us great support and really, we're playing for them. We have a really young team now, 95 per cent Ukrainians. It's an unpredictable situation for Shakhtar. We showed that we have spirit and good players, so we can be proud of Shakhtar, our country and our people.'

So does a senior player like him feel that Shakhtar are now perceived differently? 'Yes, I think so. I think now more people in Ukraine support Shakhtar. In the past, most of our supporters were from the east and south of Ukraine. But now I think Shakhtar has more supporters from all parts of Ukraine, because the club did great work with grassroots football, with social organisation. That's helped the club to achieve good results. This year, Shakhtar has helped Ukrainian people a lot during the war, helping to organise charity funds and charity games. Shakhtar represents Ukrainians all over Europe. The president has done a lot for Ukraine. I think people see that, and they see what Shakhtar does for Ukraine.'

Stepanenko and his teammates are well aware of their platform and exactly how important it can be. The growth of Shakhtar is gradual but deliberate, and much needed. 'We know that football is the most important game in the world,' he says. 'Four billion people watched the last World Cup final. So when you send your message through football, it helps a lot. We see our Ukrainian players representing with the flag, talking about the situation in Ukraine. It's important to help people in other countries understand what's going on. It helps us to receive help from other European countries, from USA, from Canada. Football is a big power in the real world.'

This was also drilled home to Adam Crafton when making his podcast series, which started with the desire to get behind the scenes at a Champions League club and wandered into something much, much bigger. What began as a football story with shards of human interest snowballed into something else; not just because of the Champions League's profile but due to the engagement and efforts of Shakhtar, on and off the field. They were the sort of efforts built on everything they've had to do for nearly a decade. Efforts they're having to make more than ever. This time, what this club and these players have to deal with is finally getting the care and attention that it merits.

They didn't quite get there in the end. The Rüdiger goal cost Shakhtar, as did Danylo Sikan's open goal miss in the return match with Celtic in Glasgow, after he was given his chance on a plate by Mudryk. It was just one of those once-in-a-footballing-lifetime occurrences you can't legislate for. By the time it got to the final group game at home to Leipzig, winning could have offered them a passage through to the last 16 – but this Leipzig was a very different team to the one they had faced less than two months before. This time, in rampant form under their new coach Marco Rose, they never offered Shakhtar even a sliver of light. It finished 4–0 to the Germans. It could have been more. Shakhtar were all out of miracles.

Months later, sat in a hotel in Antalya, the widescreen TV in the bar shows another one of those Toni Kroos deliveries wafting in as Madrid chase a late equaliser at a domestic underdog, Mallorca. Again, Rüdiger's head connects and again he lies prostrate on the floor after contact – this time, through frustration, as the ball glides agonisingly wide of the far post, the chance goes and Ancelotti's team are, this time, forced to face defeat. If only.

The victory from that night, however, was already won. 'I understood that 90 per cent of those people arrived at the stadium as tourists,' says Palkin of that October night in Warsaw. 'But when they see we are fighting, that we are playing good football, then they started to support us. They became, for these 90 minutes, our fans.'

10

Hope

'About war and football.

On this evening a year ago, I read a fairytale to the children, hugged my wife, who was already asleep, and read the news, waiting for the usual daily speech of the president. A few hours later, my parents, who live near the border with the Russian Federation and Belarus, called.

And in tears they said that they heard explosions and the Russian offensive had begun. Already in the afternoon, my parents were in the occupation, and we were preparing for the worst.

Today in Rennes, a year after the beginning of the full-scale invasion of the Russian Federation, we all felt this special moment.

We had to win, show character and [get] to the [last 16 of the Europa] League for the sake of Ukraine and Ukrainians, for the sake of our guys from the armed forces, for the sake of everyone who defends the country. This match and this Shakhtar is a reflection of the whole country. We never give up, we always fight to the last, and for each other.

Incredible emotions, fantastic [emotions] that cannot be described. I felt it for the first time in all the years I have been working in football. Everyone understood the price of victory today. And we achieved it. This is another opportunity to remind the world about Ukraine and Ukrainians, about our fighting spirit and victorious character.

Every match in Europe is a help to Ukraine.

Well done, Shakhtar. Well done to the fans who supported the team frantically throughout the match. Hearing "well done" after the game is fantastic. I am sure that one day we will hear that applause at the Donbass Arena.'

Oleg Barkov, Shakhtar media officer, tweeting in the early hours of
24 February 2023, after the Europa League victory at Rennes

Warsaw had been a good home for Shakhtar. The question was always going to be – 'how long for?'

A little longer, it turned out. Losing on Matchday 6 at home to Leipzig may have been disappointing but it had not been the end of the European adventure – it had been, as Adam Crafton describes, 'a bit of a free hit.' In other seasons, securing third place in the Champions League group, and with it a Europa League spot for after Christmas, would have been seen as the bare minimum. Not this time. Here, it was a genuine achievement.

When Shakhtar's social accounts put out a post on 2 November, the very same night as the Leipzig defeat, with a graphic of the team entitled 'Qualified – We Are Shakhtar!' it wasn't the sort of piecemeal, typical official mouthpiece approach to fan communication that many clubs employ. They meant it. It was worthy of recognition and acknowledgement, something to be celebrated and not to be hidden or diminished. Within a fortnight, the club was already promoting the sale of tickets for their next match at Legia, the first leg of the Europa League last 32 match against upwardly mobile French side Rennes.

By the time Rennes arrived in the Polish capital on 16 February, a lot of water had flowed under the bridge. Shakhtar were still over a week away from resuming domestic action after the planned three-month hiatus, but for the club, the winter break had really been no such thing. The club's board were in a constant state of movement. Preparing for the second half of the season without knowing what sort of conditions it would resume under. Preparing for another flurry of continuous journeys. Trying to prepare the squad, with any possible reinforcements, for a continuing European campaign, a joy but an obligation.

The main issue was Mykhailo Mudryk. His status had progressed with the pace of one of his now-familiar runs – smoothly, elegantly but with dizzying speed. His Champions League appearances were genuinely thrilling from the opening match at Leipzig onwards. It was utterly remarkable that a player of such an age (turning twenty-two on 5 January) and such relative inexperience (forty-four appearances in all competitions for the Shakhtar first team) should be so assured and convincing.

The delight taken in those performances against Leipzig, Celtic and Real Madrid were twofold. Seeing an extraordinary talent on an inexorable course for the top was exciting. It was coupled with the feeling that the club were getting some bonus Mudryk. He had not been expected to come this far with Shakhtar. In the summer window he had been the subject of persistent interest from Bayer Leverkusen and Brentford, with the club reputedly hoping for a fee around the €25 million mark. The player preferred Leverkusen, but they didn't meet Shakhtar's expectations, and the move didn't happen. He stayed, and how glad all parties came to be that that was the case.

In January 2023, the sale of Mudryk was finally completed. To Chelsea, rather than the mooted move to Arsenal, with the big-spending club from London SW6 committing up to €100 million in transfer fee alone (if all add-on clauses and conditions are eventually met). That's almost four times the amount he was on the block for just five months before. It was a triumph for the player, henceforth the most expensive Ukrainian footballer of all time, and for the club, squeezed into an unenviable position by FIFA's ruling on the suspension of foreign players' contracts in Ukraine and Russia following the full-scale invasion.

In a normal season, Mudryk would not have gone for such an elevated fee, but this was neither a normal season nor a normal situation. The squad being decimated made him an automatic first eleven pick. He stood out for his flair, his pace and his wit, the player most likely to make something happen. It was something especially noticeable in a side that was extremely admirable, but lacking the dazzle of previous Shakhtar incarnations. 'He was almost exotic,' suggests Adam Crafton. The seed that it could be Mudryk's autumn and winter was planted in Glasgow in summer. The winger came on for the last eighteen minutes, plus stoppages, and it was his first senior Ukraine appearance in a competitive game, having been involved (and scored) in the charity friendly in Mönchengladbach the previous month.

Oleksandr Zinchenko had stood out that day too, a semi-revelation to a British audience used to seeing him as a reserve left-back for Manchester City, but who were now bludgeoned not just with his talent, but with his ability to lead. Yet as Mudryk came on, he started to mark himself out as a figurehead in a different way. And that continued as Shakhtar stepped onto the European stage in autumn, expected to be a support act but making themselves headliners.

Part of it was the company Mudryk kept. Shakhtar were

plugging gaps in the squad left and right, and they needed to do it with Ukrainians. They brought back Marian Shved from an underwhelming spell in Belgium with Mechelen; he had struggled at Celtic too but had been prolific for Karpaty Lviv, Jovićević's old club. Oleksandr Zubkov, who had been at the club's youth academy when it was back in Donetsk, returned from Hungarian champions Ferencváros. The club were working the margins, bringing in honest, UPL-familiar players who might not have made the best sides of Lucescu or Fonseca, but who were now the order of the day.

This new team composition played into Mudryk's strengths. The team was set to soak up pressure and counter at speed in the Champions League, setting them apart amongst the competition's familiar names in an era of increasingly bold, front-foot football. In the most de facto way, Mudryk was suddenly handed the keys to his club team. With each Shakhtar attack an event, with their story of defiance having the ear of even casual European football fans, the speed demon with the shock of blond hair couldn't fail to catch the eye. He was on the main stage and didn't hesitate to turn his amp up to eleven.

He was ready. In that opening match away at Leipzig his stunning display built on the interest of those already intrigued by Mudryk, and abruptly demanded the attention of those that weren't yet. Shakhtar's tactics, birthed by circumstance, were thrusting their young attacking star into centre stage. There was already interest in him among Europe's good and great – Arsenal had made enquiries towards the end of the summer – and combined with his performances and rising profile in the full glare of the spotlight, it was only going in one direction. Repeatedly strong performances in the big games were doing wonders for Mudryk's, and for Shakhtar's, futures.

What Shakhtar must have hoped for initially is interest from England. They had that. Then, a bit of competition. Now, they had that too. Arsenal became more persistent as winter approached. 'They carried on talking to him,' Crafton says, 'so it just created this expanding market. Chelsea came as a bit of a surprise.' The 2021 Champions League winners appeared suddenly in the race, and if there was little difference between the final figures they and Arsenal were offering, according to Shakhtar, there was a difference in the speed of the payment, a crucially important detail to the Ukrainians.

The club had stuck to their guns and been rewarded. 'On the first day of the negotiation with Chelsea we asked for €100 million,' states Darijo Srna, 'and to the last day of the negotiation, we didn't change a thing.' Some will point to the fact that The Blues spent heavily in January 2023, so it must have been straightforward. Not so. Ask those involved on both sides of the deadline day deal to bring World Cup winner Enzo Fernández from Benfica to Stamford Bridge. There was payment structuring and restructuring before an agreement was finally struck late on.

It was a personal triumph, too, for Srna, as well as a business one for the club. The sporting director accompanied Mudryk on to the Stamford Bridge pitch like a proud father when the new arrival was presented to the Chelsea supporters at half-time of the 1–0 win over Crystal Palace on 15 January, a Ukraine flag draped around his shoulders and bobbing in the gentle wind. It was an unexpected way to release the news, but seeing Mudryk in the flag was a reminder of what he had achieved, in terms of sport and valuable profile as well as profit, for his club and for his country in such a short, intense time. It was a whirlwind.

'I was with him because he was alone,' Srna says, 'and I felt that he was nervous. They asked me, "Could you go with Misha?" So I went. I took two steps and I went off to the side, because it wasn't my moment. That was Misha's moment. I just wanted to help him to make those couple of steps and after the stage is for him.' As the fans in the Matthew Harding Stand cheered their new boy, Srna was lost in a moment of contemplation. 'I was proud but deep inside myself I was so sad because of the war, because of everything. You are selling maybe one of the best players in the history of Ukraine to Chelsea. And he should be with us. But because of the situation, you have to do it.'

It was simultaneously a relief for now, and a reminder that the heights of 2009–2014 – and even some of the European exploits since – are increasingly hard to touch. 'The president wasn't happy,' nods Srna, 'because really, he wants Champions League quarter-finals every year. And to have that, you need four Mudryks in the team. When we sell him we are happy for him, for the money . . . but we are not happy because we lost an important player. But during the war, we sold a player for 100 million and I'll tell you that if there wasn't a war, maybe his price will be 120 or 150. If it was a normal situation we would like to buy two or three more like him to maintain our level.'

The ambition to claw back that level burns bright. Srna and Palkin still look hard for the next generation of stars. Their phones are always buzzing. Palkin admits, though, that there are roadblocks to getting in the talent these days, even with foresight and determination. 'Sometimes they just don't want to,' he acknowledges. 'They're afraid.'

So developing one's own players is not just desirable, but integral to the new model. Mudryk will remain a beacon for the next generation(s) for a while. 'This is a good signal for all our Ukrainian players,' enthuses Srna, 'because believe me, Mudryk is not the only one. We have a lot of top talents for the future. We have signed a professional contract already with all our young players, because this generation of Ukrainian players is amazing. There is no difference between top Brazilian talent and top Ukrainian talent. The only difference is the passport. There are more Mudryks.'

They will need them. For matches, and for the market. Shakhtar drove a hard bargain in selling Mudryk to the Premier League, and how they deserved to do so. Both Palkin and Srna had been pushed to the edge by one of the unforeseen side effects of FIFA's attempts to look after, as they see it, the interests of foreign players in Ukraine and Russia since the invasion. With the option to suspend their contracts, Shakhtar have been left in a state of limbo, personnel-wise and financially. In fact, it's worse than that.

Shakhtar have harboured high-class talent for over a decade, and have continued to do so post-Donetsk. Losing a clutch of stars has been intolerable, and not just for the sporting side of the operation. So when Palkin talked about a potential €40 million loss when he and Shakhtar took FIFA to the Court of Arbitration for Sport, he was hedging on the conservative side of estimates.

'FIFA are destroying Ukrainian football,' Palkin says, bluntly. 'If you can imagine, on one day last year fifteen foreigners left. And there's nothing you can do. You cannot sell them. You cannot loan them. You cannot do sale or return because clubs are calling me going, "When are you going to pay for this player?" So from one side they released our players and from another nobody helped us to settle our business debts somehow. They are just leaving us to die alone, you know? And if we didn't go straight into the group stage of the Champions League, if we didn't sell Mudryk, we are bankrupt. Completely bankrupt. We would not exist, because the situation is catastrophic.'

Few would disagree that protecting the interests and rights of players is enormously important. Yet FIFA, in typical grandstanding, have offered little thought or care to how the clubs left behind in Ukraine can sustain themselves in these unprecedented circumstances. Shakhtar were owing sums that could rise to €70 million for players they had invested in and, in some cases, no longer had any control over. Typically, a club will pay for a player over a few years. If they buy a player for €15 million, for example, they might pay in instalments of €5 million in each of the next three years. Palkin reiterates to me that those obligations to clubs they had done business with didn't go away just because of the war.

David Neres, a statement signing from Ajax in January 2022, is perhaps the best example. 'He didn't play one game,' shrugs Palkin. 'The same with Vinícius [Tobias, not to be confused with Vinícius Júnior] who went to Real Madrid – he didn't play one game. We exchanged Neres with the debt of Pedrinho, because I should be paying Benfica up to €16 million in the year.' Pedrinho had been signed for €18 million from the Portuguese club in 2021. He played nineteen times for Shakhtar. But if it wasn't for Benfica's president, Rui Costa, being open to find a mutually acceptable solution, it could have been way worse for Shakhtar. 'I gave them Neres and they [let that] offset our debt for Pedrinho,' Palkin confirms. 'It was good that the player's agent and Benfica accepted this deal. Otherwise they could have just said, "OK, we're taking Neres for free." It could have been that we needed to pay for Pedrinho *and* they have Neres.'

Does he believe clubs interested in signing Shakhtar's players took advantage of the situation? 'Yes, completely. They understood our situation completely. We needed money to survive, to repay our debts and to pay salaries to employees and players. In respect of [Manor] Solomon I already had a transfer contract. I needed just two days to get it signed and close it. Then FIFA issued [their ruling] and *finito*.' Palkin is not sure if clubs including Lyon, who signed Tetê under the new ruling, or Fulham, who did likewise with Solomon, negotiated in good faith or played for time until FIFA offered the loophole. He certainly believes some agents attempted to manipulate the situation.

At the beginning of June, Lyon were apparently negotiating with Shakhtar for the permanent signing of Tetê, who had said on 31 March, the day of his presentation to the French media,

'Of course I want to stay at Lyon [past 30 June] and there are several people working on it right now.' On 21 June 2022, FIFA extended the suspension of the foreigners' contracts in Ukraine and Russia. 'These provisions give players and coaches the opportunity to train,' said the FIFA statement, 'play and receive a salary, while protecting Ukrainian clubs and facilitating the departure of foreign players and coaches from Russia.'

At the start of July, it was announced that Tetê would stay at Lyon under the same conditions for the 22–23 season. By the end of that deal, he would be six months from the end of his Shakhtar contract, which would expire on 31 December 2023 – for these players contracts are being suspended, not frozen, under the regulations. By that point, a player who scored thirty-one times and provided fifteen assists in 108 matches with Shakhtar, and who had long been coveted by top Premier League clubs in England, would be worth some way less than the €17 million that he cost to bring from Grêmio in 2019.

In the end, he didn't see his Lyon deal through; the team's poor form and the appointment of the former Paris Saint-Germain boss Laurent Blanc as coach in October 2022 to replace Peter Bosz (Tetê didn't fit Blanc's tactical rejig), made both parties think a separation was best. A couple of days before deadline in the January transfer window, Tetê moved again – this time to the Premier League, and to Leicester City. Did Shakhtar see a single cent out of it? Nope. One of their prime Brazilian talents had flown the nest, twice in the space of a year, but there had been no bounty à la Fernandinho or Fred. Leicester paid Lyon (that's right, Lyon) £3 million in compensation to terminate his temporary agreement with them and sign a similar one with the 2016 English champions. Officially, Tetê remains Shakhtar's player, but the reality is they now have no control over a valuable asset.

The first that Shakhtar knew about the transfer was when the pictures emerged of a smiling Tetê standing, arms folded, in his new blue and white jersey in the corridors of the King Power Stadium. 'Tetê is changing club and we don't know anything about it,' Srna tells me, his voice rising half an octave in indignation. 'We paid €17 million for him. Explain to me the logic. He will go for free and we will have lost our €17 million.' And they will be losing it at the time when they can least afford it. FIFA's announcement on 26 May 2023 that the now-infamous Annexe 7 to the transfer regulations would be continued, allowing foreigners attached to Ukrainian and Russian clubs to now suspend their contracts until 30 June 2024, promises more headaches on the way.

Srna's anger with FIFA is close to the surface. 'They say, "We are with Ukraine, we will do everything to help Ukraine,"' he mutters. Srna is full of praise for Aleksander Čeferin, who took such a hands-on role in helping those Shakhtar players (and the Brazilians in particular) get out of Kyiv in late February 2022. 'He showed he is the president of UEFA,' Srna states. 'To be the president of UEFA means you protect the clubs, protect the teams. But the president of FIFA must do the same, and he doesn't do anything. Nothing. We lost millions. We lost our houses, our apartments. Some of us lost our friends. And in the end we lost our money, and we needed FIFA to protect us at this moment. They did nothing. *Nothing.* And me, as an ex-football player and as a guy who lived in Ukraine for twenty years, I will never forget this. I'm curious because the war will one day stop. Life will continue. When someone from FIFA comes to Ukraine, what sort of welcome will he receive there? But life is long. We don't ask them to give us money. We just ask them to protect us. They don't care about us. It is painful. They don't care about Ukraine and if you don't care about Ukraine today, you're on the opposite side.'

What would it have been like, we wonder, had Ukraine qualified for the World Cup in Qatar and the omnipresent, grandstanding FIFA president Gianni Infantino been made to face a nation he has offered little thought or consideration to? 'It would have been very, very interesting,' muses Srna. 'It would be embarrassing for him. I'm not just talking about Shakhtar. [The UPL] lost seventy to one hundred players. That's not something that you can respect in the twenty-first century. If Čeferin was president of FIFA, everything would be different.'

On Friday 13 January, the Court of Arbitration for Sport (CAS) announced their decisions in Shakhtar's cases; one against the FIFA ruling allowing overseas players in Ukraine and Russia to suspend their contracts (a group of eight Russian Premier League clubs, led by Zenit St Petersburg, also appealed that ruling, in a distinct action with separate legal representation) and the other seeking €50 million compensation for loss of transfer revenues. Both appeals were rejected.

Palkin does not accept that FIFA simply don't understand Ukrainian needs. 'They understand everything,' he says. 'They are not stupid people. They are playing games. The management of FIFA has very good relations with the Russian government.' He continues without mentioning Infantino by name. The FIFA president was awarded an Order of Friendship medal by Russian president Vladimir Putin in 2019. Infantino has not returned it, despite saying publicly he is 'as devastated as everyone' about the full-scale invasion. In the same statement, he talked of his regret at having to suspend Russia from FIFA tournaments, and that when the 'conflict' ended 'we would be [in Russia] the first day to play football again, because that's what I think is needed in this country.' Little wonder, then, that Palkin is so visibly irate.

He talks passionately and with disgust about the continued snubs to Ukraine, about how it was 'almost impossible' for Ukrainians to be approved for the Hayya card, the fan permit that allowed entry to stadiums at the World Cup in Qatar, and about how 'President Zelenskiy wanted to give a speech before the final of the World Cup,' but was refused. 'They're just thinking about money.' The normally measured and poised Palkin is starting to get agitated. Understandably so.

The lack of respect that Palkin felt in the proceedings clearly infuriated him. When Shakhtar were having their day in court at CAS, he says FIFA couldn't even be pushed to send a senior delegate, instead sending a 'vice, vice, vice' director. Palkin is used to constant interviews, to stating his club's case calmly but firmly, to representing Shakhtar (and Ukraine) in a reasoned and convincing way. This time, he can't take the story any further. 'I don't want to continue anymore,' he says, gently resting his hand on the table. The indefatigable has become wearied.

The strength of Shakhtar is that if one person needs picking up, there is someone next to them to do it. The energy of Igor Jovićević has fitted in perfectly with the club's credo. In the final stages of the training camp in Antalya, he had warned that his team would have to be 'a lot, lot better' than they had shown him in the sessions and the practice matches if they were to get anywhere in the UPL, let alone in European competition. His words were heeded.

Shakhtar are a more recognisable name within the boundaries of UEFA club competition, so it is worth remembering in this situation that, nowadays, they are always the underdogs. The knockout stage of the Europa League, having stepped down from the Champions League, was going to be no different. Their opponents, Rennes, have been mapping an ambitious route to repeated European qualifications funded by owner Artémis, the investment company founded by François Pinault, whose wealth is estimated at over $42 billion by Forbes. They spent €82 million in the summer of 2022 – more than Shakhtar will spend in the next two or three years combined unless something drastically changes – on players including highly-rated Paris Saint-Germain academy product Arnaud Kalimuendo, without mentioning the loan and free signings of players including veteran goalkeeper Steve Mandanda and Tottenham pair Djed Spence and Joe Rodon, all of whom earn good salaries.

What a revelation it was, then, to see Shakhtar play not just with grit, but with enterprise and invention in the first half of the first leg. They took a two-goal lead, Dmytro Kryskiv finishing a flowing move that would fit into any era of

Shakhtar, before Artem Bondarenko just about squeezed in a penalty. Karl Toko Ekambi's second-half goal gave Rennes something to work with in the return, but not parity. On the eve of the first anniversary of the full-scale invasion, Shakhtar travelled to western France for the return. Lassina Traoré's first-half goal was disallowed for a very marginal handball decision against Mykola Matvienko. Another Toko Ekambi goal took it to extra-time where Ibrahim Salah's goal looked like it would be too much for the visitors.

That was until Jeanuël Belocian's freak, unfortunate own goal right at the end of extra-time. Just like Ruben Aguilar in Kharkiv, it was a sliver of fate doing its thing. It left Belocian in tears, less than a week after his eighteenth birthday. And after three penalty saves by Trubin, Kevin Kelsy smashed in the decisive kick in the shootout on his Shakhtar debut. On 31 January, the deadline day for most of Europe's major leagues, Shakhtar had announced the signing of the eighteen-year-old forward Kelsy, the first Venezuelan to play for the club. That entrepreneurial spirit lives on. As the clock ticked over midnight and Shakhtar acknowledged that it had been a year since their country's freedom was stolen, it was a poignant, powerful moment.

Back in the press conference room, we were reminded that these are not just fighters for a cause, but real people, with lives that matter. 'I'm proud of [my players],' said Jovićević. 'Without European competition, we wouldn't go to Warsaw. Personally speaking, if we had been eliminated tonight, I would not have seen my family until at least June.' He was visibly emotional.

Even just back from the winter break, it felt as if the team were tired and emotional. The camp in Turkey had not been easy. Antalya's awkward mix of Ukrainian footballers and Russian tourists (not to mention a few Russian teams) created an off-kilter dynamic. Incidents such as FC Minaj's fight with Russia's FC Shinnik in their hotel underlined the tension in a resort city which continues to welcome tourists from several cities in Russia. It was emotionally wearing.

After the 1–1 draw with Eredivisie leaders Feyenoord in the opening leg of the last 16, taking Shakhtar's Warsaw odyssey into March, the team had taken a pounding, even if it took a late Ezequiel Bullaude goal to salvage a draw for the Dutch. Jovićević called to mind his side's obstinate characteristics after the game. 'Even when the game is not what we wanted, and we suffered from the first minute,' he told me, 'we can stay in the game. We had problems in the squad. We were without five today. And we felt the pressure. It's very difficult to get into the game and control the game. I think today the result is better than the game. We showed many times we can play better. If we are ourselves, we can be what we want to be. They are favourites, but we can dream.'

The football Shakhtar played in Rotterdam was briefly worthy of that, arguably the most dominant they had been in Europe since before Christmas. Unfortunately, they were also 2–0 down by that point. Yukhym Konoplya's handball – in these days of various handball awards of vastly varying merit blighting the game, this really was one that would have been given in any era, and the defender knew it instantly – finished it as a contest. It allowed Orkun Kökcü the means to make it 3–0 with a penalty and Feyenoord went on to rip into downcast opponents after half-time, running up an eventual 7–1 score. It was a harsh end to a proud campaign, just as the comprehensive Matchday 6 loss to Leipzig had been.

In a sporting sense there have been a few really bad days scattered among the good ones since 2014, days when it feels as if the disadvantages, the treadmill of travelling and the departures from the staff have all become a bit too much. 'Like Igor [Jovićević] said before,' says Iryna Koziupa, 'this season is very emotional. You can't just lose by one goal if you had such great games before. So it's probably logical in some way to have such a big defeat.'

The international profile, until next season, would be maintained elsewhere. Paulo Fonseca was in Rotterdam with his wife to see his old friends and colleagues and to support Shakhtar. 'Unfortunately,' he tells me, 'I didn't bring much luck given the result, but it was amazing being with my friends and the people who are still at the club.' Fonseca is working to run a foundation for refugees with the *Federação Portuguesa de Futebol* (FPF), a sign not only that football is front-foot in its humanitarian response, but that the spirit of Shakhtar remains in those it has worked with long after they have moved on.

'It had been a very tough time,' he says, 'and every day we try and find out what's going on there. We've suffered a lot, especially my wife because of this, but we thought we could help in some way, and especially people who arrived in Portugal, and that's what we did. We helped a lot of people when they arrived in Portugal and also through this project with the Federation. The FPF president Fernando Gomes had been a big help getting us out of Ukraine, because when this happened he was among the first people who called me. He asked me how he could help me get out of Ukraine. He said he would make some calls, among them to the president of the Ukrainian Football Federation, Andriy Pavelko, who immediately said he would try and help. So much so that when we were in the hotel it was someone Pavelko had arranged who drove us to the border and helped us cross the border.'

After safe passage back to Portugal was assured, Fonseca and Gomes stayed in touch over what had happened. They were determined the story shouldn't end there. 'When I got to Portugal,' he continues, 'the president of the Federation was always in contact with me, and he invited my wife and I to be ambassadors of this initiative, which was called 'Each Club, One Family'. It was to help the children and families who arrived through the creation of jobs in the clubs and help the kids through playing football, integrating them into the clubs and into society. It was a lovely initiative by the Federation. They helped a lot of families and played a much bigger role than I did. Rita Ferro Rodrigues [a Portuguese TV presenter] also did fantastic work, and helped lots of families and lots of kids through football there in Portugal.'

That his past at the club is remembered, and considered, means so much, as Fonseca is aware. 'I've always kept a very close connection to the people of Shakhtar because I was very, very happy in Ukraine and in Shakhtar,' he says. 'I think we – my wife too because she worked for the president as the head of the press office – have always kept close links to Shakhtar. I think at the end of the day it's a way of showing support to the club and the people, and it was an extraordinary moment for me to see again those people [in Rotterdam] who had worked with me. It was fantastic, but it was above all to support them at that time.'

For Iryna Koziupa, the European season was ending where it had started, in Rotterdam. 'It helps you to see the world,' she ponders, grateful for the mental break she has been offered from the troubles back home. 'You don't stay in the war all the time. And I'm really happy that I had this opportunity to travel and to see not only great games in Champions League, but also to see how people and countries and cities give support to Ukraine.' Stepping outside the bubble is a moment in which you realise the groundswell of feeling in your favour, and it makes you understand that there really is hope. 'In every city we travelled to,' she says, 'all the time you see Ukrainian flags in the windows near the museums or government buildings. And it was like, you know, we are not alone. We have so much great support in in every country. So we really appreciate this time to see with my own eyes how it was in different countries. I spent maybe more time travelling abroad than at home.'

Sometimes vulnerability is as important as strength. Accepting the help of the collective rather than just ploughing on. And in a sporting sense at least, for Shakhtar to continue to thrive, they need their prospective rivals to do so as well. I'm reminded of Joe Palmer's words to me back in 2019. 'The challenge for me was the fact that they won, nearly all the time,' he smiled. 'I used to say, "Actually, it's good to lose every now and again," and the people at the club would reply,

"What are you saying, you're crazy!" But no, competition is important. To drive attendance, you need to be coming along thinking this could be an interesting game. If you're winning 5–0 every weekend, it's boring, isn't it?'

What we're talking about for Shakhtar, and Ukraine's future, though, is different. We aren't talking about the importance of a sense of jeopardy for entertainment's sake, or to finesse the product, for want of a better phrase. We are talking about survival.

Shakhtar have more than their share of heroic qualities, but it is simply not possible for them to keep Ukrainian football afloat on their own. Direct access to the Champions League group stage as Ukrainian Premier League champions is vital, not just for Shakhtar but for any Ukrainian team; for the financial bounty, for the platform, for publicity, to keep getting that message out there. Yet at the time of writing, Ukraine is now fourteenth in the UEFA country coefficient table. By the parameters of the UEFA competitions access list for the 2021–24 period (the set of criteria that defines which countries get which amount of placings for the Champions League, Europa League and Conference League), that would not entitle Ukraine's champions to direct Champions League group stage qualification. They would be required to enter the competition at the third qualifying round, meaning two double-headers – four matches in total – to be negotiated just to make the group stage.

That would be no easy task. Not only is there the matter of the games themselves to be won, but it casts doubt over all a club's ideas and plans for the season. There would be at least two different budgets to be set – the Champions League budget and, if the club doesn't make it, the Europa League budget. The gap in revenue is enormous and it has serious consequences for a club's recruitment strategy.

There are contributory factors to that outside of Shakhtar's control. In 22–23, Dynamo Kyiv's poor Europa League – one point from six games – was deeply disappointing after their heroics in the Champions League qualifiers. Dnipro-1, after their great season under Jovićević, dropped into the Conference League and exited in the last 32 in miserable fashion against AEK Larnaca. Vorskla Poltava slumped to defeat against AIK in the second qualifying round and Zorya Luhansk exited in the following round against Universitatea Craiova, who finished third in Romania last year. All these results count towards the UEFA coefficient table, affecting Ukraine's future participation – and Shakhtar's.

It's precarious. If Ukraine were to drop a place further in the coefficient table, the champions of the fifteenth-placed country actually has to start their Champions League campaign in the second qualifying round – so add two more matches worth of tension, insecurity and the potential for a set of players yet to hit their athletic peak (and in some cases yet to even start their domestic season) to be undercooked, still in pre-season form, and to come up short at the worst possible time. Those particular thoughts, and especially the things that Shakhtar can't influence, can wait for now, though Palkin and his staff will continue to try and future-proof the club in expecting the worst, but hoping for the best. It is, as he often says, about 'planning one week at a time.'

In the meantime, Shakhtar can help shine a little light. 'Sometimes in our country,' says Koziupa, 'it's a hell with no lights. The war bombing is this big drama and trauma of lost lives. A lot of dead people. And you have this feeling of a life that Russia stole from us. That they put our country in this nightmare. But thanks to football, like the Shakhtar story, we have some hope and a bit of normal life. Even the soldiers and the guys on the frontline . . . you ask them, "You are in the war, so is there even a place for a football?" And some of them said, "Yes."'

And the strength of feeling for this club, this club with a soul, is something. Miguel Cardoso told me that the last time he spoke to Palkin, he offered to go back and help the club for nothing. 'If you need me in this moment,' he told him, 'I'm unemployed. I'll cover my own expenses. Fly me to where you have the academy boys and I offer myself to work for free for the club for the months you need. Because this club gave me so much that I will feel in debt for all my life.'

Everything that Cardoso experienced still really lives with him. Asked about his more special memories, he replies 'the spirit with which people in the city lived in general. I have wonderful memories from all the stages I lived in Shakhtar. I have memories from Poltava that I will keep for all my life. I have memories from the first moments in Kyiv. Unbelievable memories from the first team. But my most deeply held memories are from Donetsk because these people, that's why I suffer so much every day. Because Shakhtar was not a football project. Shakhtar was a social project, most of all connected with a football club. Shakhtar was a vision of a group of people – mostly of its president – to, through football, make people happy.'

Akhmetov is the living proof of that. Even after losing all this money, he has not lost hope. His continuing charity efforts are considerable. 'Since 24 February,' says Palkin, 'the president already helped with more than €100 million. He spent to help the army, to help refugees, to help people. Now three weeks ago [when we speak in February 2023] he organised a fund called the Defenders of Mariupol. He donated $25 million to help the Defenders of Mariupol to have medical treatment, psychological treatment, and to help their families. Therefore it's another tranche of help.'

Srna also reminds me that if Shakhtar are ready to carry on, it is because of what the president built. Not one of Europe's greatest stadiums, nor one of its most palatial training centres. The spirit. 'Already we are eight years without a home,' he nods slowly. 'We are getting amazing results in the Champions League, selling players. This is what I want to say. It's the system, which is built from the president. When he bought the club he started to build a system. And this system is surviving in all conditions.'

'It's one of our biggest strengths,' Yuri Sviridov says. 'It's very important and I understand it better and better every single day.' He looks back towards the work of Palkin. 'It's basically . . . it's Sergei who did this. I mean, he built this team around him of people who share values, who share goals. It's important to have a strong team moving in one direction. And that's why I think from 2014, we don't have a single director who comes from outside. We are all from Donetsk. We share our memories, values and inspiration and hopes to come back to Donetsk. And this helps us more.'

'All those directors who we have now, 99 per cent are from Donetsk,' confirms Palkin. 'This team was built and formed in Donetsk. I took six, seven years to create this team. Every one of them feeds into our system. We are like family now, and I wouldn't want to lose any one of them. Because we've stayed together for a long time, I say to them that we have the common DNA of our club. We're with some of these directors for fifteen years, maybe even twenty. Sometimes we fail – everybody fails. It's life. But I do everything [I can] to keep us all together.'

The third weekend of April sees the final Ukrainian clásico of the season, between Dynamo and Shakhtar. It always matters. Yet the first Instagram post from Shakhtar's account after it kicks off pays tribute to the injured servicemen who have been invited to the game. 'The defenders of Ukraine and Shakhtar ultras supported the team in the match against Dynamo in Kyiv,' it reads. 'Thank you for your support and the opportunity to play football in our home country!' They never forget, and they never will.

The game was at the smaller Lobanovskyi, with its currently patchy pitch (another reminder of hard times), rather than the cavernous Olimpiyskiy, taking me back to my first impressions of Kyiv; the lush greenery surrounding the stadium, the magnificent semi-antique floodlights that loom over the trees like big metal lacrosse sticks, the fierce wind whipping into the low bowl from the adjacent Dnipro river. And Lobanovskyi's bench by the pillars at the entrance, his statue sat on one end of it, almost if he is inviting you to stop and to reflect.

On the club's highlights, there is the gentle music that they've begun to edit over the top to cover the sound of near-silence, of shrill referee whistles and inter-player exhortations. Yet it is still Dynamo versus Shakhtar. The first goal, twelve minutes in, reminds us of this, with Stepanenko's shot from range swerving just before reaching the goalkeeper, Ruslan Neshcheret, bouncing and eluding him, into the corner of the net. It is celebrated with gusto – as is Dynamo's unexpected equaliser in the final ten minutes, artfully curled in from range by Oleksandr Andriyevskyi, scuppering Shakhtar's hopes of pulling away at the top of the UPL table. It still matters. It always matters.

It mattered again on Sunday 28 May when Shakhtar sealed the Ukrainian Premier League title, beating their nearest rivals Dnipro-1 3–0 in Lviv in the season's penultimate game, having needed just a point to be sure. As the end neared, and as Shakhtar's substitutes and backroom team gathered on the touchline ready to celebrate, the two teams locked horns one last time and a fight broke out, reminding us that even in times when the bigger picture is at the forefront of the mind, egos, pride and desperate desire are still present and correct. Referee Kateryna Monzul showed six red cards – two for Shakhtar, four for Dnipro. When order was restored, Shakhtar had to find an outfield goalkeeper, with Trubin sent off and all their changes already made. A laughing Rakitskyi donned the gloves and the purple goalkeeper jersey for the final seconds of the game, much to the amusement of those gathered by the bench. Then the whistle went and, finally, it was time to celebrate.

'Every trip,' wrote Curro Galán on Instagram, 'every kilometre on the bus, every training session, every night in the bunker has been worth it. We are champions of Ukraine.' Stepanenko, having clinched it with another swing of that left foot from deep, told the club's television channel about 'the most difficult title in all my years at Shakhtar,' going back to the summer of 2010 when he and his mate Kryvtsov arrived from Zaporizhzhia. 'There weren't just eleven footballers' he said, 'but fifty players; the subs, the coaches, the technical staff, the medical staff, the administrators. Everyone has won this title.'

For Igor Jovićević, it really was the denouement. The coach had done a more than laudable job, but the club announced the termination of his contract on Saturday 1 July, with the official statement recognising his 'high level of professionalism', as well as the 'beautiful victories and unforgettable emotions' they had shared. 'Special thanks,' it added, 'are for the active civic position in support of Ukraine and Ukrainians.' Jovićević was swiftly replaced by a familiar face, one who understands the Shakhtar outlook, in Patrick van Leeuwen, returning from Zorya. Akhmetov's decision might have been based on the too-close-for-comfort title win over less resourced opponents, but history tells us it was more likely to have been the aesthetics of the team, or perceived lack of them in comparison with teams of the club's past. What mattered on the pitch before still matters now. Shakhtar standards remain Shakhtar standards, even in extraordinary times.

'Playing for Shakhtar is something special,' smiles Srna. 'And I spoke with Jádson, with Fernandinho, with Luiz Adriano, with all my teammates from before and they really have amazing memories with Shakhtar. Amazing. And I promised myself and everyone that after the war I will call all the ex-players of Shakhtar and we will play a friendly game, hopefully in Donetsk. That is our dream and everyone will come.'

He's right. They will. That core of management from Donetsk means so much, giving the club its soul. But those the club takes in, who immediately feel compelled to give back, to carry on the name and to share the stories, are vitally important too. Fernandinho, Mudryk, Fonseca, Cardoso and so many more. What Srna says is not cliché or cloying. He *is* right. Shakhtar *are* family. And they all play their part, whether working for the club's continued health day-to-day, or in just spreading the word, keeping the name out there, and keeping that link with a proud history alive. Those still at the club spend so much time dealing with reality that they need, and deserve, to have their dreams. Srna does too. After so many years of fighting to keep their dreams alive, above and beyond all reasonable expectations and possibility, who would bet against Shakhtar?

Acknowledgements

Firstly, I have to go back to where it all started, so thank you to Kevin Ashby and Andrew Haslam for commissioning me to go and discover Shakhtar, and Ukraine, many years ago. Thanks too to Ryan Baxter and Jonathan Fisher for backing me to go out and make the film on Shakhtar from which this idea really stemmed.

Thanks to Nick Ames, Adam Crafton, Andrew Todos and Iryna Koziupa for chats, thoughts, expertise and insight. My thanks also go to Paul Camillin, Carmelo Mifsud, Daniel Nanu and Emanuel Rosu for help with interviewees and pushing me in the right direction of them.

Thanks, of course, go to everyone at Shakhtar, and especially Yuri Sviridov, for their spirit of co-operation and openness.

Finally, big thanks to my editor at Little, Brown, Emma Smith, for her boundless enthusiasm for the idea, her willingness to challenge and to make this book the best version of this important story it could be. Thanks too to Lucian Randall for the edit – and last and by no means least, to my agent Melanie Michael-Greer for her constant support and attention to all the details that otherwise might have been in danger of being forgotten.

INDEX